The stories behind 50 of Eur[ope's] destinations by Terry Stevens

WISH YOU WERE HERE EUROPE

To Jac, Elis, Gruff, Owain a Moi

Be curious, enjoy travelling the world – the Odyssey of the human spirit –

but always return home safe.

GRAFFEG

DESTINATIONS

Soča Valley, Slovenia

CONTENTS

WELCOME / CROESO
PETER GREENBERG

Terry Stevens gives these destinations real world context.

He tells us its personality, its mood, and not just its reason for being, but also its resilience, perseverance and ultimate success.

Perhaps the best part of *Wish You Were Here* is that – unlike the obvious suggestion of its title – this is not a typical language-driven, promotional, bucket list guidebook. Terry Stevens gives these destinations real world context. He doesn't just present a description of a destination – be it a city or a region.

He tells us its personality, its mood, and not just its reason for being, but also its resilience, perseverance and ultimate success. Stevens' real wish here is for us to approach the world with a mission that goes beyond mere attraction or desire, but to understand these places and how they came to be, and perhaps in the process to understand our never-ending need to experience them.

Peter Greenberg
Travel Editor/CBS News

Above: Cardiff Castle and Bute Park.
Right: Berlin Cathedral.

FOREWORD
ANITA MENDIRATTA

French poet Victor Hugo once wrote, wisely and poignantly: 'There is nothing more powerful than an idea whose time has come.' How perfectly this statement applies to global travel and tourism!

Embedded within the United Nations Sustainable Development Goals, travel and tourism is now recognised and respected as an economic sector vital to sustainable, inclusive global development. With more than four million people crossing international boundaries every single day in 2019, travel and tourism accounted for over 10% of global gross domestic product and one in ten jobs worldwide. Uniquely, it has also become a means for shaping the future of nations, (re)strengthening national identity, competitiveness and participation in the global community.

Importantly, the strength of the industry's heartbeat comes from its ability to unlock cross-border, cross-cultural and cross-generational understanding – the human interactions created by tourism offering us all direct, invaluable sensitivity towards our shared world's diversity and differences in a way that inspires greater understanding, respect, and ultimately peace.

With this remarkable impact, destinations – cities, regions and nations – are working tirelessly to unfold welcome mats to travellers. Increased competition has meant that, sadly, the desire of destinations to quickly and aggressively stand out can, on occasion, result in strategically short-sighted product and/or promotion decision making that goes against the innate strengths and spirit of the destination. In so doing, tourism development can challenge the social, cultural and/or environmental fabric of the destination, creating an underlying tension between visitors and locals. Duty of care has, as a result, become a part of the DNA of responsible tourism growth made even more important by the COVID-19 pandemic.

In *Wish You Were Here Europe*, industry veteran Professor Terry Stevens applies his decades of experience and insight as a global tourism practitioner into putting a zoom lens on 50 leading destinations and their leaders. From Aarhus to Zadar, *Wish You Were Here Europe* carefully analyses what it takes to successfully not just build, but rebuild through tourism, making it a rich, practical travel guide with a difference.

Anita Mendiratta
Founder & President, Anita Mendiratta & Associates, Special Advisor to the Secretary General, UNWTO

AUTHOR
TERRY STEVENS

Professor Terry Stevens is an international tourism consultant. A love of travel and interest in landscape was inspired by a teacher of geography at Yeovil Grammar School and fuelled by fellow East Coker 'villagers', William Dampier (1651–1715), explorer, hydrographer and buccaneer, and the great 20th-century poet T. S. Eliot.

Terry arrived in Swansea to study Geography at Swansea University in 1970. After gaining his MSc in Land Management at Reading University he returned to work at the Wales Tourist Board and has lived in Wales ever since, where he learnt to speak Welsh.

After leaving university he developed tourism on some private estates before working for the Pembrokeshire Coast National Park, West Glamorgan County Council and the Welsh Historic Monuments before being appointed Professor and Dean of Tourism in Swansea and Advisor to the European Centre for Cultural Tourism in Barcelona. In 1986 he established his multi-award-winning international tourism consultancy, Stevens &

Associates, and has now worked on destination development and management in almost 60 countries around the world. In 2019, 2020 and 2021 he was honoured to receive the LUXLife award for being the Best Destination Development Expert in the World – an award that initially prompted this book. The LUXLife citation follows on the next page.

Terry has over 350 published works including *Landscape Wales* (published by Graffeg), a pictorial celebration of the glorious natural treasures and landscapes of Wales, featuring spectacular mountains, dramatic coastlines, gentle lowlands and idyllic river valleys in over 80 photographs.

Terry is originally from East Coker in Somerset and is married to Catrin. They and their daughters, Mari and Non, together with their families, all live in south Wales. He's a lifetime fan of Yeovil Town F.C. (The Glovers).

Amen Corner, Dorset.

BEST DESTINATION MANAGEMENT DEVELOPMENT EXPERT 2019, 2020 AND 2021

— the LUXlife citation (2019 to 2021)

Led by renowned hospitality industry expert Terry Stevens, Stevens & Associates (S&A) provides innovative consultancy services to clients around the world. We profile the firm and Terry to find out more about how he has driven the firm to the success it now enjoys.

Established in 1986, S&A was designed to support a wide array of clients with their destination management. Since its inception, the company has worked on over five hundred tourism development projects in 56 countries around the world – from New Zealand to Ireland and from Iceland to the Western Cape – winning numerous awards for clients and for the company itself.

Over the years S&A has been honoured to have clients including the leading international development organisations such as the European Bank of Reconstruction, USAID, the United Nations Development Program, UNESCO and the United Nations World Tourism Organisation (UNWTO). In addition, S&A have been privileged to have worked for many national, regional and local tourism organisations as well as both international blue-chip companies and many family-run SMEs.

Founder Terry Stevens has worked in the tourism industry since the late 1960's serving an apprenticeship working in bars, at festivals and in organising music events whilst at University. After university he spent time working on private estate recreation management, then had experience in national parks in the USA, Canada and in Wales as well as running tourist attractions including some World Heritage Sites.

Thanks to this expertise he is now regarded throughout the industry as an innovative thinker and a person who challenges conventions, often pushing clients to think bravely, with innovation and creativity, about the opportunities to capture the interests of the visitors and the involvement of their community to deliver sustainable destination development or individual projects.

This challenging approach is based upon a sound understanding not only of tourism trends and their implications but also upon a rigorous approach to identifying and learning from international best practice. As a result, his clients are exposed to in-depth information about the approach taken by the world's leading tourism destinations and how they are managed. Terry has developed a number of unique destination benchmarking tools which have now been deployed in the analysis of over one hundred of the world's leading destinations. This has not only given him insight and in-depth understanding of the critical success factors but also resulted in a data bank of information which is readily shared throughout the extensive global network that has been created amongst all those he has worked with.

Indeed, it is his ability to connect these networks and to bring people from different destinations and disciplines together that creates the added-value so desired of the tourism industry today. His particular area of interest and expertise is in the dynamics of destination management and helping to create effective, competent and efficient destination management organisations. He advocates for a future where tourism will be about sustainable destinations – those relatively compact, well-run

places, where tourism actually takes place and experiences are delivered.

Driving S&A towards constant excellence, Terry's work demonstrates that great tourism experiences and products tend to be located in great destinations. He works tirelessly with a wide range of managers and leaders to drive them to create a space where their business can flourish.

Since establishing S&A, sharing knowledge and connecting people is the underlying goal of the company and of Terry's work. His expertise is openly shared with anyone with the curiosity to want to know more through conference presentations, workshops and seminars; by publishing in a wide range of sources including books, magazines, journals, the S&A in-house journal, *Fields of Vision* and being involved with the development of young talent through a close involvement with a large number of universities throughout the world. Terry has regularly spoken at Global Summits including those organised by the UNWTO, The Global Wellness Institute, Stadium Business and others as well as many international conferences on all aspects of tourism development.

This dedication to sharing his knowledge proves that he is committed to ensuring that there are appropriate policies and actions in place to ensure that there is a steady supply of talented, enthusiastic and culturally intelligent people being prepared to meet the challenges and opportunities of tourism in the volatile, turbulent and unpredictable world in which tourism remains a growth industry and important force for peace and global understanding.

Looking to the future, over the coming years Terry will be focusing upon knowledge sharing and the dissemination of a lifetime's work in the assessment and identification of international best practice. This will further enhance his international reputation for excellence in the industry.

Overall, whilst Terry is proud of his own success, he believes that this award is testimony to the excellence and commitment of the highly professional destination managers who have inspired him, and as such he dedicates this success to them.

Above: Reformation Monument, Copenhagen.

CAPTURING MEMORIES
TAKING PHOTOGRAPHS OF GREAT DESTINATIONS
BY SARAH FREEMAN

An infinite and powerful storytelling tool, there's no understating the affecting qualities of travel photography. It freeze frames those fleeting moments – whether it be a sari-wearing woman scattering cremated ashes into the sacred Ganges, or a fog-shrouded heather moorland in the Yorkshire Dales, taking us right back to that place that stirred our souls, if only for a minute. In doing so, it forces us to observe what we so often bypass in our modern lives, sometimes discovering something about ourselves along the way.

I've found that instinct, above all else, has served me well. I've followed my nose down many a dusty alley (a memorable find was a toothless Puglian grandma cooking up pasta on her front doorstep) and chased the sounds of Gamelan music across Balinese rice paddies to a local temple. The list goes on. It may be a visual medium, but in reality, photography demands input from all our senses.

Factoring in the unexpected and embracing it rather than fearing it helps too. For all the planning and weather forecasting that goes into a cinematic landscape shot, a surprise storm can yield that elusive money shot. The cornerstone of a good travel photo are these serendipitous 'in-between' moments, like the bone-rattling journey to a mountain pass (I've had too many to count), which winds up trumping the peak views. The most memorable travel photos tell a story after all.

Whilst no amount of expensive gear, tuition or technical know-how can compensate for a great eye, there are a few pointers worth considering. Long exposures, for instance, can help capture dramatic nocturnal scenes like the vast Milky Way in the Atacama Desert, or freeze frame a gushing waterfall, achieved by using a slower shutter speed and lightweight tripod. In sun-sure places it's worth the early alarm call or holding out till sunset when golden hour's warm tones can transform a scene from blah to beautiful. And turning on your camera's grid feature is a good trick for reminding you of the rule of thirds. Before investing in high spec kit, it's worth remembering the advantages of having a simple point-and-shoot or iPhone for destinations that necessitate discretion or a lighter load.

No genre of photography requires the sort of jack-of-all-trades approach that travel does. People, landscape, food and architecture each provide unique portals to a destination. This is how we experience new cultures, different mind-sets,

unfamiliar landscapes and distant languages that travel engages us with.

Understanding cultural sensitivities and building a rapport with your subject are both vital for photographing people, whilst landscape demands patience and a grasp of your terrain – whether it's jungle, desert, mountain or coast, as well as an appetite for adventure. Food relies more on being led by your palette. Understand the origins of that Peruvian stew by visiting a local market, or even better, the volcanic slopes where its ingredients were cultivated. Architecture, meanwhile, can be as much about details like a centuries-old gargoyle on Edinburgh's Royal Mile, versus the vertical drama of NYC's soaring skyline. Are you painting a familiar building in a different light (think St.

Peter's Basilica being lashed by hailstones), or communicating a sense of familiarity?

The bottom line – it's not solely about capturing the conventional beauty of a place. Travel confronts us with the light and shade of life after all, whether it's a lone kittiwake chick on a windswept cliff in the Outer Hebrides or raucous carnival scene in the colourful streets of Rio. As American photographer Dorothea Lange put it, 'the camera is an instrument that teaches people how to see without a camera'.

Sarah Freeman
Travel photographer and writer

Above: Soča Valley by Sarah Freeman.

MAKING THE CUT: SELECTING THE 50 DESTINATIONS

RULE ONE: You must always give tourists a great experience
RULE TWO: Never forget rule one

Great destinations always abide by these rules. This is essential if they are to thrive in an uber-competitive world of tourism.

The aim of this book is to give the reader an insight as to what makes a tourist destination great. It gives the backstories, the planning and the people working in the destinations who ensure we have a memorable, rewarding and enjoyable holiday or business trip – and how these 50 great destinations live by these two simple rules.

The selection has been made by me alone. I do not claim that these are Europe and the world's 50 greatest destinations, but they are *great* destinations: consistently delivering fine experiences for their guests and ensuring that tourism benefits their local community. An essential requirement for their inclusion was that all of these destinations had to have been visited, on at least two occasions, by a member of the Stevens & Associates team – I have visited all of them and I have worked in them all after I have visited.

Judging what makes them great is based on a mix of scientific analysis and the personal experiences as a tourist. I hope you will be surprised by the final list and delighted to learn about places that you may not have heard of and will now be inspired visit them. When you do, I sincerely hope they live up to their reputation.

Over the past 40 years I have had the honour to work on tourism destination development in countries around the world. Destinations are,

simply put, places that people want to visit for pleasure or business or a combination of the two. We travel on our own, with family, friends or work colleagues – and we travel a lot and in increasing numbers. We are urged to travel. It is after all a basic human right. The Dalai Lama encourages us to 'once a year go someplace you've never been to before.' T. S. Eliot invites us all to undertake an 'Odyssey of the human spirit'.

For the first time in the history of mankind, in 2016 the United Nation's World Tourism Organisation (UNWTO) reported that, worldwide, there were over 1 billion international tourist arrivals. By 2030, the UNWTO predicted that this would increase to 1.8 billion. Travel and tourism was then the world's largest industry and, according to Gloria Guevara, President and CEO of the World Travel and Tourism Council (WTTC), 'In 2018, travel & tourism generated $8.8 trillion and supported 319 million jobs across the world and accounted for one in five of all new jobs created worldwide.' Then along came COVID-19 and global travel was reduced to zero. The pandemic exposed the fragilities within the sector. It put a spotlight on many things that were wrong in tourism. There will be recovery and re-growth. The opportunity is being taken to improve destination management, create better visitor experiences, and listen more to the voice of the host communities. As we go to print, many countries in Europe are recording strong tourist activity in Summer 2021. There is

still a long way to go to on the journey of recovery and the destinations in this book are well-placed to succeed.

Billions are spent each year by thousands of destinations to grab our attention and seduce us to commit to become a tourist. Our anticipation builds from the minute we start exploring the internet or consulting a travel agent. We intently take note of recommendations by trusted friends and are heavily influenced by social media posts. We are anxious to find that special place that ticks all our boxes – and there is lots of choice. Every country, territory and city in the world wants a bit of the action. The success of all this effort is judged by our experience in the destination – from the minute we arrive to the time of departure. The experiences in that place where we, the tourists, spend over 80% of our time, 80% of our budget and derive 100% of our enjoyment.

The destination is *the* most important entity in tourism. In order to fulfil its promise to us that it made in its marketing, the destination must be well-managed. Consistently delivering great tourist experiences over time does not happen by chance. It demands intelligent, well-structured, well-resourced destination management organisations. Every one of the destinations in this book has an efficient and effective organisation pulling the strings and making it all work.

I do not have much faith in the all too familiar annual lists of the so-called top places to visit or the best short-break cities of the world. Many of these rankings are subjective or based on a rather fluid set of criteria. In order to be included in this book every destination has been assessed using a unique evaluation model developed by Stevens & Associates. The model was not created to produce this book. It was developed to help us identify international best practice in destination development and the competency of the destination organisations. It has been used to evaluate over 120 destinations in the world and has helped us hone the advice we give our clients. Every one of

the destinations in the book has been visited and evaluated. In order to make it into this book that had to achieve a minimum score 160 of the 190 marks available. Clearly, they are all doing the right things to ensure that their guests have a great visit.

In addition to the obvious need to be well-managed, these destinations have other factors in common: they are relatively compact in size, easy to understand and have a sense of everyone working together. There is a clear vision, strong leadership and they innovate to stay ahead of the game often challenging the way we think about tourism. They invest in the people working in the industry and they do the right things for local people.

There could have been more than 50 but a line had to be drawn. Those that just missed the cut were: Porto and Lisbon (Portugal), Hamburg (Germany), Tallin and Saaremaa Island (Estonia), Bornholm and Skagen (Denmark) and the New Forest (England).

The list is clearly not exhaustive. It may be criticised for not including other destinations. Their time will come. Maybe this book will help them in the management of their destinations in the post-COVID-19 world.

Above: View of Fanad Head Lighthouse with Milky Way in the night sky, Ireland.

AARHUS, DENMARK

A contemporary, forward-looking city that celebrates and nurtures its traditions, heritage and quality of life

First or last in the index to an atlas? In most cases Aarhus appears at the top of indexes, however, the modern Danish alphabet puts the letter combination 'aa' after Z under the letter Å. This confusion all dates back to the Danish spelling reform of 1948, when the capital A was replaced with an A with a ring on top, so Aarhus, which had been in use for centuries, became Århus. At the time some Danish cities resisted the new spelling of their names, notably Aalborg and Aabenraa, but Århus city council explicitly embraced the new spelling. In 2010, the city council voted to change the name back from Århus to Aarhus to strengthen the international profile of the city and this renaming came into effect on 1 January 2011.

If Denmark's second city has appeared ambivalent about the spelling of its name it is definitely confident and focused upon its appeal as a first-rate city tourist destination. Aarhus is full of self-confidence, civic pride and is oozing with creativity. Bolstered by being the European Capital of Culture in 2017, the city has become an eye-catching centre for innovative architecture, culture and contemporary Scandinavian gastronomy. It is now a vibrant mix of youthful energy and with a living history giving the city an energetic beat and can-do approach.

This is a compact city. Indeed, in Aarhus, it is claimed that when a tourist is told that somewhere is within walking distance, it really is within walking distance – and it is a delightful, safe and pleasantly varied, visibly maritime city, in which to walk. A modern and efficient light rail system makes access

AARHUS●

DENMARK

Population of city: 235,000
Population of wider area: 1.3 million
Nearest international airports: Aarhus Karup, Aalborg, Billund, Copenhagen International.
Key websites: www.visitaarhus.com
www.dengamle.dk
www.aarhuscnetralfoodmarket.dk
Icons: Den Gamle By, ARoS, Central Food Market, DOKK1, the Isbjerger, Aarhus Ø, Midtbyen, Djursalnd, Aarhus Mad & Mark'd Street Food Market, Urban Mediaspace, The Frederiksbjerg Quarter, the Cathedral, The Women's Museum of Denmark, the 1,900 volunteers to help tourists.

Left: The rainbow panorama on the roof of ARoS is a spectacular artwork designed by Olafur Eliasson.

to the wider city easy and enjoyable. The city is on the east coast of the Jutland peninsula (almost the geographic centre of the country). It is located on the Bay of Aarhus facing the Kattegat sea and the Djursland peninsula, one of Denmark's most popular family summer holiday destinations.

The Bay of Aarhus provides a natural harbour, and, unlike many ports, the port of Aarhus, De Bynære Havnearealer is located within touching distance of the city centre. This is one of the busiest ports and ferry terminals in Denmark. Overlooking the Bay, on the hills south of the city, is the remnants of the Marselisborg Forest with the Riis Skov forest on the hills to the north, both offering fine walks, cycle routes and a series of lakes west from the inner city. These together with Den Permanente (a local favourite beach and promenade) make it easy for tourists to escape the city.

Aarhus was an 8th century fortified Viking settlement. By the mid-15th century it had become an important market town, however, as a result of the Swedish Wars and the Schleswig War with Germany in the 17th and 19th centuries respectively, the city's growth was severely constrained only to be released with the onset of the industrial revolution.

Today the city is an economic, innovation and cultural powerhouse and has a reputation for re-invention, challenging many traditional ideas about city development. It is encouraging innovative architectural practices by the creation of arkitekturklyngen, a cluster of architects whose work, together with that of the Aarhus School of Architecture, is injecting fresh ideas, shaping the face of the city. Nowhere is this ambition being put into practice more than in De Bynære Havnearealer, one of the largest harbourfront regeneration projects in Europe. It includes Aarhus Ø, an area of the old docks that is now a new neighbourhood with the eye-catching, white peaked, Isbjerger (Iceberg) apartment block. To the south is the Urban Mediaspace project, which is transforming the Inner Harbour from industrial uses and ferry port to a delightful urban space making the link between the city and water even stronger by opening up the last bit of the Aarhus Å River. The stand-out feature of this area is Dokk1, the amazing library of the future. It is a wonderful flexible sanctuary for those in search of knowledge, inspiration and personal development – and a very fine tourist attraction. Libraries are the visitor attractions of the 21st century.

Make sure to hire a car when visiting Dokk1 for smarter parking. The fully automated parking system gives a real insight as to what all city car parks should be in the future. Here, you leave your vehicle in a light, pleasant terminal with views of the bay, after which it is mechanically conveyed to an empty slot underground. You drive your car into a box that disappears into the ground. When you return your car is brought up to you: the ultimate robotic concierge service.

Whilst pursuing these avant-garde, large-scale projects, the city has not forgotten its heritage, its traditional city centre and all the small things that make a city a great destination – including a slice of humour. The Midtbyen area is characterised by narrow, winding, cobbled streets and a busy street life. Large areas have been pedestrianised including Store Torv, the square in front of the Cathedral, and the main shopping areas. In summer, Viking-themed pedestrian crossings appear throughout the city with green and red figures bearing axes and wearing helmets.

Aarhus has recently been crowned the best shopping city in the Nordic countries with its canal-side boutiques, bars and restaurants, the traditional stylish department stores and the small designer studios and vintage fashion shops in the Latin Quarter. Artisan crafts, handmade ceramics and jewellery fill the independent stores in the trendy Frederiksbjerg area of the city. It is also known for its musical heritage and, especially, the emergence of jazz clubs in the 1950s. In the 1970s and 1980s, Aarhus became the centre for Denmark's rock music, fostering many iconic Danish bands, and is home to a number of music festivals, including the Aarhus Jazz Festival, the SPoT Festival, and the NorthSide Festival.

In recent years Aarhus has become a city of gastronomy topped off with the opening of the Central Food Market, which is housed in the 1938 Aarhus Hall – famed for its dancing restaurant, a venue for six-day cycle races and, famously, where The Who played for less than a minute before the stage was invaded by over-excited fans in 1965. In 2016 it re-opened as a new mecca for gastronomy. Elsewhere the city has welcomed new cuisine with four restaurants gaining Michelin stars, whilst in a former garage behind the main bus station Aarhus Street Food has opened with the Mad & Mark'd Food Festival showcasing the city's fresh approach to food and drink.

In terms of attractions, the ARoS Art Museum with its 360 degree, absolutely unmissable, rooftop walkway is a rainbow-coloured halo appearing to float above the landmark museum. This totally immersive experience is uplifting, exhilarating and thoroughly unique – arguably on its own worth a visit to Aarhus. The museum itself is a delight – and vast – displaying works from Denmark's 'Golden Age of Painting' from the early 19th century together with modernist pieces and video installations. The café, restaurant and gift shop are equally impressive.

Just a short walk downhill from ARoS, in the Botanical Gardens, is the museum of Den Gamle By (The Old Town) – the first open-air town museum in the world opening in 1914 and concentrating on town culture rather than rural folk culture. Today the museum consists of 75 historical buildings collected from townships across Denmark. Besides the historic houses, there are many workshops and shops as well as a pharmacy, a school, a post office and a jazz bar.

There are some cities you love to visit. There are cities that you can simply admire in terms of the way they go about their business or tackle urban design and architecture. There are other cities where you envy the residents their quality of life. Rarely, however, does one city satisfy all of these feelings. Aarhus is the exception. It is a must-visit destination for a short break or, when combined with the exploration of Djursland, with its iconic maritime attraction of the Frigate of Jutland and the Glass Museum in the delightful historic maritime town of Ebeltoft, the Mols Bjerge National Park or Djurs Sommerland a family theme park, can become a worthwhile and longer holiday.

Bringing all these components together and forging a forward looking, innovative and highly creative approach to developing tourism is VisitAarhus. This is an extremely professional, well-managed, body that is the official tourism organisation, not only for Aarhus, but also for the whole region. VisitAarhus has developed an impressive Aarhus City card offering guests a wide range of discounts and free admission to attractions and has recruited an impressive 1,900 volunteers to welcome visitors to the city. In 2019 VisitAarhus became one of the new Danish 'super' destinations, merging with VisitDjursland and VisitSilkeborg to create one organisation under the name of VisitAarhus that is now working tirelessly to developing tourism in the region and marketing it as a world-class place to visit. So, today VisitAarhus represents the city of Aarhus, the regions of Northern and Southern Djursland as well as the nearby regions of Silkeborg, Viborg, Randers and Skanderborg ensuring a seamless tourist experience across the whole area.

ABANO-MONTEGROTTO AND THE EUGANEE HILLS, VENETO, ITALY

Time to live – the largest thermal spa area in Europe and the first preventative health destination

● ABANO-MONTEGROTTO

ITALY

Population of Abano–Montegrotto: 20,000
Population of wider area: 50,000
Nearest international airports: Venice Marco Polo, Treviso, Verona, Bergamo/Milan, Bologne
Key websites: www.visitabanomontegrotto.it; www.euganeanhills.com; www.parcollieuganei.it; www.welcomepadova.it; www.abanospa.com; www.consorziotermeeuganee.it
Icons: Colli Euganei, Arquà Petrarca, GB Hotels, Petrarch, Fango, Pietro d'Abano Spa Research Centre, Abano Terme, Montegrotto Terme, Est.

The Euganean Hills, anchored by the twin spa towns of Abano–Montegrotto, are to be found south-west of Padova. They have been attracting tourists for many centuries due to the picturesque landscape beauty, world famous thermal waters and associated mud and other spa treatments. The area is highly accessible, it has a large and diverse hotel stock, a well-developed hospitality sector and a range of heritage, cultural and activity-based attractions. The Euganean Hills (Colli Euganei) is a group of hills of volcanic origin that rise to heights of 300 to 600 m poking out from the Padovan-Venetian plain. Their name memorialises that of the Euganei, an ancient people who originally inhabited the region with over a dozen delightful, historic walled (such as Vo, Este, Monselice and Arquà Petrarca) thermal communes (such as Battaglia Terme and Galzignano Terme).

The Euganean Thermal Basin (sitting around the base of the upland area) is regarded as a unique thermal resource. In 1817 it was described as:

'Having all the happiness of the Venetian character in its waters.' Today all the spa centres of the destination have been classified with a '1 Super' qualification issued by the Italian Ministry of Health reflecting the health enhancing qualities of the hot springs. It was in the Euganean Hills, at Arquà, which now bears his name, that Petrarch (the Italian poet and scholar) found peace and harmony towards the end of his life. He discovered the village in 1369; there, he stated in his letter to posterity, 'I have built me a house, small, but pleasant and decent, in the midst of slopes clothed with vines and olives,' – a house that may be visited today.

The Euganean hills sits like an archipelago of steep-sided wooded islands rising from the perfectly flat agricultural plain and inspired the setting of Percy Bysshe Shelley's 'Lines Written

Above: Prosecco Vineyards at summer on the Euganean Hills.

Among the Euganean Hills'. Shelley likens the hills at first to an island 'in the deep wide sea of Misery', then he sees that: 'Beneath is spread like a green sea the waveless plain of Lombardy, bounded by the vaporous air, Islanded by cities fair'. Today, the whole area has been designated the Parco Regionale dei Colli Euganei offering a wide choice of recreational, natural world, historical and cultural tourist activities. This destination is part of the Veneto Region. The lower plain is both a mainstay of agricultural production and the most populated part of the region, as well as forming part of the Province of Padova, whose eponymous capital city claims to be the oldest city in northern Italy. This area is exceptionally accessible with a major motorway and rail system connecting to all the main metropolitan centres of northern Italy, especially Venice, and routes to Austria, Slovenia and Croatia.

The Hills are an extremely rural context for a highly developed spa destination, a factor of increasing importance to the area's overall appeal, having been recently n described as the 'decorative stage set', characterised by verdant green wooded slopes whose crags are capped with ruined villas, castles and monasteries. The farmlands, vineyards and market gardens of the Veneto Plain create an arcadian landscape within which the Palladian villas of the Venetian merchants (past and present) sit quite comfortably. This area has historically been the rural escape for Venetians: for recreation, relaxation and revitalisation. This is not, however, the classical Italian *campagne* landscape that inspired the Grand Tour or the 17th century Dutch Masters but an understated place whose tourism product has been finely tuned for many centuries to create a destination of the highest quality, unpretentious, but captivating.

The twin spa resort towns of Abano and Montegrotto are the focus for marketing this area led by the Consorzio Terme Euganee. These two towns have almost one hundred spa hotels between them. The 'Consorzio' is an extremely professional body. It is a private sector, not-for-profit company funded by local sales taxes and direct support from its members (comprising hotels, restaurants and the wineries). Today thirteen wineries have grouped together under the recently established Colli Euganei denomination. Wines consist of the white, with its typical straw-yellow colour and jasmine scent, the Cabernet Franc and Cabernet Sauvignon reds, the Chardonnay, the Fior d'Arancio, the very sweet yellow Moscato, the dry Pinello, Pinot blanc, Red Wine, the sparkling Serprino and the Tocai Italico.

The Consorzio now recognises the importance of the wider tourism appeal to be found in the Euganean Hills as an essential component of an inclusive well-being holiday. Thus, there is an impressive range of collaborative product development and marketing activity taking place throughout the area. As a result, the area is increasingly referred to as an eco-compatible economy. The spa operators in the area also recognise the importance of the countryside for activities such as walking and cycling and local produce (food, beverages and crafts) as part of an approach to a 'spa' holiday for the mind, body and the soul. This holistic, integrated, approach is the foundation of the new well-being concept. The traditional treatments and curative activities are being supplemented by packages that recognise guest needs to satisfy many interests with the key to success being to combine the medical products with offerings of local culture and experiences for optimal relaxation.

The past few years have witnessed a number of interesting new developments, notably: the introduction of a unique range of signature spa treatments and products known as the Abano SPA line; investment in rural trails and routes for walking, hiking, cycling and car touring; and, the opening of the amazing and extraordinary Y-40 The Deep Joy. This is a vertical 21x18 m swimming pool deep in the Euganee Hills Regional Park with 4,300 cubic ft of water at 34 degrees centigrade, allowing

guests to swim and dive (free dives, scuba diving and rescue training teams) as well use for medical research purposes.

The destination spa waters are defined as salty-bromine-iodic hyper-thermal mineral waters. The classification takes into account the high concentration of minerals and the high water temperature of approximately 87°C at the well-head. The water emanates from the southern Alps some 100 km north of Euganee. The rainwater seeps into the substrata at some 3,500 metres depth, becoming mineral rich and gaining heat. This water takes some 50 years to reach the Euganean area, where it surfaces at the high temperatures. In the Euganean spa centres, spa water is mainly used for the bath therapies, in the spa pools, in the inhalation treatments, but, above all, for maturing, keeping and regenerating the spa mud. The spa water therapies include inhalation as well as hydro-massage and Rinesi therapy.

Throughout the thermal spas of Europe mud-bath therapy has been very popular for centuries due to the proven effectiveness in solving symptoms of pain in problems tied to various complaints of the locomotor apparatus. The unique feature of the Euganean spas is specifically linked to mud-bath therapy and thermal waters making it the largest spa centre in Europe specialising in this field. The spa mud, or *fango*, from the Euganean Basin (and applied in Abano Terme, Montegrotto Terme, Galzignano Terme and Teolo) is used for therapeutic purposes.

The sophisticated research, carried out by the Pietro d'Abano Spa Research Centre, has shown that a specific 50–60 day maturation period is necessary for the hot mudpack to have the right therapeutic properties. This takes place in special maturation tanks when the mud remains in close contact with the spa water, which constantly flows at a temperature of approximately 38–40°C. The Euganean mud has been recognised as having therapeutic qualities since the 7th century BC. At that time the area was already recognised by the Romans as having important mineral properties. It is, however, the ways in which the spa waters and the mud are used together that creates what locals call the 'real wealth of Euganee'. The local authority strictly controls the licensing of the collection of fresh mud from specially created lakes in the area and the permits for spa well-heads. Every spa hotel has a specific allocation of mud as well as its own recycling and maturation tanks and well-head.

Above: Piazza Fontana at night.

ARMAGH, FOOD AND CIDER FESTIVAL, NORTHERN IRELAND

'Imagine the autumnal mists rising to meet the apple-laden branches as dawn breaks, the heady aroma of a perfect oak barrel, fermented cider, intimate 5-star dining with old friends (and new). Live our passion, hear our story, and taste our tradition!'

This is an understated, often by-passed, yet fascinating and very pleasing destination. The twin cathedrals (both named after St Patrick) sit on two hills overseeing the Mall lined by fine Georgian architecture of this compact and, historically, highly influential city of Armagh. It is regarded as the ecclesiastical capital of Ireland – the seat of the Archbishops of Armagh, the Primates of All Ireland for both the Roman Catholic Church and the Church of Ireland. It is also central to the story of St Patrick with a strong educational heritage initiated by the teachings of Ireland's patron saint and continued through the ages with the establishment of the Royal School in 1605, the Armagh Observatory in 1790 (part of Archbishop Robinson's plan to build a university in the city) and the opening of St Patrick's College in 1834. It is no wonder that Armagh has often been referred to as the 'city of saints and of scholars'.

The city has ancient roots with nearby Navan Fort – the Eamhain Mhacha – home of the famous Red Branch Knights and the Ulster Cycle of Tales. The Ulster Cycle is a series of stories from Celtic mythology telling the adventures of legendary figures such as the Irish warrior hero, Cuchulainn, and epic battles such as the Cattle Raid of Cooley, known in Irish as Táin Bó Cúailnge. It is one of the four great cycles of stories from ancient Celtic mythology; the others being the Mythological Cycle, the Fenian Cycle and the Cycle of Kings. Navan is

NORTHERN IRELAND

●ARMAGH

Population of city: 16,000
Population of wider area: 214,000
Nearest international airports: Belfast International, Belfast George Best, Dublin International
Key websites: www.visitarmagh.com; www.longmeadowcider.com; www.armaghcidercompany.com
Icons: Eamhain Mhacha, the two St Patrick's Cathedrals, the Observatory and Planetarium, 5 Vicar's Hill, the Cardinal Tomás Ó Fiaich Memorial Library, William McCrum Park and the Milford Penalty Kick, the Argory, Ardress House, Tayto Factory, Armagh Georgian Festival, Armagh Bramley apples, Loughgall, The Mall.

Right: Food and Cider Festival.

lorded as a place where myth and reality meet. It was also an important pre-Christian ceremonial site and one of the six great royal capitals of Gaelic Ireland along with The Hill of Tara, the Rock of Cashel and the Hill of Uisneach.

Armagh sits at the heart of delightfully gentle countryside brimming with apple orchards and interesting villages. This is a real borderland: at times, in its recent past, the area was notoriously plagued by incidents associated with the sectarian conflict, known as The Troubles. As much as anywhere in Northern Ireland, Armagh will be having to face up to the many uncertainties brought on by BREXIT and the future relationship with Ireland as County Monaghan is just a Milford Penalty Kick away the other side of the wriggling, currently invisible, border with Ireland.

The home of the penalty kick, which is now a fundamental feature of the rules of soccer (and has been adapted for many other sports), is William McCrum Park in the former linen-making village of Milford – 2 km southwest of the city centre. It was on this football pitch in this park that William McCrum, the goalkeeper of the home side and son of R.G McCrum of Milford House and the head of one of Ireland's premier linen manufacturing dynasties, invented the penalty kick rule. It was first adopted by the Irish Football Association in 1889 and adopted in the world of soccer a year later.

Following local government reform in Northern Ireland in 2015 Armagh has been incorporated within the council area of Armagh, Banbridge and Craigavon. It is, however, the former County of Armagh that is the main focal point for tourism in the area – although plans are afoot to develop a major new *Game of Thrones* themed attraction near Banbridge. In addition to Armagh's rich heritage appeal the destination has made its name as a centre for imaginative, innovative and extremely well-organised events and festivals.

The Council's small but very efficient and creative tourism and events team has boldly crafted a fine, diverse, year-round programme that is capturing the attention of international as well as tourists from both Northern Ireland and Ireland. The tourism team is always looking at best practice around the world for their inspiration. They have worked hard to gain the confidence and the support of local tourism operators and food and drink producers and, as a result, the destination is fast becoming a leader in gastronomy tourism. Armagh is officially one of Ireland's top foodie destinations, and Northern Ireland's most authentic food and drink experience, Armagh City and the Orchard County, now confidently and expertly showcases its international-class culinary and hospitality credentials with a major series of events. From the May Apple Blossom Weekend with activities throughout the 4,000 orchards to the wonderful Armagh Food and Cider Festival at harvest time, the area's locally grown produce is celebrated with a special focus on the apple.

The attractive, English-looking village of Loughgall, developed by the Cope family from Oxfordshire who owned Loughgall Manor, is the centre of Armagh's long-established apple growing tradition. There is some evidence that apples grew wild in Britain in the Neolithic period, around 4,000 BC to 2,000 BC, but it was the Romans who first introduced varieties with sweeter taste in the first century AD. The result was that some seeds of sweet apples were brought to Ireland during the migration of the Celts from Europe. A large apple, believed to date from about 1000 BC, has been found in excavations at Navan Fort and legend states that St Patrick planted an apple tree at Ceangoba, an ancient settlement close to Armagh. There are historical records noting that the monks of the ninth century Culdee Monasteries in Armagh also enjoyed apples as treats during festivals. By the 12th century, apple growing was widespread in County Armagh. At the time of the Ulster Plantation, in the 1600s, tenants, including those in Loughgall, were actively encouraged to plant orchards including apple, plum, cherry and pear trees. The Cope family encouraged the improvement of the farms of their tenants. Apple growing on their estate flourished and the apple industry grew to become a major factor in the economic development of the area to this day.

Loughgall is famous for the Armagh Bramley Apple, an almost exclusively British species used for cooking. It now enjoys Protected Geographical Indication (PGI) status. It did not arrive in the area until 1884 when a villager planted sixty Bramley seedlings at Crannagael House acquired from the master of the cultivar in England. Owned by the Nicholson family, Crannagael House and its grounds today form the centrepiece of the annual Armagh Food and Cider Festival.

At the time the first Armagh Bramley seedling was planted, this area was producing over 100 different varieties of apples, many with wonderful names such as Widow's Whelps, Sugar Sweet, Foxes Whelps, Strawberry Cheeks, Gillyflowers, Irish Peach, Angel Bites, Beauty of Bath, Honeycomb, Ladyfingers and the Bloody Butcher. By 1921, the Bramley apple had become the principal variety of apple grown in Armagh and today accounts for approximately 90 per cent of the apples grown and processed. For future research and breeding purposes, the Armagh Orchard Trust has planted a heritage orchard of old Irish varieties in a walled garden within Loughgall Country Park.

Alongside the Bramley apple there has been a history of cider making in this area since 1682, however, it was not until Philip and Helen Troughton of Ballinteggart House (between Armagh and Portadown) harnessed the family's one hundred-year-old tradition of growing apples to make their own brand of hand-crafted cider – Carson's – in 2006, that cider became one of the headline acts of the destination and the Armagh Cider Company became established in the marketplace. The Troughton family have now diversified into mulled cider, apple juice, cider vinegar, cider making tours and award-winning cider-laced, fun-filled dining in a converted barn.

Another well-established local family has also entered the cider market helping to consolidate Armagh's fast-growing reputation for hand-crafted, quality ciders: The Longmeadow Cider Company, a farm owned by the McKeever family who have been growing apples for three generations. Over the years they have focussed on Bramley apple production, but each generation has added to the varieties grown and passed on different methods and traditions to the next; from Peter (Senior) to Patrick to Peter (Junior) in order to grow and produce the perfect apples. Since 2014 cider has been pressed and fermented naturally by both father and son: Pat and Peter McKeever. The family originally started out with two craft ciders, Medium and Sweet, adding the matured Oak Aged Cider a year later followed by a Rhubarb & Honey cider and other berry-flavoured ciders.

The McKeever and the Troughton families are major supporters of one of Armagh's primary signature events – the Armagh Food and Cider Festival – held every September since 2014. It is a weekend overflowing with a wide range of highly seductive events right across the destination, many taking place at The Long Meadow and at Ballinteggart House. The festival organisers in Armagh's tourism and events team have enlisted nine Ambassadors (chefs, master cider makers and sommeliers) to lead the celebrations. The events sell out early in the year, such is the demand for the Bramley Banquet, the Cider Discovery tours, the cider and Irish tapas evenings, the Cooking with Fire demonstrations and, above all, the memorable Cider v Wine face-off. This takes place in an elaborate marquee, set amongst orchards, in the grounds of Crannagael House, where guests sit at long wooden tables ready to be challenged as wine experts and cider makers justify their pairing of selected wines and ciders to each of the specially curated courses. The guests are then asked to vote by shouting-out their decision after each course whether the cider or wine is the best match for each course best.

Above left: Armagh Observatory.
Above right: Long Meadow Farm.

BADEN-BADEN, GERMANY

A celebration of Belle Époque elegance with contemporary cultural and
wellness relevance — the European capital of the art of living

GERMANY

● BADEN-BADEN

Population of city: 55,000
Population of wider area: 500,000
Nearest international airports: Karlsruhe/Baden-
Baden, Stuttgart, Frankfurt, Basel (Switzerland),
Strasburg (France).
Key websites: www.baden-baden.com
Icons: Spielbank Casino, River Oos, the Trinkhalle,
Lichtentaler Allee, Kurhaus, Kurgarten,
Merkurbergbahn Funicular, Michaelstunnel,
Caracalla Spa, Friedrichsbad, Festspielhaus,
Iffezheim Racecourse, Gönneranlage rose garden,
the Panorama Trail, Mount Merkur Tower.

Baden-Baden has been attracting tourists since Roman times, when visitors arrived from across the empire to sample the mineral baths fed from 12 natural thermal springs issuing from under the Florentine Hill at temperatures ranging from 115-153°F (46-67°C). The water is rich in salt and flows at a rate of 90 gallons per minute, conveyed by pipes to the various baths and spas, most of which are located on the left (south) bank of the River Oos. These waters have properties which enhance blood circulation to the muscles and ease pain from arthritis in the joints, help stabilise the heart, remove metabolic waste and, in short, keep you fit and healthy.

It is a town of endless elegance, of fine architecture and well-managed pleasure gardens designed for promenades and public squares in which the fashionistas of the time wished to be seen. As the American author Mark Twain wrote in his 1880 travelogue *A Tramp Abroad*, the story of his journey through Europe:

'Baden-Baden sits in the lap of the hills, and the natural and artificial beauties of the surroundings are combined effectively and charmingly. The level strip of ground which stretches through and beyond the town is laid out in handsome pleasure grounds, shaded by noble trees and adorned at intervals with lofty and sparkling fountain-jets. Thrice a day a fine band makes music in the public promenade before the Conversation House, and in the afternoon and evening that locality is populous with fashionably dressed people of both sexes, who march back and forth past the great music-stand'. He added that 'After 10 minutes you forget time, after 20 minutes the world ... Where exactly? By an unforgettable visit to the Friedrichsbad! I left my rheumatism in Baden-Baden.'

Baden-Baden's prevailing reputation for quality and wellness helped the town become the playground of leading cultural and political figures as a place to visit and to live. This world-famous thermal spa destination has remained relevant and current to changing market trends over the past 150 years.

Exceptionally well located, the city sits at the heart of western Europe, almost kissing the border with France, north-east of Strasbourg and an hour's drive south-west of Stuttgart. Sitting on the floor of the forest-framed Oos Valley on the north-western edge of the Black Forest mountain range, it is the gateway to the recently designated Black Forest National Park.

The thermal springs of Baden-Baden were known to the Romans as Aquae (The Waters) and Aurelia Aquensis (Aurelia of the Waters, after Aurelius Severus Alexander Augustus) and came to prominence in the reign of Caracalla (210 AD). In modern German, a 'baden' is a bathing area, but the original name for the town, Baden, actually derived from the slightly earlier plural form of bath ('bad'). In 1931, however, the town formally adopted the

Above: Kurhaus, Baden-Baden.

doubled name, Baden-Baden, to distinguish itself from other 'Badens' throughout central Europe (notably those near Vienna and Zurich).

Its history as a spa destination can be traced from the 7th century, however, its status as a tourist destination was relatively modest until the start of the 19th century, despite being an important seat of religious and political activity. Devastated during the Thirty Years' War, with the French plundering the town in 1643, recovery as an urban centre began in the late 18th century. At this time the waters began to get a reputation for medical reasons and royal recognition resulted from a visit by the Queen of Prussia, after which the ducal government invested heavily in the destination's rebuilding and its development as a spa between 1840 and 1845. This included the construction of the Spielbank Casino, the Trinkhalle (pump room), the creation of luxury hotels, a racecourse, the arrival of the grand duchy's railway and the gardens of the Lichtentaler Allee.

By the mid-1850s, Baden-Baden was known as 'Europe's Summer Capital', frequented by royalty and celebrities from across the continent and America. Investment and development continued apace over the next 50 years to create a spa destination of world-class significance based on neo-classical architecture, grand promenades, places of worship to meet the needs of a diverse market (Greek and Russian Orthodox churches were built) and attractions for entertainment, culture and relaxation flourished, including the Kurhaus with its Kurgarten, the Merkurbergbahn funicular railway and the theatre. By 1912, the destination was hosting over 70,000 tourists.

Baden-Baden escaped destruction during both world wars for two reasons: first, there was no industry, and second, senior strategists and military personnel recognised the inherent qualities of the town and simply wanted to visit or relocate there. After WW2 Baden-Baden became the HQ of the French occupation forces in Germany and home to one of Germany's largest public broadcasting stations, as well a unique French-language broadcasting service. The French military presence remained until 1999. Unusually, the destination is known as an 'Olympic City', having hosted the XIth Olympic Congress in the Kurhaus in 1981.

The destination's 'promise' is based upon 'Urban Life in the Country', reflecting the natural setting and complex topography and micro-climate that makes it a prized, accessible and highly appealing location. From the original vision of the redevelopment process in the mid-19th century through to the current day, a succession of community leaders appreciated the fundamental importance of marrying nature with culture and design to allow the spirit of wellness and wellbeing to be fully exploited. It continues to evolve through fresh investments, contemporary ideas and innovative schemes whilst at the same time ensuring that the essential fabric and infrastructure which reflects the basis of its 150 years as a leader in the world of spas is maintained.

It has a well-oiled destination management team, the Baden-Baden Kur & Tourismus, a not-for-profit company chaired by the mayor that oversees new developments and co-ordinates marketing. Recent years have seen the growth of new leisure tourist markets from India, China and the Middle East, taking advantage of the delights of the town that European and American tourists have recognised for many years. The Russian market is especially strong, building on the long relationship that has existed since Catherine the Great married off her grandson Alexander to Princess Louise of Baden, and writers including Tolstoy and Dostoyevsky who set up base here. The business tourist markets are also increasingly realising the attraction, with international corporations holding meetings and conferences in Baden-Baden.

There is a significant and continual investment in hotels and in cultural amenities by both the public and private sectors, notably the Staatliche

Kunsthalle Baden-Baden (State Art Gallery), the Museum Frieder Burda (a sleek, white box, designed by Richard Meier and dedicated to modern and contemporary art, based on the private collection of a wealthy German publishing family), the Museum für Kunst und Technik and the Fabergé Museum.

Central to the tourism success of Baden-Baden is the dedication to providing the highest quality service standards across its hospitality, wellness and shopping facilities like the Sophienstraße, the 'Fifth Avenue of Baden-Baden'. This destination knows which side its bread is buttered. The close connection between the destination company and the municipality ensures that the municipality delivers an ongoing commitment to the maintenance of the public gardens, parks and squares and that planning procedures prioritize investment in tourism and spa developments.

One of the outstanding providers of this world-class experience is delivered by the Oetker Collection at its eloquent, five-star superior Brenner's Park Hotel and Spa – a true icon of the destination and located at the heart the town (both literally and metaphorically) in a landscaped parkland on the Lichtentaler. Positioned as 'Lifestyle: At one with nature', this lavish grand hotel concept dates from 1872, when it was established by Anton Brenner (a Baden-Baden tailor), with ownership gradually shifting to the Oetker family following their first share acquisition in 1923. This is a multi-award-winning product and has been in the Condé Naste Traveller Gold List every year for the past 20 years.

Two other icons of the destination must be mentioned: the Caracalla Spa and the Friedrichsbad, both located in Baden-Baden's Spa Quarter on the left bank of the River Oos and which deal only with day visitors. The Caracalla Spa (named after the Roman emperor Caracalla and created in 1995) is a wellness complex offering a year-round holistic wellness experience set in its

own landscaped gardens. Friedrichsbad, opened in 1877 as a 'temple of wellbeing', is an historic building and respected Baden-Baden institution located adjacent to the 'new' Caracalla Spa. It offers a unique Roman (warm waters)-Irish (cold waters) bathing experience by way of an immersive journey through a series of treatments at 17 separate stations.

Above: Friedrichsbad.

BAIERSBRONN, GERMANY

'The purpose of travelling is to get to a destination, the purpose of hiking is to travel' Theodor Heuss, First President of the Federal German Republic, journalist and political scientist, 1884–1963

Most of the leading destinations have an established profile that generates high levels of international awareness, which either places them in the forefront or allows them to reside in the background of customer's mind ready to trigger a decision to book a holiday. Other destinations will enter a tourists' consciousness, either from word of mouth recommendations from friends and family or on social media. Some places seem to appear by chance or serendipity. Truthfully, I am not really sure how Baiersbronn came to my attention.

It was certainly not through working in this part of Germany, nor was it a destination recommended by anyone. Yet, somehow, I had registered the considerable reputation of the Hotel Engel Obertal as a top-class, family run wellness hotel and had also been searching for a laid-back, rural retreat as an antidote to a few days spent in the finery and sophistication of Baden-Baden (less than an hour to the north and the starting point of the Black Forest High Road tourist route, Schwarzerwald Hochstrasse, which is celebrating its 88th anniversary in 2020.) So, it was a genuine surprise to discover this peaceful, well-equipped, well-organised, corner of the Black Forest. It is a place that meets every one of the criteria needed to be included in this selection of 50 great destinations. It was then an even bigger eye-opener to discover the unexpected news that Baiersbronn is widely regarded as the centre of *haute cuisine* in Germany.

The destination's reputation is for star cuisine is founded upon being able to boast eight Michelin Stars across three restaurants, two of which

GERMANY

● BAIERSBRONN

Population of city: 12,000
Population of wider area: 16,000
Nearest international airports: Karlsruhe Baden-Baden, Stuttgart, Frankfurt (Germany), Basel (Switzerland), Strasburg (France)
Key websites: www.baiersbronn.de; www.blackforest-tourism.com
Icons: Schwarzerwald Hochstrasse, Schwarzerwald Karte, Lumpp, Wohlfarht, Sackmann, Murg River, Hotel Engel Obertal, Vesperstuben, Hiking Lodges, Tonbach and Obertal-Buhlbach Illiminations, Wanderhimmel.

Left: Baiersbronn.

have three stars – in Michelin terms that means exceptional cuisine worth a special journey – and one two stars – excellent and worth a detour. In 2007 Claus-Peter Lumpp's 'Bareiss' became the second restaurant in the valley to receive a three star designation following in the footsteps of Harald Wohlfarht's 'Schwarzwaldstübe'; Jörg Sackmann's 'Schlossberg' owns the other two stars. The gastronomic accolades don't end with these three superstars.

It is not just these prized restaurants that generates the reputation for this being the centre of gastronomy. There are a surprisingly large number of high-end hotels for a rural destination; notably the Hotel Engel Obertal, the National Park Hotel, the Heselbacher Hof and the Schliffkopf Hotel and all have fine restaurants. In addition, the contemporary designed, family-run Wirthaus zur Sieberei restaurant with rooms, which is suspended above a trout-ladened tributary of the Murg, offers delightful indoor and outdoor terrace dining using locally sourced produce.

Baiersbronn is the main settlement serving a rural area that includes a number of small valleys with their dispersed farming communities. The town is the gateway to the main, typical Black Forest valley: forested hillsides with broad meadow bottoms and once dominated by agriculture. This is the Mitteltal valley with its collection of charming villages, strung out like beads, along the banks of the Murg River and its tributaries as it winds its way, flowing west to east, from its source (the Murgersprung) and its two headstreams (the Rechtmurg and the Red Murg or Rotmurg) to the west of Baiersbronn in the hills above the hamlet of Buhlbach, through the larger villages of Obertal, Mitteltal, Allmand and then to Baiersbronn before turning north and becoming a major landscape feature – one of the largest and deepest valleys in the Black Forest – eventually flowing into the Rhine.

This destination also has a fine reputation amongst walkers and hikers. It is known as the *wanderhimmel* – a walker's paradise with trails suitable for all levels of experience, competency, intensity and difficulty. There are many routes specifically designed for families. It is argued locally that hiking was invented in this area with Philipp Bussemer from Baden-Baden who, at the end of the 19th century, opened what was probably the first tourist information centre in the Black Forest near to his haberdashery shop. Throughout Baiersbronn there are links to the long-distance, more severe routes such as the Mittelweg, that interconnect with local footpaths that wend their way through wildflower and hay meadows, mixed species woodlands or follow the banks of the Murg and its tributaries.

Here hiking and, more recently, mountain biking, is accessible, attractive and easy with over 550 kilometres of well-maintained routes by the local tourism organisation who also ensure good way-marked trails; several with lodges offering well-deserved refreshments for walkers. Many of the trails begin and end in the village centres and a regular public bus service ensures that walkers are assured of getting back to base efficiently and cheaply. These are routes used by local people. This means that the tourist is, more often than not, sharing a walk with someone from the valley making interaction easy and thoroughly enjoyable.

A really fine additional feature of walking in this area are the most beautiful hiking lodges (such as the Löwen, the Sattelei, the Panorama, Forenellenhof Buhlbach and the Bareiss) dispersed throughout the forests of the area – all great places to stay, close to nature, family-run and offering typically good cuisine.

Baiersbronn Tourism is a well-run organisation providing the leadership and co-ordination needed to deliver a confident, highly ambitious vision for the destination. It manages an impressive network of modern, very efficient tourist information centres throughout the valleys; it organises a year-round program of events and festivals – including high-profile tennis competitions and the annual classic car rally and vintage bicycle rally – as well as overseeing the planning, the way-marking, maintenance and promotion of trails and other amenities for visitors.

One of the most delightful, unique events is the annual spectacle in the Buhlbachtal (alternating between Tonbach and the Obertal-Buhlbacj valleys) on 3 August when 50,000 candles transform the valleys into a sea of lights. For over 40 years, this has become one of the highlights of the summer when the meadows, streams and slopes are blanketed with the warm glow of the candles and all streetlights are turned off. The Buhlbach stream also becomes part of the spectacle: colourful lights in the streambed make the water shine. In the build-up to the drama, numerous volunteers work on the project with participation in the 'Night of the Year', now regarded as a local tradition. As the sun sets, thousands of visitors will gather for a few hours to marvel at the works of art.

Kulturepark Glashütte (the Glassworks Cultural Park) in the hamlet of Buhlbach, located at the western end of the Murg Valley, is another surprise package. This understated, unpretentious heritage site is a community initiative. It tells the remarkably important story of the largest and most successful glassworks in the Black Forest using creative, humorous, hand-made exhibits as well as the chance to meet local people acting as tour guides – the wonderful, highly appropriate, persistence of analogue in a digital world. During its heyday in the 18th and 19th centuries this site achieved a world-wide reputation for the invention of a pressure resistant glass champagne bottle – the 'Buhlbacher Schlegel' bottle with its inward concave base – a clever and immensely important creation by local craftsmen that transformed the champagne industry into the global phenomenon it is today. From modest beginnings, at its peak the Buhlbach glassworks was producing over two million champagne bottles each year.

This is a destination whose communities and

local tourism businesses intuitively understand the meaning of quality. There is a real spirit of adventure in terms of constantly innovating and creating new experiences and products for visitors. There is an inventiveness that was reflected in the design of the champagne bottle that thrives today represented by Heidi Seyfried, who has started a new whisky company producing a golden yellow, fruity, single malt in the village of Alpirsbach. Baiersbronn Tourism's website is a benchmark for local tourist organisations and its online magazine is a gold mine of local stories and interesting features that will whet your appetite to visit. There is an old Black Forest saying that goes something like this: 'after a fine meal relax or take a thousand steps' – well in Baiersbronn it is easy to apply either of these recommendations.

Above: Baiersbronn Classic Car Rally.

BARCELONA, CATALUNYA, SPAIN

The charismatic, sensuous and beguiling modernista capital of Catalunya

BARCELONA●

SPAIN

Population of city: 1.7 million
Population of wider area: 5.5 million
Nearest international airports: Josep Tarradella
Barcelona – El Prat de Llobregat Airport, Reus,
Girona
Key websites: www.barcelonaturisme.com;
www.cccb.org; www.macba.cat; www.tibidabo.cat
Icons: Antoni Gaudi, Pablo Picasso, Joan Miró,
Lionel Messi, Camp Nou, Futbol Club Barcelona,
Parc Guell, Montjuic, Shadows of the Wind,
La Ramblas, Barri Gòthic, Jacint Verdaguer,
Carlos Ruiz Zafón, Tibidabo, Sagrada Familia,
La Barceloneta.

Barcelona is built on a flat plain with a long Mediterranean beach and contained to the north of the Collserola Hills, topped-off by Mount Tibidabo: the city's sentinel with its own theme park and Norman Foster's Communications Tower built for the 1992 Olympics. The city's location is described in the 1883 triumphant song poem, 'A Barcelona' by Jacint Verdaguer – 'The Prince of Catalan' poets – a celebration of the transformation of Barcelona over the previous hundred years: 'La mar no te l'han presa, ni el pla, ni la muntanya, qr s'alça a tes espatlles fer-te de mantel' (The sea has not taken you, neither the plain nor the mountains that rise behind your shoulders, a mantle for your back).

Catalans would have you believe that Barcelona had a Mediterranean empire when Madrid was still an arid village on the road to nowhere. Founded by the Carthaginian Hamilcar Barca around 230 BC, it was Roman for six hundred years, then occupied by the Visigoths and the Moors. At various times throughout its history it was planned and developed by patricians and urban innovators. The first phase being the medieval expansion (Barri Gòtic) beyond the Roman walls. The second expansion took place in the area known as El Raval then, in the mid-18th century, La Barceloneta was created.

The next refashioning of modern Barcelona happened in the mid-19th century when urban planning was becoming consciously scientific and rational. This enlargement was designed by one of the greatest urban innovators of the modern era – Ildefons Cerdà. His plan for Eixample resulted in layout where people's needs for social interaction, leisure and health were all catered for in small parks and public spaces. In this area the architecture described as Catalan Art Nouveau (or modernista) blossomed. The most famous exponent was Antoni Gaudi (1852–1926). Today, the Eixample is one of the nicest areas to live in and, true to Ildefons Cerdà's dream, there's always a restaurant, shop, park, supermarket or bar in walking distance. It is one of the main shopping districts with Passeig de Gràcia, Plaça Catalunya and Diagonal Avenue with their exclusive boutiques and finery – maybe inspiring Bob Dylan's 'something fine made of silver or of gold from the coast of Barcelona' in the 1963 song, 'Boots of Spanish Leather'.

Throughout the twentieth century Barcelona entered periods of growth, the first coinciding with the Renaixença – the revival of Catalan culture, political activism and demands for autonomy. The Spanish Civil War followed by the era of General Franco, witnessed major industrial growth then decline in the 1970s. Catalan regional autonomy was secured in 1977 and with it came the determination of the city's politicians to, once again, recreate and reinvent Barcelona. The opportunity to deliver this ambition came in 1986 when the International Olympic Committee designated Barcelona (the hometown of Juan

Left: Camp Nou, FC Barcelona.

Antonio Samaranch, the IOC president) as the host city for the XXV Summer Olympiad in 1992 – the first Games after the end of the Cold War and the trigger to release a new period of inspired architecture-led regeneration.

In six years leading up to the Games the city was transformed. Thirty years on and the city still revels in change: adding new districts, enhancing old neighbourhoods and building distinctively designed cultural centres such as Els Encants Vells market hall, the Torre Glòries skyscraper by Jean Nouvel, the design centre of DHUB, Centre de Cultura Contemporanania de Barcelona, Fabra i Coats (one of ten new arts factories) Torre Diagonal Zero Zero. There are extraordinary parks to explore: Parc de l'Espanya Industrial; the 18th century Parc de Laberint d'Horta and the modern linear park that is the boardwalk of La Barceloneta.

All of this has made Barcelona the complete, charismatic, modern city known for its good living and nurturing its heritage of creativity: with surviving Roman, medieval and Gothic architecture surrounded by great 19th century avenues, wonderful Art Nouveau palaces, a bustling harbour and intimate historic neighbourhoods full of tradition and artisan foods. It is a modern city studded with great cathedrals of sport and contemporary culture intermingled with the legacies of the masters of surrealism and fine art.

This post-industrial city has well and truly reconnected with its waterfront. It is a city with a, well-documented, turbulent history, many aspects of which were prescient of the underlying tensions that still spill out onto the streets fuelled by the ever-present desire for Catalan independence; a key factor that makes this such a vital, interesting and compelling city to visit. In his 1966 guidebook, *Famous Cities of the World – Barcelona*, James Morris writes an opening statement that still resonates today: 'Barcelona feels like an explosive place giving the visitor a constant sense of volcanic energy. Her people are quick and intensely eager to express their fierce talents and emotions – it fizzes beneath the surface.'

This is a city that overflows with traditional tourist guidebooks, all setting out expected and occasionally unexpected suggestions as to how to discover the Catalan capital. Time to step away from this treadmill of information to delve into other sources to inspire your visit. The Museu Maritime de Barcelona produces trail guides exploring Barcelona's relationship with the sea whilst Rusc de Turisme publishes routes to discover the city's the traditional markets. Fans of FC Barcelona will take you on a tour of their favourite bars, restaurants and hangouts.

For a detailed historical review try Robert Hughes' 1992 epic *Barcelona*, or Tóbin's 1990 *Homage to Barcelona*, a 'sensuous and beguiling portrait of this great Mediterranean city'. There are wonderful novels that give the reader an unusual insight to the city. Try the iconic quartet by Catalan author, Carlos Ruiz Zafón. They largely lament a lost city, the city that disappeared with the Olympic Games: *Marina* (1999), *The Shadow of the Wind* (2001) and *The Angel's Game* (2008) and *Labyrinth of the Spirits* (2018). Local journalist, Sergi Doria, has published an excellent guidebook – *The Barcelona of Carlos Ruiz Zafón* – to lead visitors through the Gothic guts of the city. Maybe get hold of *City of Marvels* by Eduardo Mendoza Garriga or Robert Gwyne's rather dark novel, *The Colour of a Dog Running Away* – a title presumably influenced by Miro's 1926 surrealist-inspired painting *A Dog Barking At the Moon* (now in the Philadelphia Museum of Art) and his other works on show at the Fundació Joan Miró on Montjuic Hill.

In the late 1980s I was part of the European Foundation for Cultural Heritage in Barcelona. During this time I became a fan of two icons of the city. Firstly, Futbol Club Barcelona, after watching the 1989 El Clasico with Real Madrid at Camp Nou – 3-1 to Barça – realising that both teams are bound up with the idea of nations. Real Madrid is described in Sid Lowe's excellent book *Fear and Loathing in La Liga: Barcelona v Real Madrid*, as being the 'epitome of virility' under General Franco and Barça the 'de facto national team of the Catalans – the nation without a state'.

Today, FC Barcelona is a global brand, an icon of the city and Catalunya. The Camp Nou complex is undergoing major refurbishment. Its current visitor experience is world class; its museum is one of the most visited in Europe. Museum Director Jordi Penas Babot is now deeply involved in creating the vision for a new museum within which homage will be paid to Don Patricio – Dublin-born Patrick O'Connell – who during the Spanish Civil War saved the club from financial ruin by taking the team out of Spain to play in Mexico, Cuba and New York. His story, *The Man Who Saved Football Club Barcelona*, written by family member Sue O'Connell, was published in 2018. The Football Club is at the heart of tourism in Barcelona, being a major draw for soccer fans from around the world. Its central role in shaping the next generation of tourist experiences was confirmed in 2019, when the UNWTO and Qatar Airways, in collaboration with FC Barcelona, established the world's first centre to develop innovation in sports tourism.

The second icon that captured my imagination was a small restaurant, Els Quatre Gats, in Bari Gótic. Established in 1897 in the Martí Building by Pere Romeu, it was first frequented by Pablo Ruiz Picasso when he was just 17 years old. The bar soon became a focal point of the turn-of-the-century Bohemian spirit: Gaudí, the musician Isaac Albéniz and the artist Ricard Opisso made it the place for discussions about new ideas. Opisso's classic poster featuring these, and other, contemporary luminaries is used as the image for the menu card and website. Romeu surprisingly closed Els Quatre Ghats in 1906. It was resurrected in the 1970s then carefully restored in 1991.

Tourism in Barcelona doesn't happen by chance. It is carefully planned and managed by the

Consortium of Turisme de Barcelona – the body for promoting sustainable tourism – which was created in 1993 by the City Council of Barcelona. It is tasked with promoting activities aimed at increasing the demand for tourism and commerce; managing and performing citizen activities that benefit and improve the quality of tourism; encourage, help and make it possible to support the private sector; study the city's problems with tourism by adopting and proposing measures for solving them, and contributing to conserving the city's natural resources and social-cultural values as well as managing tourist facilities.

· ·

Above: Parc Guell, Barcelona.

BASEL, SWITZERLAND

The historic Rhineland city, today's Swiss capital of art, culture and cutting-edge architecture

BASEL

SWITZERLAND

Population of city: 178,000
Population of wider area: 530,000
Nearest international airports: Basel, Zurich, Strasbourg, Stuttgart and Geneva.
Key websites: www.basel.com; www.myswitzerland.com; www.artbasel.com; www.wickelfisch.ch
Icons: Wickelfisch, Art Basel, the River Rhine, historic ferries, Erasmus, Herzog & de Meuron, Fondation Beyeler, Basler Personenschifffahrt, the 'Rhytaxi' water taxi, Museum Tinguely, Jean Tinguely, Kunsthalle, Vitra Design Museum, the Market Square, Basler Münster (the cathedral), Kunstmuseum Basel.

Anterior, Posterior, Alpine, High, Middle, Lower and Nether. These, together with Lake Constance, define the 1,232 km route of the River Rhine from its source in the Swiss canton of Graubünden in the south-eastern Swiss Alps to the North Sea, making it the second longest river in Europe after the Danube. In its early stages, the Rhine forms part of the Swiss-Liechtenstein, Swiss-Austrian, Swiss-German and then the Franco-German border. In the centre of Basel, the first major city on the Rhine, is what is known as 'Rhine knee', a major bend where the direction of the river abruptly changes from west to north. Here, at the Central Bridge, the High Rhine legally ends and the Middle Rhine begins.

A vital navigable waterway, carrying trade, goods and ideas deep inland to Basel, the length of the Rhine has been the subject of some debate. In 1939 a convention was introduced known as 'Rheinkilometer', measuring the length of the river from the Old Rhine Bridge at Constance (0 km) to Hook of Holland (1036.20 km). However, the total length of the Rhine, including Lake Constance and the Alpine Rhine, was eventually agreed as 1,232 km in 2010 following research by the Dutch Rijkswaterstaat.

The river is the focal point of the history of Basel, having shaped the city's design, fortunes and status over time, and is key to the contemporary quality-of-life of Baselers. Today, this majestic river remains indispensable to the city's leisure activities, and crossing its breadth is an essential experience. There are five bridges in the city, and between them four iconic passenger ferries, Wilde Maa, Leu, Vogel Gryff and Ueli, that utilise the natural power of the river's current. These are still fundamentally part of the local transport system, rather than a tourist attraction.

Basel may be small in size – it is Switzerland's third largest city – but with a population of less than 200,000 it has all the charm of a small town. In terms of the impact of its creative forces, it seems that size doesn't matter, as Basel punches well above its weight, bustling with contemporary culture and cutting-edge architecture, and has inspired numerous architects, artists and writers during its history.

Although the Rhine flows through a number of cities (Cologne, Düsseldorf, Rotterdam and Strasbourg), in Basel there are multiple layers of influence beyond the obvious physical and commercial impacts that dominate the other Rhine cities, shaping all aspects of life and helping to make it one of the most liveable cities in the world. In summer, artists and art dealers descend for Art Basel and the river and riverbanks burst into activity and energy, with water taxis, river cruises, floating performance stages, barbeques, busy buvettes (riverside cafes and bars), sunbathing (Basel enjoys around 300 sunny days a year) and a clamour for the traditional bathing houses, Rheinbad Breite and St. Johann.

There is a longstanding culture of river swimming in Swiss cities, and none more so than Basel. Swimming and floating down the Rhine is now mainstream thanks to the Wickelfisch – a clever Basel invention. On summer days the flotsam and jetsam of hundreds of swimmers share the water with flat-bottomed barges and local rowing clubs, all clinging on to their Wickelfisch.

This story may have been much different, as a serious chemical accident in the 1980s had turned the Rhine in Basel into a sewer. Much was done to improve water quality, making it safe for a dip again and stimulating the creative thinking of Tilo Ahmels, whose idea was to equip Basel's swimmers with a swimming bag designed for use in the Rhine. Tilo, together with local energy operator IWB, emerged with the Wickelfisch bag that is crafted from fabric, light yet tear-resistant and distinctively fashionable, with a sealing system that is secure and absolutely

Left: Swimming in the Rhine, Basel.

waterproof. The river-floaters enter the Rhine at Solitude, below the Tinguely Museum, with most drifting 2 km on the downstream current in a buoy-marked channel just for the swimmers, between the Schwarzwald and Johanniter bridges – a fine way to experience this city.

Basel is located at the point at which Germany, France and Switzerland converge, a centre for export and import, a transport hub for Switzerland and a unique meeting place for three countries, languages and cultures. The city, and indeed Switzerland as a whole, has long been regarded as a 'safe haven', a neutral enclave avoiding the historical, political, economic and societal upheavals that have affected the rest of Europe. Basel was the seat of a Prince-Bishopric in the 11th century and joined the Swiss Confederacy in 1501, emerging as a commercial hub and an important cultural centre since the Renaissance. By the 16th century Basel was regarded for its role in learning and printing and its commitment to humanism, attracting notable freethinkers, such as Erasmus of Rotterdam, the artist Hans Holbein, philosophers Friedrich Nietzsche, Carl Jung and Karl Jaspers and the writer and poet Hermann Hesse.

This city of art and culture hosts 40 museums, the highest concentration in the country, and is where the fine heritage of its Old Town is permitted to blend with bold modern architecture. Switzerland's oldest university city (the university was founded in 1460) with its 16th-century Market Square, extravagantly decorated town hall and Romanesque-Gothic cathedral, the Old Town packs together high-end global fashion brands with small boutiques, antique bookshops and local craft shops. It is said that Baselers are tradition-conscious but open-minded at the same time, a fact reflected in the welcome given to the work of renowned contemporary architects and home of the globally sought-after Herzog & de Meuron.

This medieval city is now a centre of contemporary art. There is an extraordinary collection of internationally renowned galleries: the Kunstmuseum Basel (showing contemporary and historic art and, allegedly, the first public gallery for contemporary art in Europe), the museum Mario Botta, devoted to the kinetic animatronic sculptures and other works by Jean Tinguely, the Fondation Beyeler, designed by Renzo Piano, and the Vitra complex in nearby Weil am Rhein that includes works by Zaha Hadid and Frank Gehry's Design Museum.

Basel was the creative midwife for Art Basel, which has now become a global event. In the 1970s, Basel gallerists Ernst Beyeler, Trudl Bruckner and Balz Hilt created this international art fair. It was to be a great success from the start, attracting more than 16,000 visitors to the inaugural show, which involved 90 galleries and 30 publishers from 10 countries. The introduction of the Art Unlimited platform 30 years later created the concept of the classic exhibition booth with an open-plan environment hosting all types of contemporary media. In 2010, Art Basel saw its debut in Miami Beach and now involves Hong Kong and Buenos Aires.

In 1952, Ernst Beyeler and his wife Hildy renamed their antiquarian bookshop in Basel Galerie Beyeler, the first step towards the establishment of the Beyeler Foundation 30 years later and the opening of the Fondation Beyeler in 1997, now one of the world's most important and beautiful art museums. Based on Ernst and Hildy Beyeler's personal collection of fine works, it is located in their hometown of Riehen, a little distance north-east of the city centre. Here, the grounds of the Villa Berower offered the Foundation an essential connection with nature in a way that would harmoniously unite the architecture of Renzo Piano with art and the countryside. The museum opened in Berower Park in 1997, a landscape of old trees and lily ponds with views of cornfields, grazing cows, vineyards and the foothills of the Black Forest. It is a delightfully restful and inspiring place

to visit with echoes of Louisiana, near Copenhagen, and Hauser & Wirth, Somerset.

Back in the city is the striking, futuristic Border Triangle building at the point where the three countries of Switzerland, Germany and France meet, the outcome of a 1990 architectural competition for Swiss, German and French architects to design a vibrant meeting place of cultures. It includes a bar, event spaces, a terrace with a border-spanning view of the Rhine and, in summer, a beach area and terminus for the harbour tours by the Basler Personenschifffahrt cruise company and the Rhytaxi water taxi.

Located on the northern banks of the Rhine is the Museum Tinguely, which houses a permanent collection of drawings, paintings, sculptures and kinetic automata, which Jean Tinguely called Métamatic (quirky machines that explore the absurd side of humanity's reliance on technology). Tinguely was a prominent Swiss artist and member of what was known as the Nouveau Réalisme group.

Aspects of his work influenced the emergence of animatronics, the technology involved in the moving characters in the world of theme parks. His 1977 fountain brought a new landmark to the city. Built on the stage of a former theatre company, the work of art features ten different characters that periodically move and play with the water to mimic a theatre performance.

So, this is Basel. This is the banner under which Basel Tourism talks about its city. An organisation driven by passion, Basel Tourism is responsible for ensuring its special nature is known beyond the borders of Switzerland. Pulling together many partners and stakeholders to support this effort, including the city council and cultural institutions, it has been creating opportunities for the city's guests for more than a hundred years.

Above: Rehberger Trail, which links two countries, two communities and two museums.

BELFAST, NORTHERN IRELAND

Overcoming a troubled past using inspiring experiences and well-known stories and global icons

A re-occurring theme characterising many of the fifty destinations in this collection is their ability to confidently bounce back from difficult times. Nowhere is this better experienced than in Belfast – Northern Ireland's most important tourist asset. Once wonderfully described on a roadside sign as a city 'walled in by the mountains, moated by sea and undermined by deposits of history', Belfast remains troubled. However, in the many visits I have made over the past fifty years I have never felt unsafe. There is an inner strength, resilience and innate friendship to strangers that belies the internal tensions.

Belfast, or Béal Feirste, meaning 'mouth of the sand-bank ford', is the capital and largest city of Northern Ireland, the second largest on the island of Ireland, after Dublin, and the 12th largest in the United Kingdom, standing on the banks of the River Lagan at the southern tip of Belfast Lough.

A maritime city with an illustrious history, from the 17th century it grew rapidly and became a major port over the next two hundred years, enjoying international trade and using innovative methods of financing to facilitate enterprise and industry. Cleverly, Belfast took raw materials from around the world and converted them into important products that fuelled the linen, shipbuilding, rope making, car making and tobacco processing industries, allowing it to play a key role in the Industrial Revolution and earning it the nickname 'Linenopolis' as the biggest linen-producer in the world. It also hosted Harland and Wolff shipyard, the world's largest shipyard in the early 20th century and responsible for building the RMS *Titanic*.

NORTHERN IRELAND   ● BELFAST

Population of Belfast: 259,000
Population of wider area: 550,000
Nearest international airports: Belfast International, Belfast George Best and Dublin.
Key websites: www.visitbelfast.com; www.visitwestbelfast.com; www.visitbelfast.com/partners/visit-east-belfast; www.titanicbelfast.com
Icons: Titanic Visitor Centre, Crumlin Road Gaol, the River Lagan, City Hall, The Opera House, Political Tours, the Murals, Féile an Phobail, the Belfast Welcome Centre, An Culturlaan, the James Connolly Centre, Eastside Visitor Centre, Botanic Gardens, The Cathedral Quarter, Culture Night, Sir Van Morrison, the Van Morrison Trail, the Waterfront Hall, National Museums Northern Ireland, the Merchant and the Europa Hotels.

Left: Titanic Belfast.

Belfast was always a city of in-migration, a community whose own cultures were influenced by direct contact with the diverse people on board the ships that traded in its harbour. This gifted the people of Belfast genuine stories and exotic tales and fed its traditions of storytelling and songwriting.

Its prosperity, pride and international status is reflected in the city's great architectural statements and its financial, philanthropic, cultural and social institutions. Today, Belfast is a global centre for aerospace, food security and applied new technologies.

The fact that it remains one of the world's most appealing, fascinating and misunderstood cities arises from its many inherent contradictions: 'She is handsome. She is pretty. She is the bell of Belfast City. Albert Mooney says he loves her. All the boys are fighting for her' (traditional Irish folk song). It has been noted in the 2014–2020 Tourism Strategy for Belfast that it is a city of 'unresolved adventure, that has a disproportionate number of fearless creatives and original thinkers where creativity is contagious through many small differences.'

The tourist experience benefits from this idea of the cumulative effect of small differences, albeit that the 2012 opening of the Titanic Museum – one of the world's best visitor attractions – was anything but a 'small difference'. This £100 million transformational signature project provided the catalyst for the world to come to see that Belfast had changed, and tourism has flourished over the past ten years.

This growth has been led by the City Council, Visit Belfast and Tourism Northern Ireland having an agreed vision and plan to attract tourists nurtured during the period of renewal and fresh hope after the 1999 Good Friday Peace Agreement and the end of thirty years of 'The Troubles'. Today Belfast is up there with the best short-break leisure destinations and is a fast-growing business and conference destination in its own right. It is a must-visit destination for those doing the tour circuit of Ireland and the obvious gateway to discover the countryside and coast of Northern Ireland.

Whilst all destinations claim that they offer tourists a friendly welcome, there is something extra special about the strength of the Belfast welcome – indeed, Belfast residents have been known as the 'extra-milers', always going a bit further than you expect to make you feel special when visiting their city.

Belfast's appeal as a destination is the result of the myriad of clever, imaginative, entertaining and inspirational tourist experiences that now flourish across the city throughout the year. These are generally created by local people who intuitively understand the needs of the tourist but are sensitive to the often troubled backstory affecting their communities. Great examples are the award-winning James Connolly Centre (Áras Uí Chonghaile) and An Culturlann (West Belfast), the Eastside Visitor Centre and Crumlin Road Gaol.

The result is a heady cocktail of adrenalin-filled urban adventures on the River Lagan or the Belfast hills, challenging, unique insights into the different perspectives from all sides involved in The Troubles, and an unrivalled evening entertainment, live music and dining scene celebrating Northern Ireland's larder of fine local food and drink, and taking place in quirky, sometimes wholly unexpected venues such as roof gardens with no roofs (another of those contradictions) or a redundant warehouse or church.

This is together with a number of highly creative festivals and events, including the annual Culture Night/Culture Day held in September, a prized, unmissable celebration centred on the Cathedral Quarter. Without doubt, however, one of Europe's most inspiring gatherings takes place in the first two weeks of August. *Féile an Phobail* (Festival of the People) is now over thirty years old and is a vibrant mix of all art forms, performances,

sport and a Summer School around Gaelic culture, politics and society. In recent years this predominantly west Belfast event has embraced the broader heritage of the city.

Driving this activity is a brave, innovative group of local entrepreneurs and community leaders who have been willing to stretch their original ideas in order to create distinctive Belfast experiences enjoyed by local people as well as international tourists. These include innovative chefs such as Nick Price and Niall Mckenna, inspired hoteliers such as Bill Wolsey and Howard Hastings and urban disruptives and innovators such as Liam Lynch, as well as the many community representatives from the east and the west sides of the city.

The undoubted success of tourism in Belfast is due to the leadership provided by Belfast City Council, Tourism Northern Ireland and Visit Belfast all working in unison to create an environment in which tourism businesses can flourish and

succeed. They have worked to an agreed strategy and action plan for the past ten years with the organisations clearly understanding their roles and responsibilities. The energy and commitment of the officers and the Board of Visit Belfast in co-ordinating the collective effort to attract and service the needs of tourists is an exemplar of its type, helping to make Belfast an outstanding destination.

Above left: Belfast Pottery in Cathedral Quarter.
Above right: Mural of Sir Van Morrison and George Best, Cathedral Quarter.

BERGAMO, LOMBARDY, ITALY

Città dei mille, the wonderous city and an Italian masterpiece

● BERGAMO

ITALY

Population of city: 123,000
Population of wider area: c. 1,108,000
Nearest international airports: Orio al Serio International, Milan Malpensa, Milan Linate, Verona Villafranca.
Key websites: www.visitbergamo.net; www.vallebrembana.org; www.qcterme.com; www.sanpelligrino.com
Icons: Atalanta Bergamasca Calcio, Città Alta, Città Bassa, Giuseppe Garibaldi, Gaetano Donizetti, the funicular railways, Monastero d'Astino, the Floating Piers, San Pellegrino Terme.

● ●

Above: Città Alta, Bergamo.

On 17 September 1987, the back pages of the _Western Mail_, the national newspaper of Wales, headlined the 2-1 victory of Merthyr Town AFC over 'the Queen of provincial Italian Serie A' soccer teams, the hugely successful Atalanta.

All eyes turned to the return match. The home side won 2-0 (3-2 on aggregate), but where was home to the queen of Italian football? One year later, I found myself working in the enchanting Lombardy city of Bergamo, 40 km north-east of Milan, where Atalanta Bergamasca Calcio was formed in 1907 by students from the Liceo Classico Paolo Sarpi di Bergamo.

Bergamo is the capital of its eponymous province. _'Città mirabilissima'_ – a most wonderous town – wrote Marin Sanudo, a 15th-century Italian poet, a superlative that has not been diminished over six centuries. One of the most attractive Italian towns, better than many of its peers, it is a 'sweet town of well-mannered people' that is best viewed

from ground level to the south when travelling on the A4 motorway between Turin and Venice, or from the railway. Equally impressive are the views from a window seat on any flight into or out of Orio al Serio International Airport.

Set against the green slopes and grandiose mountains of the snow-capped Bergamo Alps on the border with Switzerland is the highly distinctive silhouette of the UNESCO World Heritage site of the Venetian Walls and Bastions of the medieval Città Alta (the Upper Town). The space-starved historic hilltop jumble of narrow streets with small piazzas and towered architecture emerges from modern expansion at its base, hence Città Bassa (the Lower Town).

Lombardy is the economic powerhouse of Italy, generating 25 per cent of all Italy's gross domestic product, with Bergamo as the economic and cultural epicentre of the eponymous province. Unfortunately, in early 2019 the city found unwanted infamy as the European epicentre of the COVID-19 pandemic. In a typical Bergamascan response, the Università Degli Studi di Bergamo pulled together 27 tourism specialists in a matter of weeks to produce a future-facing text, _Tourism Facing a Pandemic: From Crisis to Recovery_, published in summer 2020.

Since its formation in 1968, the university has led the restoration of key heritage sites in the old city and being enrolled here permits studying in some of the oldest and most impressive buildings in Città Alta. Imagine learning about the economics of tourism in the former Monastery of Sant'Agostino, or modern languages in the Terzi Palace of Saint Agatha.

The former site of the Roman settlement of Bergomum, the city became the seat of powerful duchies and a military garrison by 1182. Part of the Republic of Venice from 1428 until 1797, it was then a crown land of the Austrian Empire from 1815. By 1859, after Giuseppe Garibaldi, a leading popular figure in the Risorgimento (the Unification of Italy, completed in 1871) had conquered Bergamo, its citizens formed Garibaldi's famous 'Expedition of the Thousand' to defeat the Kingdom of the Two Sicilies. Henceforth, Bergamo was known as *Città dei Mille*.

Early 20th-century industrialisation and urban expansion necessitated a master plan, namely Marcello Placentini's, one of the most successful architects in Mussolini's Italy and among the main proponents of Italian Fascist architecture. In 1907 he won the competition to redesign the Città Bassa – the core of the cheerful modern city – thankfully retaining the imposing boulevard, the city's spine, connecting the railway station to the Città Alta. This grand statement was a legacy of the Austrian Empire and opened by Emperor Ferdinand I.

The route is served by a frequent and highly efficient bus, generally filled with noisy, polite, multinational students heading for the university and schools in the upper city. Too crowded? Then hop off at the lower station of the funicular railway for a five-minute ride that passes through the Venetian walls to the Upper Town, complete with panoramic views over the Po plain surrounding countryside and worth every cent for the return ticket. The Lower Funicular has been connecting the centre of Bergamo with the Piazza Mercato delle Scarpe (a former shoe market in the 15th century) in the Upper Town for more than 120 years and is much loved by Bergamo's citizens.

It is hard to believe that the gigantic 16th-century defensive walls that encircle the Upper Town never endured a siege. Walking the ramparts and the maze of connecting stairways and passages is a delight. Paul Fort, an early 20th-century French symbolist poet, expressed the thrill of strolling the walls of the Città Alta on a warm, sunny evening, writing: 'From the bastions, illuminated by the trembling gold of the sun; the blue moulded hills, with their languid slopes came to life in the light.'

The Mura walks are an exceptional experience any time of the day or night and any time of the year – as too is the discovery of pleasant surprises around every corner of Città Alta. Try the unusual custom of touching Colleoni's three testicles for good luck, carved on the Colleoni family's Coat of Arms on the chapel next to the Santa Maria Maggiore Basilica in the beautiful Piazza Vecchia, count the number of times the curfew bells of the Campanone chime each night at 22.00 hours or the steps to the top of the Torre del Gombito, seek out the secret ingredients of Enrico Panattoni's Stracciatella ice cream, discover the culinary delights of Bergamo's recently created m'oro cake, the delicious casoncelli alla bergamasca pasta, or the city's unique take on the early evening 'happy hour'.

This is a city steeped in culture of every dimension. Home to the world's greatest juggler and acrobat, Enrico Rastelli (1896-1931), Bergamo is known for *commedia dell 'arte*, a form of improvised travelling entertainment popularised in the 16th century that spawned the puppetry characters of the Harlequin, Pantaloon and Columbine so reflective of the Punch and Judy shows of British resorts to fine opera. This was the birthplace of Domenico Gaetano Maria Donizetti, composer of 70 operas, who during the 19th century rivalled Rossini and Verdi in popularity and spent most of his 55 years in Bergamo (his body is interred in the church of Santa Maria, his home is open to the public and an annual music festival celebrates his work and legacy). The Accademia Carrara has paintings by all the main Italian artists whilst the Galleria d'Arte Moderna a Contemporanea (GAMeC) is as good as any in the world.

For a city of its size, Bergamo has an abundance of tourist accommodation and an exceptional range of bars and restaurants in both the Città Alta and Città Bassa. In the Upper City the standout places to sleep include the Design Gombit Hotel in its medieval tower and the Hotel Piazza Vecchia whilst every other building seems to be home to a gastronomic gem.

Professor Roberta Garibaldi, a renowned expert on wine and food tourism, says of her home city that 'Bergamo is an enchanting and fascinating city, mixing modernity with its ancient roots. Our city restaurants and bars delight travellers with different culinary options, from locally based to gourmet recipes. Moreover, the recent recognition as creative city for gastronomy by UNESCO has shed light on its rich but still less undiscovered gastronomic heritage making Bergamo an appealing gastronomic destination'.

There is the classy, yet unpretentious, Rota family's Bernabò restaurant, today run by Paolo Rota, a Van Morrison fan and jazz musician, with a delightfully simple menu served in a garden setting. Pub dell'Angelo and Bergamo Alta Brewery serve local beers and wines in a traditional environment, while in the Lower City the Arli Art Hotel consistently delivers caring hospitality with a wellness spa in the heart of the retail centre, which is overflowing with fine shops, bars and restaurants. In truth, after over 30 years of travel to Bergamo, the city's hospitality has never failed.

One of the great delights of Città Alta is that within minutes of the vibrant historic streets

Above: Città Alta, Bergamo.

you can be immersed in nature, exploring the countryside and following ancient footpaths framed by dry stone walls of antiquity, the rocks of ages, on the San Vigilio hill. Start this exploration by taking the 100-year-old funicular San Vigilio's 90-metre uplift from the Sant'Alessandro Gate (at the western edge of the Upper City) to Belvedere San Vigilio.

From this viewpoint you can plot your trail down to Valle d'Astino. Forever a serene, peaceful and spiritual place, its rich biodiversity and farmland saw the establishment of the Monastero di Astino with its Church of the Holy Sepulchre centuries ago. Today, under the aegis of the Bergamo Botanic Gardens and a charitable foundation, the

historic buildings have been restored to become the centrepiece for a remarkable experiment in agritourism and sustainable rural regeneration with the Pick-Up Orchard, where locals can pick the apples and peaches, and the growing of traditional crops such as flax and hemp. It is a fitting tribute to the principles of sustainable agriculture agreed at the 43rd G7 Summit in 2017, known as The Charter of Bergamo.

This is typical of the many innovative projects taking place across Bergamo and its environs that intelligently connect heritage and culture with contemporary themes, and since 2001 the co-ordination of developments to promote tourism across the province has been the responsibility of Bergamo Turismo. It is active in curating compelling experiences for visitors as well as

Above: Porta San Giacomo.

encouraging fresh ideas. Throughout the Province of Bergamo several transformational initiatives in tourism have taken place, notably in the Val Brembana (the gateway to the Bergamo Alps) and, to the south-east, Lake Iseo.

Another example is the restoration of the 19th-century workers' village of Crespi d'Adda at the extreme southern point of the 'Isola Bergamasca', nestled between the Adda and Brembo rivers. The village was founded by Cristoforo Benigno Crespi and his son to house the workers in their textile factory, where they developed this classic company town to provide comfortable housing and services to maintain a stable workforce and prevent industrial strife. After being closed permanently in 2003 and abandoned for a decade, the factory was bought in 2013 by local entrepreneur Antonio Percassi with the intention of making it a hub for innovation and art. Besides becoming the new headquarters of the Percassi Group, with offices and centres for research, it will host the Antonio Percassi Family Foundation.

The Percassi Group are also active in Val Brembana, to the north-east of Bergamo, driving the reimagining of the historic spa town of San Pellegrino Terme. During the Belle Époque of the late 1800s and early 1900s San Pellegrino Terme was engulfed in elegance and splendour, attracting royalty, diplomats and celebrities for its therapeutic mineral springs – Leonardo da Vinci's miraculous water – the quality of its sub-Alpine setting and its extraordinary Art Nouveau Grand Hotel and Casino. Ten years ago, the Percassi Group announced plans to recreate the Belle Époque era for San Pellegrino Terme in an extraordinarily ambitious scheme involving, with a new spa complex designed by French architect Dominique Perrault as its centrepiece. These plans have been fulfilled with the opening of the bold QC San Pellegrino Terme Spa and associated lifestyle hotel, mirroring the elegance and style of the past but given modern, contemporary expression.

The spa gave its name to one of the world's best-known brands of mineral water (now owned by Nestlé), with annual global sales of over one billion bottles. Since 1899, Sanpellegrino Group has been synonymous with the highest quality mineral waters: Aqua Panna and S. Pellegrino are quintessentially 'Tastefully Italian', encouraging the group to be active in nurturing young chefs and promoting Italian cuisine to accompany their drinks.

The concept of the dispersed, or decentralised, hotel – *albergo diffuso* – is an Italian solution for sustainable tourism in small rural communities, one of the early adopters of this idea being Albergo Diffuso Ornica in the hills of the Brembana Valley. Here guests are hosted in lodgings spread throughout the ancient village, organised through a single reception, exactly like a hotel: Cà del Cirillo, Cà Hius, Cà Tolae, Cà di Giustì, Cà di Lesandre (reception). It is also possible to stay in newly restored huts (*baita*) surrounded by nature, once home to farmers and animals.

Located between Bergamo and Brescia is Lago d'Iseo, the fourth largest lake in Lombardy. It is a low-key summer resort and has never possessed the allure of its more famous neighbour, Lake Como. For 16 days in 2016, Italy's Lake Iseo was reimagined by the internationally acclaimed artist Christo through the creation of a walkway across the lake connecting the islands of Monte Isola and San Paolo. The walkway of yellow fabric was carried on a floating deck that undulated with the movement of the waves of the lake and was known as the Floating Piers. The project was anticipated to attract 300,000 visitors, but over the course of the 16 days the area welcomed 1.2 million visitors. The legacy of the project is the transformation of the area, with greater collaboration between its communities.

BERLIN, GERMANY

'Wir Sind Das Volk: Wir Sind Ein Volk'
(We are the people: we are all one people) The words to be engraved
on the wall of the Freedom & Unity Reunification Memorial

● BERLIN

GERMANY

Population of city: 3.75 million
Population of wider area: 6.1 million
Nearest international airports: Tegel, Schönefeld
Key websites: www.visitberlin.de;
www.messe-berlin.de; www.du-hier-in.berlin;
www.fc-union-berlin.de
Icons: Tiergarten, Charlottenburg, Mitte, Messe,
Berlin Wall, Checkpoint Charlie, S-Bahn, U-Bahn,
Brandenburg Gate, Olympiastadion, Schloss
Charlottenberg, Friedrichshain, Fernsehturm,
Alexanderplatz, 1.FC Union Berlin, Museum Island.

For the past 50 years, for one week in March, Berlin morphs into the tourism capital of the world. *Internationale Tourismus – Börse* **(ITB Berlin) attracts organisations representing destinations from every corner of the globe and thousands of tourism professionals travel for this extravaganza at the massive Messe Berlin.** The the idea for a dedicated site for fairs and exhibitions was first proposed in 1822. Fifty years later Messe was developed at its present location in the north-west suburbs of Berlin then totally reconstructed in 1946. Today, known as Berlin ExpoCentre City. For many people working in the tourism industry their annual pilgrimage to ITB is as much about the opportunity to see how Berlin continues to drive its own tourism agenda as much as it is to sell their own destinations.

After the fall of the Wall in 1989, Berlin needed to reinvent itself. The result resonates with locals and visitors from around the world as Berlin has emerged as a constantly evolving, tolerant, open city, overflowing with history you can touch. It is a rebellious city attracting rebellious and talented people, acting as a magnet for creatives, artists, designers and entrepreneurs. This shift has not been without its difficulties. In the euphoria of the post-unification years there was a heady over-expectation for the city that soon gave way to disappointment as the sheer scale of the reconstruction became apparent. Rising unemployment, the delay in making Berlin the capital of the new Federal Republic and, with the last of the Russian, French, US and British troops departing in 1994, Berlin's unique role in the Cold War came to an end. So, after decades of being different, Berlin was becoming just another European city having to face up to the realities of managing urban growth and the über-competitiveness of the global investment and tourism markets. However, underpinning these challenges was the Berliners' love of freedom born of a place that knows only too well what a lack of freedom means.

Q BERLIN is a new event that reflects this DNA. It is a unique annual event about freedom and responsibility – two hugely prescient topics affecting the governance of the world's major urban centres that have special resonance in this city. Q BERLIN premiered in 2017 as a forum of debate and discourse with speakers that have included Nobel Peace Prize Laureate Muhammad Yunus and star architect Rem Koolhaas and the young Chinese multimedia artist Cao Fei with their ideas offering new perspectives on the pressing issues of today. This event was conceived by the City Council and is curated and organised by visitBerlin.

visitBerlin is the city's tourism body responsible for promoting Berlin around the world. Its work successfully captures the special qualities and character of the city presenting the brand of Berlin as a place of freedom, tolerance, openness and creativity; a city that, through visitBerlin's activities, work and governance, is inspiring people to think with an open mind. It is a dynamic, well-resourced, well-managed organisation that is powered by more than 200 creatives, market managers, journalists, sales experts and service providers – making it one of the largest destination organisations in the world – all focused on telling the Berlin story – from walled city to world city – and regularly breaking new ground with its marketing.

Its objective is to ensure that Berlin is depicted as authentic with a unique character and lifestyle; where tourism development takes place in harmony with the interests of the citizens by encouraging tourists to visit local neighbourhoods. visitBerlin is tasked to survey residents' acceptance of tourism by evaluating new tourist activities and overseeing their implementation with the aim to evolve innovative approaches that support a long-term, sustainable culture of welcome by curating a network that brings all interested parties together to agree on future initiatives under the title of 'Heir in Berlin' – a citizen engagement programme to develop ideas for Berlin's new approach to tourism development.

Since 2016, visitBerlin has been regularly touring local neighbourhoods discussing 'Berlin and tourism' and encouraging new ideas amongst the residents of Charlottenburg, Mitte, Neukölln, and Schöneberg. As a result, visitBerlin is now implementing some of these ideas: the annual 'Experience Your City' (Erlebe Deine Stadt) weekend where Berlin residents are invited to take a short city break in the city where they live); an annual survey on the perceptions of tourism; the travel app 'Going local Berlin'; and, reviewing how New York, Vienna, Barcelona and Copenhagen's solutions for sustainable tourism development.

This means that, when visiting the city, tourists are now encouraged to explore and discover the lesser known neighbourhoods: to enjoy local markets and participate in local culture, sports and to spend money in family-run shops, bars and restaurants. The lesser known of Berlin's two Bundesliga football clubs, 1.Football Club Union

Berlin (the rebellious club for the rebellious city), has been one of the first to respond to the call to draw tourists from the usual hotspots. Another peripheral experience is the former Templehof Airport, situated in the south-central area of Berlin. Dating from 1923, the airport ceased operating in 2008 amid great controversy, leaving Tegel and Schönefeld as the airports serving the city,. During the 1930s, the Nazi government began a massive reconstruction of Templehof making it one of Europe's iconic airports. It consolidated its iconic status when in 1948/49 it was the centre of the Berlin Airlift and was renowned for its main building that was once among the top 20 largest buildings on earth – housing the world's smallest duty-free shop. Now known as Tempelhofer Feld, it is a popular city park hosting some major events and festivals, including the Berlin Marathon and the FIA Formula E Championships. In 2015 it became a temporary refugee centre welcoming over 1,000 displaced people. The current plans are for Templehof to evolve as a creative centre for the city with a visitor centre.

All great cities have their signature events – events whose very nature express the ambitions and character of the host city. For Berlin, as a progressive world city influencing and shaping international opinion, there are a number of stand-out events including Berlin's largest open-air event, the Karnaval de Kulturen. The International Green Week Berlin, established in 1926, presents trends in food, agriculture and gardening from a global perspective. Especially popular with families is the hands-on farm offering a behind-the-scenes look at modern agriculture. Each year, a different country is named the partner of Green Week Berlin and is invited to advertise its products and specialities at the fair – in 2020, this was Croatia. In January, since 2007, the latest international fashion trends are presented at Berlin Fashion Week. Sustainable fashion, along with fashion and technology, are the latest trends in the spotlight in an event where the highlights are the 70 fashion shows by the top designers and the different themed fashion shows.

The most obvious of the signature events for this city first took place in 2019. This was a momentous anniversary for the city – the 30th anniversary of the 'Peaceful Revolution and the Fall of the Berlin Wall'. During the '7 Days: 7 Places' anniversary celebrations one million guests visited the city. The programme generated worldwide attention for one of the most emotional moments in German history and allowed visitBerlin to present Berlin as a contemporary, vibrant and innovative city with its reinvention continuing apace. The Futurium is Berlin's centre for shaping the future. This unique building hosts an exhibition with vivid scenarios, an interactive hands-on laboratory and a lively forum to debate visionary ideas to feed the discussions about the future of Berlin. Elsewhere, former industrial buildings (such as the Berghain power station, the old Greissmuehle and the Ritter Butzke factory) have been re-imagined as nightclubs. Art is everywhere: from the pavement embedded *stolpersteine* (stumbling stones) marking the former residences of victims of Nazism to the Eastside Gallery of murals and graffiti along 1.3 km of the former Berlin Wall and significant investment has reinforced the rich cluster of museums and galleries on the UNESCO World Heritage listed, Museum Island.

Interesting re-invention of places abound throughout the city. PLUS Berlin is one such example as a new take on a youth hostel. It is housed in a 100-year-old neo-Gothic building creating a 700-capacity hostel attracting corporate and business travellers as well as the backpackers with its arty design and stylish décor and the luxury of an indoor pool and sauna. The Opera Bar and 24-hour restaurant provides great social spaces with good food and drink. PLUS is found in Friedrichshain, one of Berlin's most lively neighbourhoods filled with arty cafés, cool bars and quirky shops and is a short walk from the EastSide Gallery.

Another fine example of the city's willingness to

re-think and re-invent its assets is at Berlin's first Jewish Girls' School, which was brought back to life in 2012 after years of dereliction, when two of the city's cultural innovators came up with a clever concept that honours the building's past with added new artistic and culinary energy. In 2010, Michael Fuchs, the Berlin gallery owner, came across a dilapidated building for his new restaurant and gallery concept. The building opened in 1930 as the city's Jewish Girls' School. Fuch's idea was to create a space with multiple eateries and galleries. Today, Eigen + Art, Camera Works, along with The Kennedy's museum, have set up outposts on the building's upper floors, in rooms where girls had their lessons. Restaurant Pauly-Saul and the attached Pauly-Bar is there with its rustic German cuisine together with the Kosher Classroom café on the ground floor which completes the gastronomic content of *Haus der Kunst und Esskultur* (House of Art and Dining Culture) on Auguststraße in the Mitte District.

Above: Reichstag dome.

BILBAO, THE BASQUE COUNTRY, SPAIN

From an industrial powerhouse that fell on hard times to a surprising, culture-driven 21st-century city

Bilbao is the capital of the Basque Autonomous Community. Founded in 1300 on the banks of the Nervion River, some 15 km from its estuary and seaport, it is Spain's sixth largest city. Since the late 1990s Bilbao has become the byword for the successful regeneration and reimagining of a post-industrial city. The Guggenheim Museum Bilbao, which opened in 1997, is one reason for its metamorphism from a bleak, decaying, formerly industrial city to one of the world's leading centres for culture, innovation and quality of life. The oft-quoted 'Guggenheim Effect' undoubtedly helped create a new image, boosted civic self-esteem, attracted millions of visitors and generated significant economic uplift but there is so much more to this success story – the renaissance of the city is founded not on this single project but on a comprehensive long-term plan, the Guggenheim being one of the engines that has changed the perceptions of the city amongst tourists and residents.

There are seven provinces straddling the border between south-western France and north-eastern Spain which can properly be called 'Basque'. On the death of General Franco in 1975, the Statute of Autonomy of the Basque Country of 1979 (Estatuto de Gernika) saw the four Basque provinces in Spain constituted as the Basque Autonomous Government with its own parliament. The Basque Country was the first autonomous community in Spain to have a regional planning strategy approved by its regional parliament – a tool which was key to the success of the regeneration of Bilbao and

Population of city: 350,000
Population of wider area: 875,000
Nearest international airports: Bilbao, Santander, Biarritz (France).
Key websites: www.bilbao.net; www.bilbaotourismo.net
Icons: Ibon Areso, Sam Mamés Stadium, Guggenheim, Frank Gehry, Nervión River, Abandorbarra District, 'fosteritos', Athletic Bilbao, the Uskalduna Palace, Dolores Palacios; Ria de Bilbao Maritime Museum; Iberdrola Tower, the Zubizuri Bridge, Santiago Calatrava.

• •

the reconceptualisation of the Basque Country as a European 'city-region'. This was designed to create a system of complementary 'capitals', with Bilbao becoming an economic, tourism and financial centre driving Donostia-San Sebástian, the elegant focus of culture, gastronomy and tourism,

Guggenheim Bilbao museum, over the Nervion river.

and Vitoria-Gasteiz becoming the political and administrative capital.

The transformation of Bilbao has been based upon a bold, imaginative and well-articulated vision which has been creatively executed with the major capital investments associated with regeneration being used as the way of marketing the city. Throughout the process political commitment has been unwavering. Stakeholder and community support is palpable. The impacts are obvious. The quality is outstanding. According to Paddy Woodworth, the author of *The Basque Country: A Cultural History – The Landscape of Imagination*: 'What makes the Basque Country really fascinating is that a traditional culture persists in a heterogeneous society which today exudes a dynamic, post-modern energy.' The reinvention of Bilbao has become a cosmopolitan model for the 21st-century city of cultural services and information technologies. The 'Guggenheim effect' has sent ripples into the remotest Basque villages – including Elciego and the City of Wine described later in this book.

The Basques have long been at the cutting edge of Iberian history, culture and commerce. Basque kings were prominent in supporting global exploration and Basque iron mines kick-started the Spanish industrial revolution. During the late 19th and early 20th century Bilbao flourished, its economy focused almost entirely on textiles, iron and steel and shipbuilding. Woodworth states that 'Bilbao is not only the womb of Basque nationalism but also the midwife of Spanish socialism and the mother of an industrial and financial oligarchy'. However, the effects of the transformation of the world economy during the 1970s were especially detrimental to these former driving forces of industry. Bilbao soon became a city dominated by its decaying heavy industries, a city of muddy slums and an obvious brutality. It had become a city described by Woodworth as having 'a pock marked look made frantic by the ceaseless all-in wrestling match of greed and misery'. The Nervión River sucked the persistent mists down from the surrounding hills, forming lung-choking smog. The river had a reputation as being a navigable sewer – along with Tokyo, this was the most polluted city in the world. By the turn of the century there was nothing but ruination along the river: a decaying, rusting, sluggish landscape.

As former mayor Ibon Areso notes, the transformation was born out of necessity: 'In the face of a declining situation similar to that of other former industrial areas in Europe and other regions of the world, Bilbao had to commit itself to finding a new model for the future, while starting from the existing one'. Seven years later the City and, especially the Abandorbarra District, had been reimagined and became a global exemplar of regeneration. Newspaper headlines declared: 'Wow Bilbao, the transformation of a tough city'.

When I first met Ibon Areso in 2007 he had the wonderfully relevant title of First Deputy Mayor and Co-ordinator of Infrastructures and Spaces of Opportunity, having been appointed in 1987 to oversee the preparation of the new General Urban Development Plan for Bilbao. This determined, visionary politician – later to become mayor of the city (2014–2015) – and architect (graduating from Barcelona's School of Architecture in 1970) has been a key figure throughout the transformation of the city over the past 35 years. His longevity in this post, married to the continued desire of the citizens to see the city evolve, is fundamental to making Bilbao the multi-award-winning destination that place it is today. The story continues. A second transformation is now taking place, shifting Bilbao from a friendly city to an intelligent and even more creative city – the more creative the cities are, the more prosperous they are. Bilbao is now exploring how best to harness the power of the interaction between art and technology as the basis of its new economy and future prosperity.

From the outset the work to transform the city was unglamorous: basic roles and responsibilities had to be considered; policies, plans and mechanisms of governance had to be agreed;

sources of financing the bold ideas had to be found. These essential building blocks took time before the main interventions of change could happen. For many the opening of the Metro in November 1995 was the first of the major events injecting momentum to the transformation of the City. The access to the metro is provided by *fosteritos*, glass structures affectionately named after the architect who designed them, Norman Foster. These modern-looking tunnels stand attractive alongside the modern and innovative interior of the stations. For Areso, one of the most significant milestones in the upgrading process was the transformation and recovery of the Nervión River and finding a way of reuniting the city with its rehabilitated river, turning it into the main structural element of the new city, bringing together leisure spaces, housing complexes and, of course, the extraordinary architectural projects as well as improving international accessibility and interior mobility with investment in the Airport, the Port of Bilbao, the motorway system, waterfront green tramways and delightful promenades and waterfront parks brimming with children's play areas and cafes.

Of fundamental importance to the whole concept was the establishment of Bilbao Ria 2000 in November 1992 to focus efforts to transform the riverside areas of Abandoibarra and Ametzola and to deliver the Guggenheim. Even within the original General Plan for the City in 1989 the scope for a museum was identified. Its location had to be strategic (hence near the Ria in Abandoibarra) and the architect internationally prestigious (hence Frank Gehry). The project was presented by Gehry in 1993 and the Guggenheim Museum Bilbao opened in October 1997. This was followed by a swathe of major architectural statements involving global stars of architecture and design. Indeed, the city has now won five Pritzker Awards for Architecture. Established by the Hyatt Foundation, these are global awards recognising excellence. Bilbao's winners are: Rafael Moneo for the Deusto University Library in Abandoibarra; Zaha Hadid for the Master Plan for the Zorrotzaurve Peninsular; Norman Foster for the Metro; Frank Gehry for the Guggenheim and Alvaro Siza for the auditorium of the Basque Country University in Abandoibarra.

Other major architecture and design statements include: the Uskalduna Palace – the Conference and Music Hall designed by Frederico Soriano and Dolores Palacios; Ria de Bilbao Maritime Museum; the Zubiante Shopping Centre; Iberdrola Tower by Cesar Pelli; the Gran Hotel Domine Bilbao by Inaki Anrrekoetxea; the Meliá Bilbao Hotel by Ricardo Legorreta; the Zubizuri Bridge by Santiago Calatrava; the Pedro Arrupe Footbridge and the Euskaldvna Bridge and the BEC – the Bilbao Exhibition Centre. At the same time Bilbao had to enhance the Museum of Fine Arts, the Arriaga Theater and the Campos Eliseos Theater, the Euskalduna Music and Conference Hall, the city libraries, the opera season, create golf courses, and turn the old Alhóndiga building into a new cultural, social and health venue.

The city's main soccer club, Athletic Bilbao, has also been part of the reimaging of the city. The club's spaceship-looking, bulbous, multicoloured new 53,000 all-seater San Mamés stadium, complete with its museum, now forms a key feature of the city's riverfront visually balancing the presence of the Guggenheim a few kilometres to the south. Since its opening in 2010, the stadium has hosted the European Rugby Challenge Cup final and was selected as one of the venues for the UEFA Euro 2020 soccer tournament, with Spain playing all of their home group games in Bilbao (the first time the national team has played in the city for over 50 years). Replacing the beloved 100-year-old stadium of Athletic Bilbao – known in Spain as the La Catedral – was a challenge for architect César Azcarate but was rewarded by winning the world's best new sports building. The design features thousands of plastic panels, which cover the stands, roof and facade and can be illuminated at night. This has created an urban landmark over the river and creating another new iconic building for Bilbao.

BLED AND BOHINJ, JULIAN ALPS, SLOVENIA

'This second Eden full of charm and grace'
(France Prešeren, 1800-1849, national poet of Slovenia)

Slovenia is one of the youngest European countries, having become an independent state in 1991 after the collapse of the Yugoslav federation and in 2004 (the same year as Bled celebrated its 1000th anniversary) Slovenia became a full member of the European Union.

This compact country has a varied landscape stretching from the Adriatic Sea to the Alps. Triglav Mountain in the Julian Alps is the highest Slovene mountain and forms the backdrop to Bled, some 50 km north-west of Ljubljana (the capital city) and Slovenia's largest lake, Bohinj. Bled is situated on the north-eastern edge of National Park. The town has one of the most dramatic settings of any destination in Europe enjoying a mild climate, a strong cultural heritage and a long tradition of welcoming tourists. Today, Bled accounts for almost a quarter of all international tourists to the country. And it is easy to see why.

Bled has achieved international acclaim and a global reputation for its natural beauty and setting. It is a picture-perfect image with its 14th-century church of St Martin, the pilgrimage Church of the Assumption of Santa Maria on Bled island in the middle of the Lake and the impressive 11th-century castle perched on a cliff buff topping Grad Hill on the north shore of the Lake and the backdrop of the Julian Alps. This, combined with its reputation as a thermal spa, has meant that Bled has attracted royalty, politicians, art lovers and sports people and international tourists for over 150 years.

Left: Glacial Lake Bled.

● BLED & BOHINJ

SLOVENIA

Population of Bled: 53,000
Population of wider area: 60,000
Nearest international airports: Jože Pučnik Ljubljana, Zagreb, Klagenfurt.
Key websites: www.bled.si; www.slovenia.info; www.tnp.si
Icons: Bled Castle, Villa Bled, Bohinj Valley, Triglav National Park, France Prešeren, Pletna boats, Fijakerji Horse drawn carriages, Garden Village Bled, Grand Toplice Hotel, Ojstrica Hill, Vintgar Gorge, Vogel Cable Car, Janej Fajfar (Mayor of Bled).

Pilgrims have been travelling to Bled to St Mary's Church since the eighth century. The rich earnings from pilgrims gave the residents of Bled a higher standard of living in the Middle Ages than their neighbours. This trend continued with the initial planned development of tourism in Bled in 1854 when Dr Rikli recognised the curative benefits of the Lake, the thermal waters and the Alpine air, climate and sunshine. Rikli built modest wooden huts to accommodate his 'guests' and a large health centre on the Lake shore. The well-being and curative regime that was applied by Rikli was strict and intense, resulting in many guests 'reportedly' leaving early. As a result, the local community recognised the potential to create other products that would entertain and provide health guests with a reason to stay longer in Bled.

The destination quickly earned a reputation for innovation, invention and quality service standards. Old pilgrim pubs were converted to quality inns and hotels. By 1900 the bed stock of Bled exceeded 1,000. In 1902 various members of European royalty were holidaying in Bled and in 1903 Bled received the Gold Medal at 'The International Exhibition of Spas' held in Vienna for the 'most beautiful spa of the Austro-Hungarian Empire'.

The downfall of the Austro-Hungarian Empire and the incorporation of Bled into the new Kingdom of Yugoslavia failed to dent the appeal of the destination for royalty, politicians and artists from across Europe. In the 1930s Bled boasted over 1,500 bedrooms, 20 tennis courts and a golf course. After World War II Marshall Tito constructed his summer residence (now the four star hotel Villa Bled owned by the Brdo Estate) on the site of the former Royal Summer Villa at the south end of Lake Bled. Tito hosted a constant parade of leading figures from Eastern Europe and independent states creating a reputation and profile for Bled. New hotels were built such that, by the late 1960s, over 2,300 hotel bed spaces existed. From the early 1970s Bled together with Bohinj grew in popularity with the core European markets, especially Austria and Germany as well as the UK.

The 20 km cul-de-sac of the Bohinj valley, which runs to the south-west of Bled is known as 'the oasis in the Alps', its string of small communities located along the Soča Bohinj River flowing into Lake Bled. Bohinj has a very strong responsible tourism ethic and is an award-winning model for sustainable tourism best practice. This is the destination's main skiing area, with cable car facilities at Vogel offering dramatic views over the Julian Alps. Bohinj has strong heritage connections, being the location of the first ironworks in Slovenia. It is rich in folklore and legends and is the birthplace of the Slovene 19th century national poet, France Prešeren. The valley, despite being a dead-end for motor vehicles, is at the mouth of a railway tunnel built in 1906 to connect the northern side of the Julian Alps with Trieste and Piran on the Adriatic.

Triglav National Park and the Julian Alps are widely recognised as one of the most dramatic ranges within Europe. The park was conceived in 1906 to conserve the landscape and its unique habitats for over 5,500 species of flora and fauna in the Park – the 'best known' animals are the chamois, eagle, bear and the lynx.

So, there is a lot going for this destination – probably the most wonderful setting of any destination in Europe: numerous unique heritage and cultural experiences (such as the fijakeri horse drawn carriage rides around the Lake shore and the flotilla of wooden pletna boats plying their way from the shore to the Island church and its wishing bell) as well as a wide choice of places to stay from grand historic hotels and modern apartments to innovative glamping with tree houses at The Garden Village. This is a centre for world-class rowing competitions and its annual Festive Promenade around the Lake takes this 'fairy tale' setting to new levels of wonderment.

Within touching distance of the centre of Bled is the ability to climb Ojstrica, Mal and Velika Ostojnica Hills to secure the most dramatic views; the Vintgar Gorge is a easy family adventure; and there are over 40 different outdoor adventure activities for all seasons. Bled Castle offers visitors an extraordinary range of participatory experiences (using a medieval printing press, bottling your own wine and historical re-enactments) as well as some of the best dining with unparalleled views.

This is a well-organised destination where the community clearly understands that tourism is vital to its economy, notwithstanding some local concerns of over-tourism at peak times. The

destination is constantly innovating in developing fresh and creative ways to attract and entertain guests. Its heritage as a tourist destination is clearly present today. The Bled Hotel School ensures a constant supply of customer-focused young people whilst the IEDC Bled School of Management delivers inspiring programs attracting leadership talent from around the world to its lakeshore centre. Leadership is key to the success of the destination with a highly committed, charismatic Mayor, Janez Fajfar, and dedicated team of tourism experts working closely with the Slovenian Tourist Board to meet the challenges of managing tourism in a hugely popular destination.

Above: Glacial Lake Bled.
Right: Pletna rowing boat and Bled Castle.

BORDEAUX, FRANCE

Capital of wine culture and UNESCO World Heritage City now driving innovation with contemporary architecture and *The Man Who Measures the Clouds*

FRANCE

● BORDEAUX

Population of city: 256,000
Population of wider area (Bordeaux Métropole): 783,000
Nearest international airports: Bordeaux-Mérignac, Bergerac-Dordogne-Périgord.
Key websites: www.bordeaux-tourisme.com; www.bassins-lumieres.com; www.laciteduvin.com; www.bordeaux-fete-le-vin.com; www.bordeauxwinetrip.fr
Icons: Château d'Arsac, Port of the Moon, Euratlantique, the old Bordeaux, La Cité du Vin, Stade Matmut Atlantique, FC Girondins de Bordeaux, MÉCA (Maison de l'Économie Créative et de la Culture in Nouvelle-Aquitaine) and Fonds Régional d'Art Contemporain, Aquitaine Museum, the Seeko'o Hotel**** Design, Quays of the Garonne River, the Bassins à Flot, Arrêt sur l'Image, Le Garage Moderne, Les Bassins de Lumières, Miroir d'eau, Palais-de-la-Bourse, the Public Garden.

Viticulture and wine production is a creative process. It is an industry that is embedded in lifestyle, all about terroir, about provenance, with the wines bearing the characteristics of their place of production. This is an industry that has long recognised its symbiotic relationship with tourism; wine tourism formed part of the 'Grand Tour' for Europe's aristocracy, while wine trails first became an official part of the tourism offer in Germany in the 1920s, but it was not until the 1970s that wine tourism emerged as a special interest aspect of global tourism.

Wine tourism exudes innovation and creativity and the industry has embraced the challenge to be competitive by combining the culture of producing fine wines with gastronomy, contemporary art and architecture to provide delightful, compelling visitor experiences, setting new standards for the rest of the industry to follow.

One of the most significant trends in its development of the past ten years has been the involvement of internationally renowned architects to design a new generation of wineries, wine museums, wine cellars and wine hotels and spas. These bold creations speak to the interests and ambitions of many tourists, and also satisfy the progressive desires of a new breed of owners.

Before the COVID-19 pandemic, France attracted over 10 million wine tourists each year, with Bordeaux its epicentre and the most famous wine region in the world. The great wine brands, the design of the wine bottle and the concept of the château were born in Bordeaux, its heritage and traditional culture of wine dating to the 4th century.

Today there are 65 appellations, over 112,000 hectares of vineyards and the biggest volume of the world's most expensive wines comes from the region's great châteaux: Lafite, Mouton-Rothschild, Latour, Margaux and Haut-Brion and Pichon-Baron. However, just as this city has been transformed, so too has its wine culture. Nowhere are the modern dynamics of wine tourism better expressed than in Bordeaux – the Port of the Moon and of the Région Nouvelle-Aquitaine.

In the 18th century, the city was one of the most important harbours in the world, but at the turn of the 20th century this river-port city straddling the Garonne River in south-west France was looking rather tired and lacklustre. Once described as being 'the very essence of elegance', the city had lost its veneer. Centuries of industrial grime had to be removed from its ornate medieval churches, baroque palaces and Art Nouveau town houses, but its majestic past needed more than spit and polish – it had to be reinvented. Over the last 20 years,

Bordeaux's metropolis has been undergoing an outstanding urban and economic metamorphosis, a spectacular renaissance that has made it a city to be admired and desired, and now finds it bursting with civic pride and confidence. This is a story that has echoes of the revitalisation of other post-industrial waterfront cities in this book: Bilbao, Nantes, Cardiff, Aarhus, Linz and Copenhagen.

This success has been built on with an ambitious and atypically French urban regeneration agenda, with major projects renovating the built heritage, the bold, imaginative development of whole new districts, such as the Euratlantique, south of the city centre, along with exciting new architecture by world-renowned designers. La Cité du Vin by XTU Architects, opened in 2016, is an appropriate new cathedral celebrating the heritage of wine; Herzog et de Meuron's Nouveau Stade de Bordeaux,

Above: Miroir d'eau.

currently also known as the Matmut Atlantique, is the home of Ligue 1 club FC Girondins de Bordeaux, Richard Rogers designed the new County Court and the 2019 Bjarke Ingels' MÉCA (Maison de l'Économie Créative et de la Culture in Nouvelle-Aquitaine) on the banks of the Garonne is a gateway to the new Euroatlantic district. The Design Hotel Seeko'o by local design firm King Kong is a modern punctuation mark on the historic Quai de Bacalan.

The Bassins à Flot is full of innovative art galleries, including MECA, Arrêt sur l'Image and Le Garage Moderne. Les Bassins de Lumières opened in 2020 as a new venue for immersive digital art in a former WWII German submarine base, allowing visitors to get up close and personal with the works of Monet alongside Yves Klein and INFINITE blue. The Miroir d'eau, the largest reflecting pool in the world, has become ever more relevant as a symbol

Above: Cité du Vin.

of change, continuing to delight residents and visitors on the Quai in front of Palais-de-la-Bourse along with other new parks and gardens.

Hybrid creative outlier projects in formerly abandoned areas of the city also represent an alternative Bordeaux. The Darwin Eco-System is an urban farm evolving in a former military barracks, La Chiffonne Rit is a collective of artists and musicians and Les Vivres de l'Art includes a collective brewery in an art gallery. All these developments are connected by futuristic trams as well as hybrid buses, a bike-sharing scheme and the BAT Club riverboat shuttles. The traditional fat-laden cuisine has given way to a new generation of chefs and kitchens, with ten Michelin-starred restaurants now in the city.

This all means that Bordeaux is attracting fresh, young talent. A centre for research and innovation, this new vitality is underpinned by the University of Bordeaux, which feeds both a dynamic start-up local scene and world-scale clusters of aeronautics and health sciences alongside the wine industry. In 2017, a new TGV high-speed train link reduced the travel time to Paris to just two hours.

These achievements have resulted in awards and recognition as European best destination in 2015 and best city in France for quality of life. There is a desire to make Bordeaux an exemplar of sustainable urban tourism development and in 2019 Bordeaux Metropole Tourism and Convention Bureau joined the Global Destination Sustainability Index, a movement to engage, inspire and enable urban centres to become better places to live and better places to visit. Bordeaux wines are also part of this movement, anticipating and adapting to climate change, water issues, and societal demands by preserving resources, safeguarding the ecosystems, and developing biodiversity.

It is the wine sector where the most exciting heritage-meets-art-and-architecture concepts are appearing. There are the large-scale, contemporary, sculptures amidst the vines at Château Smith Haut Lafitte where a metallic sphere spreads out like a vine flower transforming into a grape and the bronze hare by Barry Flanagan sits above the lines of cabernet. But, for me, there are two outstanding examples of vine meeting modern art.

At Château les Carmes Haut-Brion, the only château located in the city (there are another 20 in the wider area), the visionary urbanist, property developer and alchemist Patrice Pichet has re-imagined the original Domaines des Carmes (the Order of the Carmelites) vineyards and their traditions of craftsmanship, working with nature to create a place of wonderment. The domaine remains a green oasis in an ever-expanding city, the gravel, clay and sandy soils being perfect for growing cabernet franc, cabernet sauvignon and merlot on both banks of the Peugue River. Pichet, an admiring neighbour for years, acquired the land in 2010 then appointed Philippe Starck and Luc Arséno-Henry to design an extraordinary new cellar, reflective metal emerging like the bow of a ship from the bed of the Peugue. It is a nod to the heritage of wine export and vessel within which contemporary artists (Ava Starck, Sergio Mora, Beniloys, and Collectif la Douceur) are invited to use the vats of wine as their canvas.

Settling in 26 hectares of vineyards some 30 minutes north of Bordeaux is a very different and highly personalised approach to the world of wine designed for both beginners and connoisseurs. While Château d'Arsac is one of the oldest estates in the Médoc and boasts a near-1,000-year history, it is home to a remarkable modern art collection, inspired by the passion of estate owner, Philippe Raoux, heir to four generations of wine growers and merchants and the owner of four vineyards including Château d'Arsac. Every year since 1992, the estate has acquired an artwork signed by a major contemporary artist, including Bernard Pagès, Claude Viallat, Bernar Venet, Pierre Buraglio, Jean-Michel Folon, Niki de Saint Phalle, Mark di Suvero and César.

In 2020, Philippe Raoux added *Le Voleur de*

Bicyclette (The Bicycle Thief), created by Romain Barelier, which marks the start of a surprising walking trail through the Sculpture Garden. The Philippe Raoux collection in Arsac of 31 art works is the largest private contemporary sculpture collection in south-west France. Château d'Arsac visitors can immerse themselves in a world where history, art and winemaking intertwine, visiting the Blue Cellar, the Sculpture Garden, and tasting the wines. For Philippe Raoux, the project is 'about touching the very soul of wine: the shared knowledge and pleasure. It is a meeting of cultures: of wine, of gastronomy, of art and of music.' The highlight of the art works on my visit? Undoubtedly the Jan Fabre bronze sculpture *The Man Who Measures the Clouds*, a poetic metaphor of the relationship between man and nature.

• •

Above: Philippe Starck's cellar at Château Les Carmes Haut-Brion.

Bregenz, floating stage on the Lake Constance, Bregenz Festival.

BREGENZ AND BREGENZERWALD, VORARLBERG, AUSTRIA

Nature and life meets contemporary design and architecture

BREGENZ &
BREGENZERWALD

AUSTRIA

Population of Bregenz: 30,000
Population of wider area: 60,000
Nearest international airports: Zurich
(Switzerland), Munich and Fredrichhshafen
(Germany), Innsbruck (Austria).
Key websites: www.bregenzerwald.at;
www.bregenz.travel; www.bregenzerfestspiele.com
Icons: Festspeilhaus, Bregenz Opera, KUB,
Horizon Field, Village bus shelters, Frauenmuseum
Hittisau, Wälderbähnle Forest railway,
Pfänderbahn, St Martin's Tower, The Cheese Road,
Seepormenade, Kunsthaus Bregenz.

In 1991, tourism was stagnating and agriculture based on ageing family farms was in decline, and there was an overriding sense of competition between small enterprises. It was decided that the only way forward was through a joint strategy that brought together agriculture and tourism, driven by co-operation between young tourism entrepreneurs and young farmers. Based on this philosophy, the initiative 'Natur und Leben (Nature and Life) Bregenzerwald' was started. The revival of tourism began with a simple idea – a creatively designed themed cheese route.

The plan was designed to build up the image of the area, for tourism, agriculture and related rural products, under the common identity of 'nature and life', in order to increase the use of local agricultural and handicraft products and skills, thereby strengthening the viability of farms and the local communities; to make people aware of the critical role of the farmer as creator and custodian of the cultural and tourism landscape; to

bring a contemporary style of architecture, design and culture to the area thus making it an attractive place to live, work, study and visit, helping to reduce out-migration and attract and retain talent; building networks between producers, designers, processors and sellers, for marketing, motivation and training; and, to encourage direct consumption of local produce, reducing the costs and pollution of transportation, and ensuring a fresh, quality experience for all consumers including visitors. And it has worked – mainly because this is an area where local people understand good quality and well, thought-out ideas. It is a lively and spirited place yet peaceful and tranquil.

The region of Bregenzerwald, with Bregenz the capital of the State, is located on the shore of Lake Constance (The Bodensee). It forms the western part of Vorarlberg sandwiched between Switzerland and Liechtenstein to the south and Germany to the north. The destination is approximately less than two hours from Zurich and Munich. There is a highly efficient and well-connected international railway service to Bregenz which is fully integrated (ticketing and timetabling) with the local bus as well as the boat services on Lake Constance.

Bregenzerwald is a series of cul-de-sac valleys. It is compact, covering an area of just 1,700 km², embracing 22 rural villages (the largest being Egg, Hittisau and Bizau). This is a gentle landscape of rolling hills and wooded valleys rising to the higher ground inland and further to the east in the state of Vorarlberg where there are the classic winter sports resorts, notably Lech and Zurs am Arlberg.

The economy of Bregenzerwald is based upon the three pillars of agriculture, tourism and artisan handcrafts. Agricultural enterprises are predominantly small scale and specialise in cattle, dairy farming and cheese production. The Alpine farming gives rise to local customs and traditions as well as shaping the landscape. By the early-1990s it was realised that the Bregenzerwald economy needed to be revitalised. For centuries, Bregenzerwald had been an isolated community

Bregenz looking towards
Bregenzerwald.

suffering from out-migration with over six thousand people a day commuting out of the valleys for work in the 1990s. Low wages and high dependency upon micro businesses resulted in the area being designated an EU 5b Area (Mountainous and Disadvantaged). Something had to be done. The result was the establishment in 1992 of the 'Nature and Life Bregenzerwald' initiative by Bregenzerwald Tourism and five years later 'Regional Development Bregenzerwald plc.' Regionalentwicklung Bregenzerwald GmbH was founded to develop new ideas and tourism activities starting with a big opening of the 'Cheese Route Bregenzerwald' consisting of many events in 23 communities and the establishment of new programmes at the College for Tourism in the village of Bizau.

At the heart of the current tourism proposition is a courageous blend of modern architecture, design and contemporary art with traditional craftsmanship embedded in nature and rural life. This combination permeates all aspects of tourism. It is based upon an appreciation of art, beauty and place that is pragmatically applied to create highly distinctive tourist experiences. For example, in 2012 the KUB in Bregenz curated 'Horizon Field' – an installation of one hundred life-size figures by the artist / sculptor Anthony Gormley across the hills in Bregenzerwald. This was an extreme example as to how this contemporary culture approach is applied to the themed hiking and walking trails, the panoramic walks, the summit tours, the cultural routes, the village bus shelters through to the design of dairies, architecturally innovative bathing huts on the lake shore, tourist information centres, hotels, cultural centres and museums – of which there are five in the destination in addition to the internationally renowned contemporary arts centre and Festival Hall in Bregenz. The small village of Hittisau is the home to Europe's only museum dedicated to 'The Contemporary Woman'. This modern architectural statement has been built as part of the new fire station for the area.

In the 1980's the Vorarlberg School of Architects decided to break away from the Austrian National Chamber of Architects in order to bring a new form of locally inspired architecture and aesthetics to Bregenzerwald. The 'Nature and Life' programme became the perfect vehicle where they could implement this vernacular but contemporary approach. As a result, over the past 15 years, Bregenzerwald has become a focal point and highly respected centre for modern architecture based upon strong bold lines, the use of local timber and stone and clear functionality.

Over the past 10 years following the decision by the destination to adopt this focused approach to tourism there has been a burst of investment by local families: for example, the Hotel Post has been a family-owned and managed hotel since 1958 but has now been re-invented as a boutique and luxury wellness hotel together with the Hotel Krone, Romantik Das Schiff, Gams Hotel Bezau, Wellness Linde, the Damulser Hof and the Sonne Lifestyle Hotel.

Local agricultural produce is promoted to visitors in a number of ways: regular culinary weeks with local products held by restaurants; annual tasting and selling exhibitions; boutique 'Bauernkasten' for agricultural produce, located in restaurants and hotels; and the special 'Bauernfruhstuck' (farmers' breakfast) available in cafes, hotels and restaurants across the destination.

Bregenz is the cultural hub and centre of Vorarlberg and drives the cultural many of the cultural initiatives of Bregenzerwald. In addition to the KUB, the international standard contemporary arts centre, there is the extraordinary Bregenz Festival and opera, which has been running since 1946. Its most iconic feature is the biannual outdoor opera held in July and August on the world's largest 'floating stage' situated on Lake Constance at the waterfront in Bregenz. Every two years a different opera is produced by an internationally renowned director and supported by the Vienna Symphony Orchestra which relocates to Bregenz for the duration of the Festival.

The newly developed harbour area in Bremerhaven.

BREMERHAVEN, GERMANY

Transformation of a struggling cold-water port into the wonder of the German north coast

● BREMERHAVEN

GERMANY

Population of city: 115,000
Population of wider area: 300,000
Nearest international airports: Bremen, Hamburg
Key websites: www.bremerhaven.de
Icons: Havenwelten – Harbour Worlds, Columbus Quay, Alfred Wenger Institute, Klimahaus, German National Emigration Museum, German National Maritime Museum, SAIL, Sail City, River Weser, Zoo am Meer.

Throughout this book there is a recurring theme of places that have, out of necessity, re-invented and undertaken a journey of recent transformation in order to become a great place to visit. This is the remarkable story of the transformation of Bremerhaven from an economically deprived coldwater port, on the eastern bank of the River Weser, some 50 km north of Bremen and 30 km from the open sea, with very limited touristic appeal in the mid-1990s, into a thriving, vibrant and attractive tourism destination. The transformational process took place over a period of 15 years and was supported by a unique public sector collaboration involving financial and political support of the Federal, State and Local governments and driven by strong, determined civic leaders who put in place a radical new way of working together to make it happen.

The vision was based upon the development of a cluster of, family-friendly visitor attractions in a small area, all built around the maritime heritage and marine expertise embedded in the DNA of the local community and the research expertise in the town's university and associated research institutions. The result is Havenwelten (Harbour Worlds), an attractive well-defined area adjacent to the commercial centre of Bremerhaven.

The German Federal Republic has 16 states (Länder) – three of which are city states. For historic reasons Bremen is one of three city states in Germany (along with Berlin and Hamburg). The State of Bremen is formed by the cities of Bremen and Bremerhaven (and formally known as The Free Hanseatic City of Bremen) with Bremerhaven also functioning as a city in its own right. Both cities are completely surrounded by the State of Saxony.

Although there had been a smaller settlement in the area since the 12th century, the city of Bremerhaven was effectively founded in 1827 by Bremen as an enclave to ensure future access to the North Sea with its economy dominated by three economic pillars: international trade, shipbuilding and fishing. Employment and population peaked in the 1930s.

A cruise ship terminal was originally built as a base for the express trans-Atlantic, 'Blue Ribbon' winning steam ships built by Norddeutscher Lloyd (today Hapag-Lloyd AG), the SS Bremen, SS Europa and SS Columbus and, as a result, It has been a major port for emigration in Europe – between 1830 and 1974 seven million emigrants departed through the city's harbour. This gave rise to the Columbus Quay being known as 'the quay of tears, hope and happiness.' Although Bremerhaven was very heavily bombed by Allied forces during WWII vital areas of its port remained undamaged. In the post-war period the city revived and flourished until, firstly, the decline of deep sea fishing in the 1970s and after the Cold War the repatriation of US Armed Forces from the city; then, secondly, the economic crisis of the mid-1980s. This resulted in the collapse of major companies and severe economic crisis in the State of Bremen, which in turn resulted in unprecedented levels of unemployment in

Bremerhaven in 1985 with the city recording its lowest population ever. Today the city is the largest city on the North Sea Coast of Germany, and its economy is flourishing.

It was not until 1975 that the first tourist activity really took off, when Buro Bremerhaven-Werburg begun its work to promote the seaport as a destination. It was in the early 1990s that the first ideas to develop the city as a major tourism destination really developed momentum based on land around the Old Harbour and the Weser Dyke. The original idea was for an 'American-style' entertainment district. Early proposals for an extravagant 'artificial world' produced a huge community outcry that the city's maritime heritage story was being ignored. Further plans by international consultants ended in stalemate with a public referendum on the future plans for tourism resulting in City Council deciding 'to take the fate of Bremerhaven into its own hands' by setting up its own tourism development company. So, just 20 years ago the remarkable journey of transformation began in earnest. By the end of 2000 the City Council had approved the masterplan for the area with the Havenwelt as the focal point for tourism. In 2003 the regeneration program began with full public support and was re-christened 'Havenwelten'. As Mayor Jörg Schultz said: 'I was delighted with the idea of opening up the city towards the water, revitalising derelict industrial sites and showing he people of Bremerhaven 'we can do it.'

From the outset the transformational process was planned as a partnership with success was predicated upon all the public sector organisations and bodies (federal, state, municipality) working together with the private sector investors, developers and operators in a unique way. Over the period 2004 – 2014 the original vision for Havenwelten regeneration was achieved making this city one of the most interesting and surprising tourism destinations in Northern Europe. The key building blocks of this success are:

- Klimahaus Bremerhaven 8° Ost, which is widely regarded as 'the greatest attraction of Havenwelt – the symbol of a city that has re-invented itself.'. It is the most strikingly beautiful of buildings. Its external form looks as if it is the most glamorous, futuristic, cruise ships moored in the harbour. Indeed, the key to the success of the Klimahaus is probably that people just love it inside and outside. The experience is based on a unique journey around the world following the 8° of longitude involving an emotional, interactive, immersive journey through five continents showing how weather and climate changes affect our way of life. The idea for the project dates back to 2000 and a concept involving the Bremerhaven-based Alfred Wegener Institute for Polar and Marine Research. Innovative building design and the use of environmentally sound technology and building methods have created an exterior that is also a light art installation. It is stunning. On opening it was hailed as 'a flagship of German environmental policies' – later endorsed by Chancellor Merkel who enthused that, 'you simply have to go there.'

- The German National Maritime Museum, located in the Old Harbour, which is officially the National Maritime Museum of the Federal Republic of Germany and highly regarded as a scientific and research centre of excellence as well as a visitor attraction. Although originally established in 1975, the Havenwelten project created the opportunity to extend and expand the Museum to include a range of ocean-going coastal vessels, a recovered U-Boat and the opening of the 'Seute Deern' – a large wooden sailing ship – as a restaurant serving theme meals and banquets.

- The Mediterrano Shopping Centre with a covered retail experience in a Mediterranean style. It was originally a controversial development project seen by residents as out-of-character and appearing to be contrary to the overall design

principles for the regeneration of the area. In 2008 it opened and today its characteristic rooftop dome has become one of the icons of the city.

- The design for the Bremerhaven SAIL City was inspired by its spectacular location on the Weser Dyke and the city's maritime heritage. This is a remarkable 'spinnaker-shaped', 150-metre-high, twenty-storey building containing a hotel, offices, the STROM restaurant, conference centre all topped with a crow's nest of a viewing platform.
- The Zoo am Meer dates back to 1913, when it opened as The North Sea Aquarium. Its focus has always been upon a mix of Nordic and aquatic animals and it had specialised in breeding Polar Bears. By the 1990s the Zoo was outdated. In 2004 it re-opened as a 'zoo without bars' and it was re-named 'Sea Zoo Meer'.

- The German National Emigration Centre was the first new attraction to open in the Havenwelten area and soon won 'European Museum of the Year'. The idea of a museum dedicated to German emigration had been greeted with scepticism for many years, however, a locally-led 'Friends' group was established to promote this project to recognise the lives of the 7 m who emigrated through Bremerhaven between 1830–1974.

Above: The Klimahaus.

CARDIFF, WALES

Victorian coal metropolis for the world to 21st-century contemporary capital for Wales

On the bookshelf are three collectors' items, *maent yn eistedd wrth ymyl ei gilydd*, sitting side-by-side. One is the 1946 Ward Lock Illustrated Red Guidebook *Cardiff and South Wales*; next to it is the official program for Cardiff City v Real Madrid in the first leg of the European Cup Winner's Cup quarter final, 1971; and third, my wife's book on Iorwerth C. Peate in the Writers of Wales series by the University of Wales Press. Put them together and you have the building blocks of my love of Cardiff.

My first experience of Cardiff (capital of Wales since 1955) was on 10 March 1971: a visit to Ninian Park to rock and roll with a crowd of 50,000 celebrating the Bluebirds beating Real Madrid 1-0 in the European Cup Winner's Cup. The trip up from Swansea with a university friend included a pre-match glass of the exotically named, Italian-influenced soft drink sarsaparilla, made with Charlie Jones' secret recipe in his bar in Morgan's Arcade – one of Cardiff's many Victorian arcades. Post-match

Cardiff Bay.

WALES

CARDIFF

Population of the city: 480,000
Population of wider area: 1.5 million
Nearest international airports: Cardiff Wales, Bristol International, Heathrow, Birmingham International.
Key websites: www.visitwales.com; www.visitcardiff.com; www.cardiff.gov.uk
Icons: The Principality Stadium, Wales Millennium Centre, Cardiff City FC, Cardiff Rugby, Cardiff Arms Park, Cardiff Devils Ice Hockey, Cardiff Castle, Castell Coch, Bute Park, St David's National Concert Hall of Wales, the Coal Exchange, Cardiff Barrage and Bay, Rivers Taff, Ely and Rhymney, Llandaff Cathedral.

it was back to the Great Western Hotel, an imposing 19th-century Gothic building next to Central Station, the regular venue for Cardiff's legendary Icon Jazz and a pint of the equally iconic, locally brewed Brains Dark. Heady times.

Iorwerth C. Peate's outstanding achievement was to be the visionary who created the National Folk Museum at St. Fagans, just north of the city centre, that opened in 1948 on land donated by the Earl of Plymouth that included St. Fagan's Castle and acres of woodland and farmland on high ground overlooking the city. Peate, who promoted the academic study of folk life, dreamt of an open-air museum in Wales based on the Scandinavian model, where the visitor could view the way of life of past ages 'to provide a strong foundation and a healthy environment for the future of their people', linking history to the present, not preserved under glass. Although formally branded as the Wales National Museum of History, the folk of Wales still fondly refer to it as St. Fagan's, THE Welsh Folk Museum, and it remains a popular and well-loved visitor attraction. You can change a name, but you cannot change an ideal. It was in this estate filled with collective national memories, traditions and identity that this Englishman first worked in Wales.

The Ward Lock guidebook, published just after the war, described Cardiff as 'the metropolis of Wales and the first coal port in the world with much to interest the visitor in its broad streets, covered arcades, fine public buildings and its pleasant parks and gardens'.

Many of the broad streets in the city centre are now pedestrianised. Tree-lined Cathedral Road, with its 19th-century villas, is an impressive drive into the city centre. The avenue links historic Llandaff, birthplace of Roald Dahl, with its early Christian heritage and Eglwys Gadeiriol Llandaf: the Cathedral Church of Saints Peter and Paul with Saints Dyfrig, Teilo and Euddogwy. Dating from the Norman period, the devastation of the cathedral on 2 January 1941 caused by the explosion of a German landmine resulted in its rebuild in the 1950s, its spire a prominent landmark to the north of the city.

Local writer Peter Finch describes Cardiff as 'the lozenge-shaped city with water to the south, hills to the north, a city of rhomboid sprawl with not one but three rivers running through it' – the Taff, a river once blackened by industry that now runs with salmon and trout, the Ely and the Rhymney. Fishing for salmon in the centre of a capital city? Now that is a very 'diff experience. Its physical development was constrained by Caerphilly Mountain, the southern escarpment of the south Wales coalfield and the Bristol Channel, the 3 m rise and fall of its tides belying the fact that Cardiff became a great harbour.

Muscular plans for the city have appeared regularly, even before the first million-pound cheque changed hands in 1904 in the famous Cardiff Coal Exchange. The Exchange building opened in 1888 as the Coal and Shipping Exchange to be used as a market floor and office building for trading in coal in Cardiff, later becoming a hub of the global coal trade and the city's prosperous shipping industry. Today, it has been transformed into a boutique hotel whose impressive trading hall is a unique venue for events and has hosted gigs by the Arctic Monkeys, Manic Street Preachers, Stereophonics and Van Morrison.

As the Ward Lock guidebook states, Cardiff was a city of fine public parks. It still is, especially Bute Park and Llandaff Fields, one of the city's finest Victorian legacies – Cardiff is essentially a Victorian invention. At the end of the 18th century, Cardiff was little more than a small market town that had hardly changed over three centuries, complete with its medieval street plan enclosed by the borough walls and overseen by its castle – a Norman keep on a Roman footprint – but was to be transformed during the course of the 19th century. The metamorphosis was fuelled by the exportation of coal that created wealth for a few, notably the Bute Family, especially the 3rd Marquis of Bute, to enact a bold vision for the city. His plans for boulevards, covered arcades, broad sweeps of greenery, fine villas and eclectic architecture define the contemporary city.

The vision was brought to life by the architect William Burges and the designer William Morris. The collaboration gave the city an exotic makeover and the reimagining of not one but two fantasy castles – Castell Coch and Cardiff Castle. Bute's patronage created distinguished architecture at the domestic and civic levels, peppered with statement buildings such as Park House, the Coal Exchange, Insole Court, the Great Western Hotel and, of course, the splendid covered arch-roofed arcades filled

with independent boutiques, specialist shops and workspaces for the city's creatives.

The 20th century brought the monumental to Cardiff. Earlier plans for Cathays Park, hitherto agricultural land, to become the civic centre were curtailed until Lord Bute agreed to sell 60 acres of the park to Cardiff Corporation in 1898. In less than 10 years, City Hall, with its wonderful Gallery of Welsh Heroes, and the Law Courts had been opened. The grand neoclassical statement of the National Museum of Wales came some 20 years later, followed by Glamorgan County Hall, the Temple of Peace and Cardiff University.

The youthful tradition of the saltwater city looking outward to the world with modern aspirations underwent another reinvention in the 1990s, bold legislation dramatically transforming the desperate wasteland of the abandoned docks and steel mills of south Cardiff. The 1960s had seen the wholescale destruction of large areas of the Bay and the displacement of the community, followed in the 1970s and '80s by a new influx of refugees from conflicts around the world. The potential to regenerate the area to mirror what had happened in Baltimore Harbour in the USA would be limited by the tidal nature of Cardiff Bay, exposing unappealing mudflats as the backdrop for future development. However, this inspired new legislation in 1993 to construct the Cardiff Bay Barrage across the mouths of the Taff and Ely rivers and create a 200-hectare freshwater lake in time to celebrate the opening of the Senedd, home of the Welsh Government, and the Wales Millennium Centre, now one of the world's leading cultural venues, in 1999.

Water taxis ply the Taff from the Castle to Mermaid

Left: Sign at Tafwyl, Cardiff.
Above: The Merchant Seaman's Memorial in Cardiff Bay.

Quay in the Bay. The Norwegian Church, the Pierhead Building, pubs with fine maritime names, robust and solid buildings that were banks and a Customs House together with historic coal stathes emerging from the water of the Bay are reminders of the once great seaport. These echoes of the past mix with a vibrant collection of modern restaurants, bars, the Techniquest Science Centre and a showcase of Welsh arts and crafts at Craft in the Bay.

Cardiff never made it to be European Capital of Culture in 2008. That was disappointing, but it stirred the desire of the capital to celebrate its rich Welsh culture, the multicultural lives of its port city residents, its international status and its many languages. The Welsh language flourishes, as it should in the capital city. Few cities the size of Cardiff can claim to have hosted a Champion's League final, the Rugby World Cup, the Cricket World Cup, be home to first-class soccer, rugby, ice hockey and cricket teams and have a heritage in baseball. The city has welcomed NATO, hosted the National Eisteddfod of Wales (the pre-eminent celebration of literature, music and poetry in the Welsh language), Tafwyl has become the city's annual expression of all things Welsh and the BBC Cardiff Singer of the World has been the launchpad of many global opera stars. The Principality Stadium, the city's cathedral of sport, located on the eastern bank of the River Taff touching the city centre, is a Mecca for some of the biggest bands in the world, including the Rolling Stones, Bruce Springsteen, Tina Turner, Beyoncé, Spice Girls and Rod Stewart.

Local heroes ride high in Cardiffian's hall of fame. Among the many there is Percy Bush, a Welsh international rugby player and local schoolmaster until 1910, who became British Vice-Consul in Nantes and was awarded the Médaille d'Argent de la Reconnaissance Française, his pacifist sister, Ethel Maud, known for her 'selfless devotion to World peace, who gave herself with reserve of the cause of peace and the ideals of the League of Nations' – whose Welsh HQ was on Cathedral Road – the pugilist Peerless Jim Driscoll, poets

R. S. Thomas and Danny Abse, Ernest Willows, the aviation pioneer, songstress Shirley Bassey and the legendary blues guitarist Vic Parker, both from Tiger Bay, Cardiff's aforementioned historic docklands.

Trevor Fishlock, one of Wales' most loved English-language storytellers, says of Cardiff, 'this is a genial city on a human scale, intimate, easy and coherent – a sense of opportunity and history. The salmon-stream Taff rambles through the heart of the city drawing the whole story of Cardiff together – from the valleys, through Tiger Bay to the drama of the reinvented Cardiff Bay. Cardiff is the necessary city, integral with Wales and speaking with Wales' distinctive voice to Europe and the world.' He is right, and this is all part of what makes the place great for the visitor.

It is a city that invites its guests to wander and explore its village-like neighbourhoods, stroll through Roath Park with its 1915 lighthouse, constructed in the lake with a scale model of the *Terra Nova* ship to commemorate Captain Scott's ill-fated voyage to the Antarctic that departed from Cardiff in 1910, or take a water taxi across the Bay, stepping out over the River Ely on Pont-y-Werin to Penarth – Cardiff's seaside resort. Pontcanna, just off Cathedral Road, has the Halfway pub – no surprise, as it is located halfway between the city and Llandaff – and has become a Welsh-bohemian hub of artisan shops, interesting eateries and art studios. The multicultural Canton neighbourhood has a bustling art scene, with The Printhaus artist community and Chapter Arts Centre complemented by interesting places to eat along Cowbridge Road East.

In 2021, Cardiff Council announced plans for the next phase of the development of this most liveable and attractive of capital cities. As a result, Cardiff will continue to evolve as a better place to live and a great place to visit, with new amenities, attractive walking and cycling routes and well-designed public spaces all helping to drive the economy and reputation of the wider city region and to flourish in its embrace of the Welsh language and culture of the nation it serves as the capital.

Llandaff Cathedral, Cardiff.

CATALUNYA, SPAIN

An homage to Catalunya: modernity with history, rural with cosmopolitan, coastal with mountains, artisan with style, tradition with innovation

CATALUNYA

SPAIN

Population of city: 1.7 million
Population of wider area: 5.5 million
Nearest international airports: Josep Tarradella Barcelona – El Prat de Llobregat Airport, Reus, Girona.
Key websites: www.act.gencat.cat; www.catalunya.com; www.barcelonaturisme.com
Icons: Costa Brava, Barcelona, Costa del Maresme, Costa de Garraf, Costa Daurada, Terres de Lleida, High Pyrenees Antoni Gaudi, Pablo Picasso, Joan Miró, Futbol Club Barcelona, Penedés.

Catalans are one of Europe's most ancient of peoples who, over the centuries, have enjoyed varying degrees of sovereignty, endured waves of external influences (from the Iberians and the Celts to the Romans, Visigoths and the Moors) and have developed their own distinctive character, language, laws, institutions and identity.

Since 1983 and the passing of the Linguistic Normalisation Law, the process of reinstating use of Catalan has been accelerated such that today 68% of the population speaks Catalan. In the Welsh language there is a popular phrase *Yma o hyd* – meaning 'against all the odds we are still here' – for the Catalans *encara som aquí* evokes the same sentiment.

Catalans take pride in the fact that they are amongst the longest living people in the world, which they attribute to good environmental conditions: a healthy diet, good health and social services and a lifestyle that balances hard work with plenty of leisure time. They have traditionally placed high value on the fact that they have distinguished themselves with their capacity for enterprise, improvisation and innovation within the context of a well-developed civil society. The ability to innovate perhaps best characterises Catalunya. From being a pioneer of the 19th century revolution it is now leading with innovation in tourism.

Catalunya is one of the autonomous communities of Spain. Approximately two thirds of the total 7.5 million population live in the Barcelona metropolitan area which covers about a tenth of the total land mass of the region. Catalunya has a wonderfully varied landscape: from the Pyrenean Mountains in the north-east and a 580 km coastline with over 300 beaches stretching from Cape Creus in the north to the highly important wetland habitats of the Ebro Delta in the south. The region is divided into 41 counties and 944 municipalities and is considered to be the economic motor of the country. In recent years its economy has been significantly more competitive than much of the rest of Spain, each year generating more than 20% of Spain's wealth, but with only 15% of the population.

There is a strong tradition in the arts. It is noted for many highly acclaimed artists: Salvador Dali, Joan Miro, Antoni Tapies, Picasso; singers and musicians such as Josep Carreras, Pau Casals, Jordi Savall; architects (Gaudi and Bofill) and its many theatre companies. It also has a strong tradition of sport and the successful bid to host the 1992 Olympic Games (see the section on Barcelona) was testimony to the generations of Catalans who had worked for sport and culture. In 2020 Agència Catalana de Turisme (ACT), in partnership with the United Nations World Tourism Organisation, hosts the World Congress on Sports Tourism as part of the 'Themed Year of Sports Tourism' for Catalunya.

It is widely acknowledged that the Government of Catalunya together with the Catalan Tourist Board – the official tourism organisation – is a global

Above: Mountains of Siurana, Priorat.

leader of fresh ideas about sustainable tourism. It is also a leader in how to develop tourism to benefit the more rural and peripheral areas of Catalunya to balance the historical dominance of Barcelona and the coastal resorts. These strategies are also addressing the much-publicised issues of residents' fears and anger about over-tourism in Barcelona. The Executive Director of the Catalan Tourist Board, Patrick Quell Torrent, is clear about the way forward: 'Over-tourism means that Barcelona must diversify and broaden its offer to avoid 'hard concentration of tourism'. Barcelona, therefore, needs Catalonia and Catalonia, of course, needs Barcelona to strengthen their joint and single visitor experiences. This is a time to work together as never before. Barcelona as the capital city is an expression of Catalunya… our accent, our message, identity and singularity. Our Catalan experience is forged and rooted in the mountains, the countryside, the fishing villages with the concept of Barcelona being the main vehicle and "exhibition centre" to showcase Catalunya. Barcelona is an expression of the region and driver of identity and Catalunya is the land of Barcelona. This means we have two strong brands working together.'

2017 was the year that over-tourism, with all its negative implications, hit the headlines as the residents of Venice, Bruges and Barcelona took to the streets in protest about too many tourists spoiling the quality of life. Catalunya rose to the challenge of how to tackle this issue whilst Patrick Quell Torrent was President of NECSTouR – the Network of European Regions for Sustainable and Competitive Tourism. In Spring 2018, during the European Year of Cultural Heritage, the 'Barcelona Declaration – Better Places to Live: Better Places to Visit' was launched (in cooperation with Europa Nostra, European Travel Commission and the European Cultural Tourism Network). The Declaration sets out guidelines to improve management of tourism to help destinations in Europe meet the Sustainable Development Goals (SDGs) of the United Nation's World Tourism Organisation.

At the same time as Catalunya was dealing with the world seeing images of its citizens protesting about over-tourism, it was plunged into a more profound period of upheaval that, again, demanded the attention of the world's media. In October 2017, the Catalan Government held a referendum on full independence from Spain. The Catalan people voted in favor of independence. The Government of Spain determined this referendum to be 'illegal' and sent in armed police to quash the celebrations taking place across Catalunya and to arrest the leaders of the Catalan Government. Images of the resulting violence taking place in well-known tourist areas of Barcelona went viral requiring the Catalan Tourist Board to take bold actions to reassure tourists about their safety and ensuring normal service would be resumed as soon as possible with an intense programme of innovative marketing and new product development.

Modern tourism started in Catalunya at the beginning of the 20th century, but its expansion really took place from the 1950s onwards with the increasing demand for holidays in a Europe reborn after the Second World War. Tourists were seduced by the climate and the extraordinary quality of the beaches, the natural and cultural landscapes and the modern resorts. It was the birth of mass tourism on parts of the coast in the 1960s, together with the exceptional growth in Barcelona due to the 1992 Olympics, that put Catalunya firmly on the tourism map of the world, becoming one of the world's leading tourist destinations.

The first phase of 'modern' tourism development in Catalunya came as a result of the highly successful, international mass sun and sand tourism model which, by the 1980s, had begun to show symptoms of obsolescence, with quantity still prevailing over quality. Then in the early 1990s came the amazing and unexpected success of Barcelona as a tourist destination following the Olympics. This success was especially notable given the fact that there was actually no plan in place to take advantage of the Olympics and, ironically, it has subsequently been suggested that, without

Barcelona's success, tourism in Catalunya may well have been in decline for some time.

The most recent phase of tourism development has been the increasing focus on the countryside of the interior and of the mountains. There is now a strong and extensive network of tourist accommodation in these areas together with the growth of active and adventure tourism, winter snow sports, eco-tourism, golf and cultural tourism. The recent emergence of Catalunya's highly innovative gastronomy has been very impressive. Food and drink are fast becoming a major feature of tourism and a key influencing factor in tourists deciding where to holiday. The culinary experience has recently been joined by an equally strong wine tourism – especially in Penedés, the coastal hill area south and west of Barcelona. This is the most important wine-producing area in Catalunya with over 200 wineries producing a diversity of wines. The Penedés Denominación de Origen Protegida covers dry, sweet and sparkling styles in all three colours (red, white and rosé), including Cava, the flagship sparkling wine of Catalunya. The Familia Torres is an exemplar of a visitor experience. The family has lived, planted vines and crafted wines in their Penedés vineyards for over 150 years and is now setting a new standard for wine tourism with their highly personalized signature wine experiences.

The foundations for the future of tourism in Catalunya emerged from the 1998 'Tourism Strategy for the 21st Century'. This demanded a 'serious commitment from everyone involved, including business owners, the authorities at all levels and society at large in order to offer quality experiences with their own Catalan style and made available in a protected, clean environment'. Eight geographic areas (brands) were identified as the focus of tourism marketing and development: Costa Brava, Barcelona, Costa del Maresme, Costa de Garraf, Costa Daurada, Terres de Lleida, High Pyrenees and Central Catalunya. Clusters of different types of tourism products were created;

businesses were encouraged to make larger commitments to marketing using new technologies. Greater cooperation between the public and private sectors was essential. Catalunya was to specialise in tourism relevant for future markets, namely: sport, gastronomy, health and well-being, design, architecture and artistic creativity. The strategy was clear: 'Catalans are no longer content just to pander to those seeking the three S's – sun, sea and sand and selling them Mexican sombreros and Spanish bull-fighting posters, things that have nothing to do with Catalunya. The Catalans see themselves and their country as deserving better.' Tourism is seen as a platform for projecting Catalunya to the world, reinforcing its identity and making a major contribution to the economy. Quality will prevail over quantity. The tourist is respected as a 'temporary citizen' and, in return, the tourist will gain a better understanding of, and respect for, the culture and heritage of Catalunya.

Above: Parachuting in Costa Brava.

COPENHAGEN, DENMARK

Creative, contemporary and cool — challenging traditional forms of tourism and re-inventing how visitors can experience the greater Copenhagen area

DENMARK COPENHAGEN

Population of city: 603,000
Population of wider area: 1.7 million
Nearest international airports: Copenhagen.
Key websites: www.visitcopenhagen.com; www.tivoli.dk; www.cph.dk; www.copenhill.dk; www.wonderfulcopenhagen.dk
Icons: Spiseloppen, Tivoli Gardens, Bakken, Reffen, Louisiana Museum of Contemporary Art, Rosenborg Castle, Kronborg Castle, The Black Diamond, Christiansborg Palace, Nyhavn, Nordatlantens Brygge, The Little Mermaid, Opera House, NOMA, Localhood, The Gaol in Slutteigade, BaNanna Park, Bus 5A, Genetically Modified Paradise, Burial Ground for the Homeless, The Reformation Monument and Absalon in Vesterbro.

Alliteration rules and positive adjectives abound. Copenhagen – city of contrasts, cool, cosy, clean, clever, compact, collaborative, cycling and customer friendly, crime-free, cultured, café-society, creative cuisine, charming, Christianhavn, Copenhageners, Christiania, Christiansborg Castle, cruise ships, CopenHill, city region and (Hans) Christian Andersen.

Copenhagen has come a long way since the late 1980s, when it was a city in decay, industries were closing down, and the city was close to bankruptcy. Very few international tourists visited the city, there was little investment and scant development. However, in 1992, the city came under state administration and started to plan European Cultural Capital in 1996. A master plan of the closing down of industrial areas was created. The state invested heavily in infrastructure: the, now infamous TV celebrity Øresund bridge to Sweden; the Copenhagen Metro; expanding Copenhagen Airport; and the new city of Ørestad. In order to

finance some of these investments, harbour areas close to the city centre were sold to hotels, banks, and other commercial enterprises. The city has been re-invented. Today, Copenhagen is one of the most important centres of modern design in Europe, and, as we will see, Copenhagen has also re-invented tourism.

Leading 20th century Danish and international architects and designers were invited to lead the regeneration program: Arne Jaconsen, Jôrn Utzon, Verner Paton, Bjarke Ingels, Henning Larsen, Sir Norman Foster, Daniel Libskind and a host of talented young Danish studios. The results are stunning. The Black Diamond (The Royal Library and National Library of Denmark) is the 1999 sculptural monolith sitting on the waterfront built

Left above: Nyhavn.
Above: CopenHill, Amager Bakke, the artificial ski slope and recreational hiking area.

of black granite, glass and concrete as an extension to the original 18th century building designed by Schmidt Hammer Lassen. Facing the Black Diamond on Holmen Island and surrounded by canals is the dramatic – and costly – Opera House. It was inaugurated in January 2005, donated by the AP Møller and the Chastine Mc-Kinney Møller Foundation and designed by architect Henning Larsen. Close by is the Royal Danish Playhouse completed in 2008 and designed by architects Boje Lundgaard and Lene Tranberg.

Innovative, creative, quality design permeates all parts of the city and beyond, touching new, large scale projects such as Den Blå Planet (the National Aquarium) in the suburb of Kastrup as well as the smaller interventions such as the boardwalks of Havegade and Havnwbade (Harbour Baths) at Islands Brygge along the waterfront leading to the Black Diamond or the Gro-spiseri rooftop farm. Another example is the Danish National Maritime Museum, which opened in 2015, where the story of Denmark as one of the world's leading maritime nations is told in dramatic architectural settings designed by BIG – Bjarke Ingels Group. The Museum is set deep inside a former dry dock in the newly renovated Culture Harbour Kronborg in Elsinore overlooked by the neighbouring the majestic Kronborg Castle – Hamlet's castle and a UNESCO World Heritage Site.

The same architects were responsible for the remarkable CopenHill project which opened in 2019 just west of the city centre on the roof of an ultra-efficient waste-to-energy plant providing power to over 300,000 people – part of Copenhagen's plan to be a carbon neutral city by 2025. The Amager Resource Centre now has an artificial ski and snow-boarding slope on its roof. It is a centre for running and other outdoor activities. Its chimney stack blows 'smoke rings'. The cleverness of this project does not stop there. A partnership has been established with Ski Circus Saalbach Hinterglemm Leogang (see Saalfelden-Leogang in this book) to provide 'taster' sessions for the 750,000 Danes who

already travel to this part of Austria for their winter sports holidays.

Copenhagen is not all about the new build re-invention. At the heart of the city is the world-famous Tivoli Gardens, which opened in 1843 and is the second oldest amusement park in the world, the oldest being Dyreharsbakken, commonly referred to as Bakken, that pre-dated Tivoli by 260 years opening near Klampenborg (about 10 km north of central Copenhagen) in 1583. Tivoli is the acknowledged inspiration for the stories of Hans Christian Andersen and Walt Disney, who made many trips to learn about the planning of theme parks: noting the magical nostalgic rides and the gallopers; the design of the 1914 wooden roller coaster; the importance of a range of eateries and the need for on-site hotels (at Tivoli there is the eponymous Tivoli Hotel and the luxury Nimb). Disney also recognised that the continued success of Tivoli was based on constant renewal, re-invention and investment as well as offering year-round appeal and a seasonal programme of events. The founder of Tivoli, Georg Carstensen, originally named the park The Tivoli and Vauxhall Gardens after le Jardin de Tivoli in Paris and the Vauxhall Gardens in London – both popular public gardens – announcing on its opening in 1844 that 'Tivoli will never be finished': a statement reiterated by Walt Disney on the opening of Disneyland in Anaheim (California) in 1955.

The Free State of Christiania is in many ways a microcosm of the city – a place that pushes boundaries, challenges convention, encourages experimentation, drives sustainability and welcomes tourists. In 2006 its own development plan was awarded the Initiative Award of the Society for the Beautification of Copenhagen and the plan received positive attention from the City Council and the Agenda 21 Society for its sustainability goals and democratic process. Each year over half a million visitors pass through its gates. Founded in 1971 on the site of the former military barracks east of Christianhavn, this unique social experiment

is home to some 1,000 residents committed to an alternative way of living with their own system of governance, schools, shops, self-build houses and workshops. Throughout its 50-year history there have been periods of turmoil. The community has never been fully adopted by the city. Christianians, and their way of life, are tolerated and admired in equal measure. Despite many eviction notices and threats of demolition it is still here; and recent surveys show that two-thirds of Copenhageners want it to stay. When Pusher Lane, also known as 'The Green Light District', a street renowned for dealing of soft drugs, was closed, one of its structures was moved to the National Museum of Denmark as an exhibit.

Upon entering one of the two gateways into Christiania visitors are greeted with a sign that sets the tone for the experience: 'Dear Friend have fun, don't run (it causes panic) and remember buying and selling hash is still illegal.' There are some really very pleasant surprises for the visitor:

guided tours; the ALIS Wonderland is a very fine skateboarding park; and, there are five cafes and restaurants catering for all tastes, notably Café Nemoland and Spiseloppen (literally meaning 'Eat the Flea') which is a well-respected, classy restaurant boasting a daily menu created by chefs from around the world. Next door is Den Grä Hal – a large hall formerly the riding school for the Royal Artillery – now one of a number of venues on site that has hosted leading bands and performers, including Bob Dylan, Blue and Portishead. Unsurprisingly, there is a music bar called Woodstock.

In many ways Reffen, Copenhagen's new 'nesting box for entrepreneurs and global street food', has some of the DNA of Christiania and a lot of the spirit of the highly acclaimed PapirØen (Paper Island) street food circus housed in a former paper

Above: Opera House.

making factory near Christiania which closed in 2017. This brilliant concept, developed by organic farmer, Reffen Jesper Møller, combines gastronomy (with over 50 chefs from 17 different countries with contemporary culture, design and crafts. It has rapidly become the go-to place to be seen in the city.

It is Copenhagen's desire to re-invent tourism which has captured the world's imagination. It was provoked to re-think tourism in the city as a result of the much publicised concerns about over-tourism and its impact on the quality of life of residents as well as the experience for tourists in Venice, Bruges and Barcelona. As a result, Wonderful Copenhagen published a bold new plan for 2020 titled *The End of Tourism as We Know It* introducing the idea of localhood. The plan opens with the reassuring statement: 'What comes after the end of tourism? Localhood for everyone. Don't worry, the sky isn't falling. Wonderful Copenhagen places people at the centre of its vision and imagines that the destination's future will be co-created by residents, industry, and visitors to seek a solution in which tourism can provide a net benefit to locals and visitors alike. By declaring 'localhood for everyone,' Wonderful Copenhagen encourages its destination to think of its visitors as temporary residents, instead of as tourists. As a resident, you are part of the community, and you contribute to it. The shift here is that the tourism industry can also help visitors add value to the community, instead of asking permanent residents to exchange their quality of life for money.'

Wonderful Copenhagen is the official destination management organisation tasked with promoting and developing business and leisure travel to the Greater Copenhagen Capital Region for the common good. The radical shift demanded in *The End of Tourism as We Know It* moves the agenda from marketing and promoting to others to the idea of promoting through others thus enabling all kinds of local partners to build experiences based on that one thing that sets the destination apart and yet pulls everyone together in a shared sense of localhood. This means that there is value added by visitors thus creating a future beyond tourism and offering something much more interesting and personal. It is a future of hosts and guests and the shared experience of localhood. A future that is about new solutions through collaboration and the shared ambition of co-creating sustainable and long-term value for the destination.

Wonderful Copenhagen will enable the destination to be shared more by increasingly inviting visitors to explore the destination's neighbourhoods: the quintessential lively and creative 'Bros' of Vesterbro (the former red light district; now cool, authentic family living with hip fashion, shopping and nightlife); the culturally diverse Nørvebro and the elegant Østerbro. There are also the gritty, up and coming former industrial districts of Refshaleøen, Nordvest and Sydhavnen or the waterfront living of Christanshavn, Nordhavn and Amager or the architectural hotspot of Øerstaden. Venturing just 30 minutes north of the city gets you to Louisiana Museum of Contemporary Art – one of the most beautiful museums in the world. It is based around an historic villa set in landscaped gardens and parkland with views across the Øresund to Sweden. It takes its name from the first owner of the property, Alexander Brun, who named the villa after his three wives, all called Louise. The museum was created in 1958 by Knud W. Jensen, the owner at the time, and is today a formidable interaction between nature, architecture and art by 20th century greats such as Picasso and Henry Moore.

- -

Right top: Henry Moore sculptures in the Sculpture Park, Louisiana Museum of Modern Art.
Right below: Skovtårnet Camp Adventure.

CORNWALL, ENGLAND

Boardmasters, artists and writers inspired by rugged coastlines

The County of Cornwall, or Kernow in Cornish, is one of the Celtic nations and occupies the tip of the south-west of England's extended peninsula, bordered by the sea on three sides: to the north and west by the Atlantic Ocean and to the south by the English Channel. Its easterly land border with the county of Devon follows the course of the River Tamar, part of which is a World Heritage Site due to its historic tin mining activities. The Tamar's source on Woolley Moor is less than 6 km from the north Cornish coast but it flows south across the peninsula into Plymouth Sound. In 2014, Cornish people, together with their language and culture, were granted minority status under the European Framework Convention for the Protection of National Minorities, giving them recognition as a distinct ethnic group.

Cornwall is regarded as an area that pioneered modern tourism. For over a century it has been in the Premier League of England's most popular tourism destinations, enjoying a strong image, a good reputation and high levels of awareness for wholesome family holidays. The coming of the railway in the 1850s provided the essential platform to realise the county's tourism potential, eventually seeing the journey time between Penzance and London slashed from two days by road to 12 hours in the 1860s, then to six hours in the early 20th century.

In June 2021, a small group of powerful world leaders known as the G7 headed to Cornwall, giving the luxury Carbis Bay Hotel and Estate in St. Ives a global profile. Built in 1894 by the renowned Cornish architect Silvanus Trevail, the Carbis Bay Hotel became a beacon of the rapid emergence of Cornwall as a holiday destination. Trevail, later to become President of the Royal Institute of British

GREAT BRITAIN

● CORNWALL

Population of Truro city: 19,000
Population of wider area: 566,000
Nearest international airports: Bristol, Exeter, Cornwall Newquay.
Key websites: www.visitcornwall.com; www.visitengland.com
Icons: Truro Cathedral, Newquay, St. Ives; Bude, the Eden Project, the Tate St. Ives, Barbara Hepworth, St. Michael's Mount, the Cornwall National Maritime Museum, Tintagel Castle, Bodmin Moor, River Tamar, St. Ives School of Art, Boardmasters Festival, Padstow, the giant Cormoran, Daphne du Maurier.

Architects, also designed several other iconic Cornish hotels, including the Headland Hotel and Atlantic Hotel, Newquay. The Carbis Bay Hotel was immortalised by Rosamunde Pilcher, the prolific local author of romance novels (with global sales of

over 60 million), appearing as The Sands Hotel in her novels *The Shell Seekers* and *Winter Solstice*.

Rosemunde Pilcher's popular writing follows in the tradition of other fine storytellers whose narratives are set in Cornwall, fuelled by folktales and legends of King Arthur and his alleged castle at Tintagel, St Michael's Mount and the giant Cormoran, and the Mermaid of Zennor.

Sir Arthur Quiller-Couch, author of many novels and works of literary criticism, was born in Bodmin; Daphne du Maurier lived near Fowey with her novels including *Rebecca*, *Jamaica Inn*, *Frenchman's Creek*, *My Cousin Rachel*, and *The House on the Strand* famously set in the county. Rather less appealing is the fact that Cornwall provided the inspiration for 'The Birds', one of her terrifying series of short stories, made famous as a film by Alfred Hitchcock. Conan Doyle's 'The Adventure of the Devil's Foot', featuring Sherlock Holmes, is also set in Cornwall. However, it is Winston Graham's series *Poldark*, Kate Tremayne's Adam Loveday

series, Susan Cooper's novels and Mary Wesley's *The Camomile Lawn* which continue to raise the county's profile.

David Cornwell, who wrote espionage novels under the name John le Carré, lived and worked in Cornwall whilst the late poet laureate Sir John Betjeman was a great fan of the county and is buried in the churchyard at St Enodoc's Church, Trebetherick. A summary of the local literary heritage would not be complete without a mention that Thomas Hardy's drama *The Queen of Cornwall* (1923), the second act of Richard Wagner's opera *Tristan und Isolde* and Gilbert and Sullivan's operettas *The Pirates of Penzance* and *Ruddigore* all take place in Cornwall.

A poignant, emotionally charged piece of writing inspired by the place is to be found on the Southwest Coast Path that edges the entire

· ·

Above: St Ives.

peninsula. Walking part of the trail on the cliffs between Pentire Point and The Rumps (a twin-headland promontory with an Iron Age fort) is a simple stone plaque marking the spot where another poet laureate, Laurence Binyon, wrote 'For the Fallen' in 1914. The stanza, more popularly known as 'The Ode', is familiar to us all: 'They shall grow not old, as we that are left grow old. Age shall not weary them, nor the years condemn. At the going down of the sun and in the morning. We will remember them.'

The 2021 cluster of G7 politicians followed in the footsteps of artists and surfers in beating a trail to Cornwall. For centuries, artists and writers have orientated to attractive, rural, often peripheral coastal locations, inspired by the quality of the landscapes, the peace and tranquillity of the area, the availability of cheap accommodation and local raw materials and relative remoteness together with the ability to lead a bohemian lifestyle. In the later years of the 19th century, artist colonies

emerged around the world in such liminal places, establishing creative clusters of global nomads.

The gathering of a small group of Romantic poets with William and Dorothy Wordsworth in the English Lake District was an early forerunner of a phenomena that would be repeated in Kirkcudbright (Scotland), Skagen and Bornholm (Denmark), Santa Fe (USA), Katwijk (Netherlands) and Rovinj (Croatia). In the 1960s and 1970s, further creative clusters formed around rock musicians in Laurel Canyon (California) and Woodstock (New York State), while today there are thriving artist colonies in Nida (Lithuania), Yadda (New York State) and Worpswede (Germany).

Although not universally welcomed in their host communities due to what may be described as a 'clash of cultures', these artistic colonies did create awareness of a place and forged a legacy of creativity that survives today, as is the case with Rovinj (described in this book) and Cornwall.

Just as with the G7 political carnival, it was St. Ives' small-town charms, rugged coastal scenery, big skies and seas, rugged cliffs and wild moorland that have seduced artists from around the world. J. M. W. Turner set the trend, first visiting in 1811 and again in 1813, making sketches of the town, harbour and coast. Outdoor painting flourished in the second half of the 19th century, benefiting St Ives, with its artistic equilibrium of daylight hours, mild climate and plenty of subject matter year-round. The 1887 arrival of the railway added to its appeal, bringing accessibility and the potential to send completed works of art back to London. Redundant fishermen's net lofts with their sea views were ideal for conversion to studios and the flow of artists to Cornwall began.

Whistler arrived in 1883 with two students. Four years later, an art school was opened by Louis Greer and Julius Olsson, a gallery was established and the St. Ives Arts Club was founded as a meeting place for musicians and writers as well as artists. The arts colony would attract visitors from around the world.

In the late 1970s through until the mid-1990s, tourism in Cornwall struggled as European sun, sand and sea destinations became readily available whilst Cornwall's tourism industry suffered a downturn in fortunes characterised by low-spending visitors, tired products and lack of investment – it needed more than scones with strawberry jam and clotted cream. However, good times were to return through transformation and renaissance at the end of the 20th century, triggered by a bold, imaginative plan to revive tourism. With strong industry leadership, visionary entrepreneurs and lots of serendipity, good things happened.

• •

Left: Trewithen Gardens.
Above: Tate St Ives.

The vision required the creation of at least three iconic, international-quality visitor attractions to draw in internationally renowned leisure brands, growing the local food and drink product, building upon the heritage of art (the St Ives School) and its surfing and maritime tradition and improving access by air by opening Cornwall Airport in Newquay. By 1999 annual visitor numbers to Cornwall had grown significantly. Fifteen years later, Cornwall was named the UK's Favourite Holiday Destination for the seventh consecutive year by the British Travel Awards.

The first years of the 20th century saw the fruition of much hard work and tenacity in a succession of wins, especially in the creation of new attractions. Some strong foundations for later changes had been set earlier and by 1980 the Tate group of galleries started to manage the Barbara Hepworth Museum and Sculpture Garden in St Ives, later deciding to open a permanent gallery on the site of the town's former gasworks. Completed and opened in 1993, the iconic building overlooking Porthmeor Beach helped set the tone for further projects, such as the National Maritime Museum of Cornwall in Falmouth, and encouraged the influx of quality restaurants heralded by Rick Stein's investments in Padstow.

The Lost Gardens of Heligan and the associated TV series about their restoration brought much-needed confidence to the area and witnessed the emergence of the charismatic impresario Sir Tim Smit KBE, co-founder of the highly acclaimed, transformational and award-winning Eden Project, near St Austell. Eden began as a dream in 1995 and opened its doors to the public five years later, since when more than 19 million people have come to see what was once a sterile china clay pit that morphed into a place of 'world-class horticulture', 'symbolic of human endeavour', adding almost £2 billion into the local economy.

For the surfing community, Cornwall has become legendary. As a peninsula, Cornwall's

position between the Bristol Channel and the English Channel has two swell-facing coasts, each with their own prime conditions and characteristics. As a result, the shoreline with its iconic surf towns of Newquay and St Ives is referred to by surfers as a 'veritable swell magnet', with Newquay the self-proclaimed wave capital, having some of the most reliable beaches for surfing, surf schools and hosting the annual Boardmasters Festival in August.

The resurgence of tourism in Cornwall has been co-ordinated and overseen by Visit Cornwall, a tourism industry-led community interest company established in 2015 as a contemporary reinvention of the more traditional model of a destination management organisation that had existed for 30 years or more. The new body has been able to harness the wealth of expertise and resources of Cornwall County Council alongside the agility, dynamism and experience of the private sector, continuing to grow Cornwall's visitor economy and ensuring it remains Britain's number one holiday destination.

Left: Epidauros II, Barbara Hepworth sculpture, St Ives, Cornwall.
Above: Surfing in Polzeath beach.

DONOSTIA–SAN SEBASTIÁN, BASQUE COUNTRY, SPAIN

The Basque Belle Époque beach city of *pintxo* and beaches framed by nature and the Pyrenees

Population of city: 187,000
Population of wider area: 436,000
Nearest international airports: Bilbao, Biarritz.
Key websites: www.euskadigastronomika.eus/en;
www.donostiakultura.eus;
www.sansebastianturismoa.eus;
www.gipuzkoaturismoa.eus/en

Icons: Txotx Cider Houses, the Festival of Tamborrada, San Sebastián International Film Festival, San Sebastián Gastronomika, the Basque Culinary Centre, Arzak restaurant, mountaineer Edurne Pasaban Lizarribar, Real Sociedad de Fútbol, fashion designer Cristóbal Balenciaga, Albaola (the Sea Factory of the Basques), Urumea River, Kursaal, Maria Cristina Hotel, Lasala Plaza Hotel, Monte Igueldo, Monte Urgull, Isla de Santa Clara.

DONOSTIA-SAN
SEBASTIÁN

SPAIN

Above: La Concha Bay, San Sebastián.

Just 20 kilometres from the French border, an hour north of Bilbao and 90 minutes north-east of the Basque capital, Vitoria-Gasteiz, is the exuberant, classy, decadent and seductive resort of Donostia-San Sebastián – the haunt of writers, artists, designers, architects and chefs. Here, in the elbow of the Bay of Biscay, natural beauty meets Basque culture and unrivalled local cuisine.

Historically the Basques were great seafarers, pioneering the seaway to the New World, whilst San Sebastián spearheaded the idea of the using the sea for leisure and pleasure. Albaola, the Sea Factory of the Basques in the sailor's town of Pasaia (east of San Sebastián), tells this history.

In 2016 this was the European Capital of Culture and is today the undisputed gastronomy centre of the Basques, what the *Telegraph* Travel magazine called a 'glutton's heaven', with the second most Michelin stars per capita in the world – seven – one with two stars and three with three. The sheer diversity of ingredients and combination of taste

makes *txikiteo*, or *pintxos* (tapas) hopping, an essential journey of culinary discovery. According to Javier De La Hormaza of Basco Fine Foods, the Gilda could be the first ever Basque *pintxo* – it has a strong, salty and pickled flavour and can be found in most bars in the city. The *pintxo* was created in the 1940s by brothers Blas and Antxon Vallés in their newly opened Bar Casa Vallés, where wine was served with plates of olives, guindilla peppers or salted anchovies, and when, according to legend, a regular customer started to combine all three together. The name comes from the eponymous 1946 film starring Rita Hayworth, in which her femme fatale character, Gilda, has the same attributes as the *pintxo*, a little sexy and spicy.

The port and resort city has had a roller-coaster history, being razed to the ground many times, the last being in August 1813. Its story has been wonderfully summarised in Paddy Woodworth's *The Basque Country: A Cultural History* (Signal Books, 2007), where he observes that the Basque coast may fly the flags of revolutionary icons today, but it was historically a magnet for reactionaries from both sides of the border at the end of the 19th century, as well as the Habsburg Queen Maria Christina and Europe's high society. Spain's neutrality in World War I allowed San Sebástian to be the last outpost of the Belle Époque, attracting prestigious arts companies and the dilettante. Even Franco, who loathed Basque nationalism, spent every August from 1940-1975 in the resort. In the post-war years San Sebástián was described as having an air of languid decline, likened by the Dutch journalist Cees Nooteboom to 'a painted lady of a certain age, reclining on a sofa. She had known better days, yet the former glory is still evident.'

In more recent times it witnessed its own Belfast-like 'troubles', with often violent campaigns by the Euskadi Ta Askatasuna (Basque Homeland

Above: La Concha Beach in San Sebástian.

and Liberty), or ETA, for Basque independence. This culminated in the International Conference to Promote the Resolution of the Conflict in the Basque Country – more widely known as the Donostia/San Sebastián International Peace Conference on 17 October 2011 – organised by the Basque citizens' group Lokarri and including leaders of Basque parties as well as international personalities known for their work in the field of politics and pacification. This event was seen as a prelude to the end of ETA's violent campaign for an independent Basque homeland, and three days later the group announced the 'definitive cessation of its armed activity'.

Today, San Sebastián is undoubtedly Basque and has been re-invented as another vision of Basque ambition. It is still a storehouse of Art Noveau and German Jugendstil architecture, yet it sweats and celebrates Basque culture in so many delightful ways, the contradictions of the past sidelined by the pull of its social life, landscape and setting, which now attracts a new cosmopolitan guest list.

Put altogether, this must be one of the most picturesque of all coastal resorts in Europe, offering three scallop-shaped bays with golden beaches, 5 km of renovated promenade, turquoise seas and the towering green headlands of Monte Igeldo and Urgull providing the most memorable views of the city, separated by the wooded Isla de Santa Clara. A century-old funicular lifts you to the summit of Igeldo, with its vintage amusement park and viewpoint overlooking the sweep of La Concha, the classy, leisurely beach and its stylish promenade, and overseeing *The Comb of the Wind* collection of sculptures.

Above: San Sebástian old town.

With Bilbao continuing to grab attention and the international uber-artlisters in the Guggenheim dominating its reimagined waterfront, San Sebastián duly celebrates contemporary culture in the Kursaal (Los Kubos) gallery on the river's edge and puts the work of its own iconic sculptor Eduardo Chillida centre stage in the city. Chillida's *Comb of the Wind* (*Haizearen Orrazia* in Basque) is located at the end of the Ondarreta beach at the foot of Mount Igeldo in the western area of San Sebastián. One of Chillida's most celebrated sculptures, installed at the edge of the sea in 1977 in a series of terraces built of pink granite and three anchor-like iron shapes welded into rocks is today one of the most visited spots in the Basque Country to enjoy views of sea and, on stormy days, hear and feel 20 ft waves pound against the cliffs in a spectacular natural show.

Born in San Sebastián on 10 January 1924, Chillida grew up near the Biarritz Hotel, which was owned by his grandparents, and had been the goalkeeper for Real Sociedad, San Sebastián's La Liga football team, until a serious injury ended his promising career. After studying architecture at the University of Madrid, he discarded architecture for art in Paris, returning home in 1951. Here he worked with iron under the tutelage of local blacksmiths, forging a series of sculptures entitled *Anvil of Dreams*. His works, inspired by his Basque upbringing, many being titled in the Basque language, Euskera, have found placements at the UNESCO headquarters in Paris, the ThyssenKrupp building in Düsseldorf, the Yorkshire Sculpture Park and a courtyard at the World Bank, Washington.

Dramatic large-scale outdoor sculptures by Basque artists feature prominently around the city. On the La Concha promenade is Chillida's *Homenaje a Fleming*, a tribute to the discovery of penicillin. Jorge Oteiza's *Construcción Vacía* (Empty Construction) stands like an echo of *Comb of the Wind* at the base of Monte Urgull, while *Sagrado Corazón*, Federico Coullaut's 1950 statue of the

Sacred Heart, sits at its peak, appearing to stand guard. The heights of Monte Urgull are encircled by a coastal path linking the old fishing port and, ironically, the aquarium on the south with the north side of Parte Vieja and Zurriola beach. On the Zurriola promenade, looking at the sea, is the installation *Bakearen Usoa* (Dove of Peace) by Nestor Basterretxea. This sculpture was built in the 1980s with the purpose of symbolising the commitment the city has to peace, freedom and coexistence. Finally, a boat trip to the Isla de Santa Clara allows you to enter an empty and roofless chamber in the lighthouse to experience Hondalea. This work by Cristina Iglesias incorporates the peculiar geology and ecology of the Basque coast and the wild waters of the ocean that surround the island.

Tasting the Basque culture is a rallying call of Basquetour. The aim is to make the Basque Country one of the world's leading gastronomy destinations by creating a diverse and unique range of products and services related to Basque food and wines, suitable for all audiences and using local products and recipes. There are now more than 750 companies as part of Euskadi Gastronomika that promotes culinary experiences, products to buy and restaurants or bars to eat at. Its Gastromaps are the envy of many destinations in the world, celebrating the work of all the food and drink interests, including the Basque Academy of Gastronomy, Gipuzkoa's hospitality industry association, Biscay's hospitality industry association, Ciderlands Makers & Lovers, Basque Beer, Gasteiz On, Gastromuseums, Sagardi Group, Jakitea, European Cheese Route, Cider Route, Sagardun and SEA Hostelería. The Basque Culinary Centre in San Sebastián is a pioneering academic institution, training and educating in Basque gastronomy as well as engaging in research, innovation and promotion.

The city's tourism team is leading the way in asking visitors to adhere to the basic rules for a

conscious, responsible and sustainable way to enjoy their city. Guests are invited to say *kaixo* and *agur* (hello and goodbye in Basque), to discover authentic places with a *donostiarra* (a local), to be environmentally considerate, to get around using public transport, on foot or by bike, to shop in traditional local stores, explore the city's neighbourhoods and to respect the sleep of the residents. Step out beyond Gros with the Zurriola beach and surf schools, the classic promenade of La Concha and the narrow lanes of the Parte Vieja (Old Town) to discover Igeldo, Antiguo, Loiolako Erriberak, Amara, Miramon, Aiete, Egia and Parte Vieja.

Donostia San Sebastián Turismoa coordinates a year-round program of festivals and events. The eponymous San Sebastián Day on 20 January sees the 24-hour-long Festival of Tamborrada (drums), while the Classical Music Fortnight in August is a less boisterous affair. The annual San Sebastián International Film Festival, begun in 1953, takes place in September and is now one of the most important film events in the world, welcoming great directors, actors and national and foreign producers and spawning other film-related festivals. The classic María Cristina Hotel, the sentinel overlooking the river and the Kursaal cubes, has hosted some of the greatest movie stars of all time while they attended the festival. Creating cocktails in the hotel's Dry Bar is a true performance – one of its specially created cocktails pays homage to the Academy Award-winning actor Bette Davis, who stayed in the hotel, with the drink composed of Champagne, orange liqueur, brandy, sugar, angostura and gold dust. In 2021 the tourism team also launched an interactive tour of the city to visit the filming locations in Woody Allen's *Rifkin's Festival* and explore his universe.

Above: Sculpture *Peine del Viento* (Spanish) / *Haizearen Orrazia* (Basque), San Sebástian.

ELCIEGO, CITY OF WINE RIOJA ALAVESA, SPAIN

Star-architects re-imagine classic wineries and viticulture

In the search for innovation in tourism and the drive for higher quality products and experiences the wine producers and growers are leading the way, setting new standards for the rest of the industry to follow. This should not be a surprise. Viticulture and wine production are inherently creative processes. It is an industry that is embedded in lifestyle. It is all about terroir, about provenance, with the wines bearing the characteristics of their place of production.

This is an industry that has long recognised its symbiotic relationship with tourism. Wine tourism formed part of the 'Grand Tour' for Europe's aristocracy. Wine trails first became an official part of the tourism offer in Germany in the 1920s but it was not until the 1970s that wine tourism emerged as a special interest aspect of tourism development. Today wine tourism is a fast growing, high-value and value-added sector of tourism. As the number of wineries and wine destinations increases so too has the demand for wine tourism. For example, in Italy there are almost four thousand vineyards offering tourist experiences with dedicated wine tourists to the country increasing from 4.5 million in 2007 to over 6.5 million in 2010.

Increasingly, wine regions understand their appeal to tourists and that it is the whole 'winescape' that attracts tourists who want to go beyond the 'cellar door' moving away from simply 'selling' their produce in simple tasting sessions in cold wine cellars. It is now about the total experience that combines the best that the wine industry can offer with those from local agriculture,

ELCIEGO

SPAIN

Population of city: 2,000
Population of wider area: 12,000
Nearest international airports: Bilbao, Biarritz, Santander and Zaragoza.
Key websites: www.rutadelvinoderiojaalavesa.com; www.elciego.es; www.enoconocimiento.com
Icons: Marques de Riscal; Frank Gehry, Santiago Calatrava, River Ebro, Dinasti Vivanco, Toloño Mountains, pintxos, The Wine Route, Racimo Tourist Train, Bodegas Ysios.

landscape, artisan food producers, design and craftsmanship – a shift from a focus of wine production to the aesthetics and experience of the winescape.

Today, both 'old world' and 'new world' wine growing area are becoming ever more innovative in their strategies for marketing and product

Marques de Riscal Hotel, a
Frank Ghery building in Elciego.

development to attract tourists. Initially, the pace was set by the 'new world' wine destinations but in the past ten years the 'old world' destinations have become exciting, imaginative and creative in their approach. None more so than Rioja Alavesa in the Basque Region especially with the involvement of the Valencian architect Santiago Calatrava at the Bodegas Ysios (2001) and the extraordinarily sensual design of the Marques de Riscal winery and hotel by Frank Gehry, who had been instrumnental in re-imagining Bilbao and Elciego.

Here, in line with one of the most significant trends in the tourism industry, has been the involvement of internationally renowned, star-architects in the creation of new wineries, wine museums, wine cellars and wine hotels and spas. This results from that link between wine and contemporary design and architecture in terms of lifestyle and affordable luxury and the creative insight of the new generation of wine producers. Some of the best examples of this trend include: Zaha Hadid's involvement at the Lopez de Hernandez Winery, Norman Foster's Bodegas Portia in Ribera Del Duero near Madrid, Herzog and de Meuron's Dominus Winery in California and Steven Holl's involvement with the LOISIUM initiatives in Austria.

Close to the south-western boundary of the Alava–Araba Province of the Basque Region is an area known as La Rioja Alavesa. It forms the border with the region of Rioja to the south and together forms the Rioja 'controlled designation of origin' wine growing area, along the valleys of the Ebro and Rio Oja rivers defined to the north by the white scarp edge of the Toloño Mountains. They have been growing vines here since the Roman times and, today, there are over four hundred vineyards in this small land area whose wine appeal is enhanced by an attractive rural landscape of small villages and relatively unspoilt, undulating countryside. It is a compact area comprising 23 historic villages and four small towns. Sprinkled throughout this

landscape are a number of wineries that have pushed the boundaries of innovation with their visitor experiences in addition to Ysios and Riscal with the Real Laguardia winery visitor centre by the French architect Philippe Mazieres; the Villa Lucia Wine Thematic Centre in Laguardia; and the Dinasti Vivanco Museum of Wine Culture at Briones.

At Elciego (Eltziego in Basque), founded in 1067, the Gothic Renaissance tower of the church of San Andreas oversees the Plaza Mayor and the extravagant creation of the 'City of Wine' (*Ciudad del Vino*) by the winery of Vinos Herederos del Marques de Riscal – the vision of chair of the company, Alejandro Aznar Sainz.

The City of Wine sits below the bluff on top of which sits the village church of San Andreas and consists of four elements that come together to create a mini-destination within the destination: the winery within the original 19th century buildings with 21st century visitor centre, tours, tasting rooms and restaurant; tours of the vineyards and the landscape of oeonology; the Hotel Marques de Riscal (opened in 2006); and La Caudalie Vinotherapie Spa. The centrepiece and cornerstone of the initiative is the instantly recognisable Hotel Marques de Riscal, consisting of a series of rectilinear elements, clad in sandstone, combined with sweeping panels of gold and pink titanium, and mirror finish stainless steel used to create a building that has captured the imagination of the world's press and discerning tourists around the world.

The hotel is lifted above the site on columns to the same height as the church, providing breath-taking views of the vineyards and the distant mountains. Distributed throughout the three upper levels of the building are guest bedrooms/ suites, a wine tasting room, restaurant and outdoor dining terraces, and conference facilities. A connecting bridge links the main building with an extension housing more bedrooms and the Caudalie Vinotherapie spa. The beauty of the hotel is enhanced by the fact that the warm colouring of the stone changes throughout the day with the movement of the sun and the unusual decorative canopies of coloured titanium, whose flowing contours and colours symbolise flowing wine, or perhaps a flamenco dancer.

The winery of Marques de Riscal is one of the oldest wineries in the Rioja wine producing area. Importantly, the winery has a history and tradition of innovation and providing both direction and leadership for the local wine industry. In 1860, for example, it was one of the first wineries to introduce Bordeaux wine-making techniques involving French winemaker Jean Pineau. In 1972 it was the first Bodega to make white wine under the Rueda label and was one of the first in the area to open for visitor tours. Indeed, until the turn of the century, the wineries in the region had not been generally open to the public; the City of Wine and investments by other wineries have redefined and invigorated the destination.

For example, over one hundred of the wineries now participate in the 'Wine Route', that was originally established 20 years ago by the Association of Spanish Wine Cities, an organisation created to encourage new, innovative, types of wine tourism ideas. The route allows tourists to delve into the lifestyle, gastronomy and culture of the destination. There are also 18 way-marked walking and cycling routes through the vineyards and the Sierra de Toloño countryside; the Racimo tourist wine train has been introduced; concerts and places to stay sit within vineyards. At the new Rioja Alavesa Eco-Campus where tourists can learn about all aspects of wine production and consumption. Many of the festivals reflect an aspect of the heritage of wine and local culture (such as Elciego's 'Waving of the Glog', 'The Shepherds' – a civic religious dance – or the Euskadi Food Festival). Other events are set within the vineyards such as the Rioja Wine Run (October) and the Rioja Alavesa Half Marathon (June). The signature Basque Rioja cuisine and, especially the pintxos, is inescapably linked to wine:

Frank Gehry's Boutique Hotel Near Eltziego

try lamb cutlets with vine shoots or veal cheeks cooked in red wine.

On the right banks of the River Ebro, just a 20 minute drive north-west from Elciego, is Briones, one of most beautiful of medieval villages in Northern Spain. On the outskirts of the village is one of the very best wine museums in the world, siting alongside the Vivanco Bodega in an expansive and specially created landscape overlooking the broad sweep of the Rio Oja valley Opened by King Carlos in 2004 this is a modern complex, housing and interpreting all facets of wine-making. Outside is the Bacchus Garden with one of the world's biggest collections of different grapes compiled by the Vivanco Family, owners of one of Rioja's leading wine companies, which has been in the industry here for four generations since 1915. They established the not-for-profit Foundation that owns and manages the Museum as a 'means to give back to wine what wine has given the family'. Importantly, however, the investment in the Museum was conceived by the family as an 'ambitious and original business initiative of international status'. It is without doubt a beautiful contemporary building and a museum collection representing 40 years of obsessive collecting by the family, which is world-class by any standards.

FANØ ISLAND, DENMARK

Denmark's holiday island with authentic experiences fuelled by the sea, the wind and nature

'We are Islands but never too far, we are Islands. Islands never been to before and we climb so high to where the wild birds soar' from the song *Islands* **by Bonnie Tyler with Mike Oldfield.**

There is a universal lure surrounding our perceptions and idea of islands as special places to escape from reality: an adventure. We are geared to expecting islands to be special, relatively remote places – evocative, malleable, erotic, exotic, mysterious, self-contained, peaceful, special cultures and easy to understand – as represented in books such as William Shakespeare's *The Tempest*, Daniel Defoe's *Robinson Crusoe*, Jonathan Swift's *Gulliver's Travels*, Johann David Wyss' *Swiss Family Robinson*, Jules Verne's *Mysterious Island* and Patrick Barkham's *Islanders*. Islands are featured in films and TV shows, such as *Love Island*, *Castaway*, *Live and Let Die*, *Blue Lagoon*, *Stromboli* or *Red Turtle*. BBC Radio even has a long-running radio program called *Desert Island Discs*. Abba, the Swedish pop super group, notoriously escaped to the island of Viggsö in Stockholm's archipelago to write their hit songs whilst artists as diverse as Harry Belafonte (with *Islands in the Sun*) and Van Morrison (*Coney Island*) eulogised about them. In the past few years a and a new generation of writing has emerged plotting our love affair with islands, including the wonderfully titled *Atlas of Remote Islands – Fifty Islands I have not visited and never will* by Judith Schalansky.

There are three islands in this book that I have visited. One, Losinj, is a warm-water island off the coast of Croatia and the other two are cold-water

DENMARK

● FANØ ISLAND

Population of city: 3,500
Population of wider area: 116,000
Nearest international airports: Billund, Copenhagen International.
Key websites: www.visitfanoe.dk; www.geocaching.com; www.fanosommercup.dk; www.visitdenmark.dk
Icons: Wadden Sea, Nordy, Galgerev sand bank, Sønderho, Seals, Kites, Oysters, Fanø Bryghus, Rindby Strand, Sönderho Kro, Sommercup, Knit Festival.

islands: Arran in the Clyde Estuary in Scotland and this – the Danish island of Fanø. The vast majority of all tourism trips to islands takes place on the warm-water islands of the Mediterranean, the Caribbean and the Pacific. The cold-water islands, of which there are thousands in Europe alone, rarely feature as 'must-visit destinations', however,

both Fanø and Arran should not be missed.

Fanø is a remarkable Island, which is well-managed and has a very efficient local tourist board. The Island has many extraordinary, endearing features: its long, clean and wind swept sandy beaches; its wildlife and seafaring culture as well as a high quality of life; the special community spirit and personality; and, the hundreds of summer vacation homes. It is a destination offering peace, solitude and the chance to get close to authentic island life. In 1940 the island was under German occupancy and during World War II Fanø, due to its strategic location, formed an important part of the Atlantic Wall created by the Third Reich with over 300 wartime bunkers constructed on the island – many of which still exist today, including the graffiti garlanded 'Be Free' bunker.

The island has a small number of charming, historic small towns and villages, two of which were among the most wealthy and influential in Denmark during the 18th and 19th centuries when this tiny island was once a maritime 'superpower'. There have been sailors on Fanø for many centuries travelling widely for employment, but from the 1760s the people of the island started their own shipping companies and building ships on Fanø with a total of nine shipyards in Nordby and Sønderho. From 1768 to 1896, a total of 1,100 ships were built on the island. As wooden ships were replaced by those made of iron and steel in the 1880s the industry declined with the last Fanø ship built in 1896. The maritime era brought wealth and inspiration from other parts of the world to the island and many of the beautiful mansions built by the captains can still be seen together with a lot of the traditions, the dances, the music, the costumes and the traditional food of the maritime era.

The island's 'capital' and ferry port is Nordby, complete with its own seal colony in the harbour,

Above: Kites on Ringby Strand.

situated at the northern end of the Postvegjen main road that runs down the spine of the island connecting with the historic, very atmospheric village of Sønderho. This is the island's most southerly community and is recognised as Denmark's most beautiful village with its crooked streets and Fanø Art Museum, Hannes hus, Sønderho Mølle and Sønderho Kirke as well as many old, well preserved buildings from the 18th and 19th centuries, including the Sønderho Kro, a cosy storied 1722 inn with an elegant restaurant built when Sønderho was the dominant shipping town of the west coast of Jutland. The harbour and shipyard area was situated in a small sheltered bay in the north-eastern end of Sønderho. The entry was, however, eventually sanded up and today the area is filled with meadows and the cries of seabirds. This all makes for a very fine destination for families with children of all ages, nature lovers and those active outdoor sports enthusiasts.

Fanø is the northernmost Danish Wadden Sea Island just of the coast from the city of Esbjerg and is separated from the mainland by a channel spanning just one kilometre at its closest point to the mainland and five kilometres where the 12-minute ferry ride from Esbjerg takes place. The island is long and thin and compact – just sixteen kilometres long and three kilometres wide – made up of heathland, small pine forests interspersed with pastureland and great dune systems backing on to expansive sandy beaches of Bad Beach and the strands of the Rinby, Fanø and Sønderho. Depending on the directions of the winds it is possible that, on these sea-washed shores, hidden amongst seaweed and shell fragments visitors will find the 'gold of the North Sea' – Amber. A local tip to help find this gem is to watch where the seagulls congregate on the foreshore.

The island earned fame between 1919 and 1923 because of the long, straight and quite firm sandy beach used to host yearly motorcycle and car racing events, until a tragic accident killed a local boy and put a stop to further events. It is still possible to drive your own car on the main beach and there is even a public bus service operating along on this beach. A 2 km guided walk over the intertidal sands to the Galgerev sand bank, just off Sønderho Strand, takes tourists to one of the largest (up to 700) seal colonies in the Wadden Sea area. At all states of the tide there is always a 100 metre-wide channel between the human observers and the seals ensuring that they are not disturbed.

Just off the eastern shoreline, from October to Easter, there are organised guided tours to go oyster hunting at the Fanø oyster beds where participants can pick native oysters before returning to shore to prepare and eat them. During these tours, visitors can also do their bit for the environment by helping to remove non-native Pacific Oysters. This gourmet dish is one element of the Island's growing reputation as a centre of North Sea gastronomy whilst the Fanø Bryghus is brewing some beers that are interesting, with new brews including a chocolate milk stout, spiced saison, and a rauch (smoked) beer.

Island communities have always had to be innovative, creative and inventive to survive. This imaginative approach is evident in many of the tourism experiences. For example, tourists are urged to try mountain climbing on Fanø. Whilst that may seem like a joke the tourist association has established a geocaching trail called The Big Five. The five big mountains are in fact sand dunes. Once conquered, families have the possibility of getting a certificate at the Tourist Office, which states that they are officially Fanø mountain climbers.

In Mid-June on the large beach on the west side of the Island, there will be thousands of kites filling the sky with designs of giant animals and cartoon characters. Fanø is a kite flyers' paradise due to the wide beach and stable wind conditions. Club Fanø arranges kite-building workshops for children all year round. Kite flying is also a sport. Most of the summer season from April to October, kite flyers come to Fanø to set up their kites. These

come in all shapes and sizes, from small traditional handheld kites to huge kites that are fixed to the ground and those that pull surfboards across the waves or karts across the sands. An international centre for the development of kite flying and kite flying equipment is now being planned.

Some of the Island's other events are similarly different and unusual. The annual Knit Festival devised and organised by local designer, Chirstel Seyfarth, has been running for almost a decade and now attracts in excess of 10,000 visitors for the weekend knitfest – a sister event has now been established at Loch Ness (Scotland). The Fanø Sommercup is a wonderfully glorious and unique weekend football competition, open to all skills, levels and genders. It is akin to Glastonbury Festival meets the amateur soccer meets music, food, art and, of course, plenty of local beers.

Fanø is located in the Wadden Sea National Park, which stretches from Blåvandshuk in the north of its border to the salt meadows of Tønder in the south. It is a unique natural area that includes the Wadden Sea, the islands of Fanø, Mandø, and Rømø. The Wadden Sea area became a national park in 2010. In 2015 it was designated as a World Heritage Site by UNESCO. Over the next few years there will be a new initiative to develop a co-ordinated approach to tourism development for the Danish Wadden Sea. Bird watching will be one of the main experiences. The plentiful fish stocks and mud banks of the Wadden Sea make it one of the world's most crucial areas for birds. Every year, 10–12 million migratory birds pass through the Wadden Sea either on their way to or from their breeding grounds in northern Scandinavia, Siberia or Greenland. The best place to observe the migratory birds in the spring and autumn is at Hønen, near Sønderho.

Above: Cottage in Nordby.

FLANDERS, BELGIUM

State-of-the-art thinking that poses important questions about what successful tourism will look like in the future

There is much to be admired about tourism in Flanders: from the way it is organised and marketed to the types of experiences available to visitors – and the new way they are thinking about the future of their tourism industry. The promotional slogan for Flanders is 'State of the Art'. A bold statement that demands that the Region lives up to the explicit promise that everything is cutting edge. It backs this up with another eye-catching claim: 'Flanders is a region of creators – headstrong, sustainable, skilled and helpful people who have been passionate about knowledge and expertise for centuries. It is a story of pioneering and high-profile skill – in the past and present, as well as in the future.' The bar is set high. There is an expectation that tourism in Flanders will be cutting edge; that Visit Flanders will be pushing the boundaries of how tourism is managed – that traditional conventions can be overruled. There is clear evidence and many examples of this happening in Flanders. There is also still work in progress but, in the main, a tourist will encounter innovative experiences that will stir their emotions and potentially change the way they think about culture, art and life in general.

Visit Flanders is the official destination organisation for Flanders and Brussels. It works hard to develop tourism and visitation to the Region knowing that people decide to make trips when a destination provides something meaningful to them and they hear positive recommendations. Tourists can be motivated by a passion or by personal and emotional connections. It is these demands and interests of visitors that guides and informs the work

FLANDERS
● BRUSSELS
BELGIUM

Population of Bruges: 118,000
Population of wider area: 11.5 million
Nearest international airports: Brussels Airport, Brussels South Charleroi, Amsterdam Schipol.
Key websites: www.visitflanders.com; www.mas.be
Icons: Bruges, Antwerp, Brussels, Ghent, Mechelen, Ostende, Flanders Fields, Ypres, Flemish Masters, Ronde van Vlaanderen, Museum aan Strom, River Scheldt, Rik van Looy and Roger de Vlaeminck.

of Visit Flanders. The existing markets for Flanders include people who are passionate about beer, Flemish Masters' fine art or cycling, and the intense emotional connections associated with Flanders Fields' World War I history and the commemorations that marked the 100 year anniversary of the end of hostilities.

Historically, Flanders covered a larger area

than today, embracing parts of north-east France – indeed the lesser-known French Flanders, is now beginning to wake up to its tourism potential. This chapter focuses upon the Flanders – one of the three Regions of Belgium. It is the northern portion of Belgium made up of five provinces with the main cities of Bruges, Ghent, Mechelin, Leuven and Antwerp. Flanders is the political heart of modern Europe. It has been strategically important and influential over the centuries as a place for trade, culture and scientific ideas and has witnessed the most unbelievable horrors of the 1914–1918 Great War.

This is a compact region (just 13,500 km²) but one of the most densely populated in Europe. It is mainly flat land with has a small, 70 km long, stretch of sandy beaches and numerous resorts along the North Sea coast. The official capital of Flanders is Brussels (an official bilingual enclave within the Flemish Region) although the Brussels Capital Region has an independent regional government,

and the government of Flanders only oversees the community aspects of Flanders life in Brussels such as (Flemish) culture and education. Flanders has figured prominently in European history since the Middle Ages. In this period, cities such as Ghent, Bruges, and later Antwerp, made it one of the richest and most urbanised parts of Europe, trading, and weaving the wool of neighbouring lands into cloth for both domestic use and export. A sophisticated culture developed, with impressive achievements in the arts and architecture. The region thrived during 19th-century industrial revolution. Modernisation and investment in the second half of the 20th century allowed the Flanders' economy to flourish making Flanders one of the wealthiest regions in Europe.

With the eyes of the world focused on Flanders during the hundredth anniversary of this conflict the four years of commemorative events were delivered

Above: Museum aan de Stroom, Antwerp.

with great sensitivity, integrity and no shortage of inspirational, state-of-the-art experiences organised by Visit Flanders and its partners. They took advantage of this global interest to pioneer new ways of telling difficult stories to visitors. Flanders Fields is a place where family heritage and world history converge. The region of Flanders in Belgium is the site of significant World War I battles, including the battles of Passchendaele and Messines. The conflict and the scars it left behind continue to affect Flanders and its society today. It is a significant element of Flanders' history and its DNA. Today, many visits are made to Flanders Fields as a symbol for peace and a memorial to all who lost their lives.

Understanding that many families with relatives who served in World War I and individuals deeply interested in the history of this major world event would want to visit Flanders Fields during the anniversary years, Visit Flanders prepared to appropriately greet and support these visitors. During 2017's anniversary of the Battle of Passchendaele, past and future visitors shared their stories of remembrance on Visit Flanders' social media channels. The Facebook audience grew to 140,000 people who shared individual posts resulting in over two million interactions and meaningful conversations. Most importantly, Visit Flanders was able to affect many lives by helping people learn about the war and its legacy, explore personal heritage, and encourage them to come to Flanders Fields. It allowed visitors to share individual family histories and honour relatives who served during the war and provided an opportunity for people to discover their own history. Visitors continue to travel to commemorate their loved ones, to remember, to learn about the war and discover travel opportunities.

The challenge for Visit Flanders to deliver the war anniversary in a respectful manner has now been replaced by new challenges to keep up with the fast-moving demands of the tourist and counter concerns about over-tourism in the historic centre of the city: a UNESCO World Heritage site. The residents of picture perfect Bruges – the 'Venice of the North'- with its labyrinth of canals of the Hansa district, market squares, whitewashed alms-houses, cobblestone paths, brick archways, stone churches, lace boutiques and galaxy of fine restaurants are now concerned about managing the peak times when the small city is swamped by tourists. With a population of 19,500 people living in Bruges centre it attracts nearly nine million visitors per year. That amounts to about 126 visitors per day per 100 residents, During the height of the main tourist season there are often three times as many tourists as residents in the city on any given day. This means that over-tourism is recognised as a potential threat by local residents who fear possible negative impacts if visitor numbers continue to rise at their current rate. As a result, an experiment is taking place to involve locals in decisions about the management of tourists in the city.

Elsewhere, something very interesting is happening in Antwerp. This port city is traditionally famous for its diamond trade and it is now a contender, along with Copenhagen, as one of the cities in Europe that has embraced stylish, contemporary architecture and design to make its mark in the modern world as a good-looking city. This isn't a new accolade. Antwerp was one of the greatest, richest, cities in Europe in the 1500s. A century later, the iconic Flemish Baroque painter Peter Paul Rubens along with Anthony Van Dyck made Antwerp their home. In more recent years, the city has become world-renowned for the famous 'Antwerp Six' – a group of fashion designers who graduated from Antwerp's Royal Academy of Fine Arts between 1980–81. It also retains a busy diamond trade and a cluster of new architectural gems: including the Richard Roger's designed Court of First Instance and the jenga-looking Neutelings Riedijk Architects 2011 red sandstone and glass Museum aan Strom (MAS) – the Museum of the River.The design has been inspired by the 19th century warehouses typical of the area. Its galleries tell the story of Antwerp and the world and how the world came to Antwerp. From its roof there

are fine 360° views of the city.

Flanders is well-suited for cycling. Bikes and cycling are part of the heritage and DNA of Flanders. It is the home of cycling legends Eddy Merckx, Rik van Looy and Roger de Vlaeminck. The region hosts many different types of cycling competitions. There are 100 themed bike tours, 500 cyclist-friendly accommodations and 13,000 km of cycle trails and, at Oudenaarde located on the left bank of the River Scheldt, is the unique museum of the Tour of Flanders / Ronde van Vlaanderen. Visit Flanders is cleverly integrating cycling tourism with wider economic development based upon growing the cutting-edge bike and cycling equipment design and manufacture in what has become known as Flanders Bike Valley. For a very enjoyable insight into cycling in Flanders read Harry Pearson's 2020 book *The Beast, The Emperor and the Milkman.*

The organisation is in the process of taking a critical look at the future of tourism in Flanders despite the fact that, according to the accepted success criteria, the tourism policy in Flanders is currently very successful. Important questions are being asked: how, for example, can you ensure there is a healthy balance between the interests of residents and visitors? How do you honour and maintain the natural richness and historical authenticity of the Region and its communities? How do you ensure that our Flanders remains a pleasant place to live, do business in, and visit? How can tourism ensure that all the communities continue to thrive in such a way that genuine hospitality goes without saying? What would happen if we could strengthen this positive power of tourism? So that visitors would feel like a welcome part of the local community and go home feeling appreciated, with a desire to return?

Visit Flanders new initiative to try to answer these questions is 'Tourism Transforms', which places the community at centre stage as the 'place keepers' to create a tourism policy of the future. The tourism of tomorrow will be different, whether we like it or not. Flanders aims to create a new way of tourism that matches the challenges of the future and establishes a positive balance for the traveller, host and place. It is clear that the tourism of tomorrow will be rooted in local communities: in neighbourhoods, villages and cities that thrive and, as a result, enjoy welcoming visitors.

Above: Cycling in Flanders, Muur van Geraardsbergen.

GORIŠKA BRDA (THE BRDA HILLS), SLOVENIA

A bucolic rural idyll of verdant rolling hills creating a symphony of cherry orchards, vineyards, world-class wines and hilltop villages

It is time to shed the tagline of Goriška Brda being 'Slovenia's Tuscany'. This is Goriška Brda, full-stop. An award-winning 'Green Destination', it commands attention without needing to be likened to anywhere else. The appeal of this rural gem is up there with the best in the world, yet it is so easily bypassed as tourists head for the Dalmatian and Istrian coasts, the resorts of the Venetian lagoon, or the mountains and lakes of the Dolomites or the Alps.

In truth, its anonymity is its saving grace. Goriška Brda presents the travel writer with the classic conundrum – celebrating a special place while concerned about jeopardising that destination's ability to cope with any increase in visitor numbers. I feel that this dilemma is more prescient for Goriška Brda than for any other destination in this book. Consequently, this chapter has been approved by the Slovenian Tourist Board.

This compact, glorious area of Slovenian countryside in the south-western corner of the country, just 72 square kilometres, is locked between the Soča Valley to the east, the Alps to the north and the Italian border to the west and south, its rolling hills overlooking Trieste and the Adriatic and the rich agricultural lands of the Friuli plains. This is a verdant place, a tapestry blanket of orchards, vineyards, cypress trees and olive groves capped with hilltop villages, castles and belfries.

Some of the world's top 100 winemakers are to be found here amongst the 600 wine producers in this patch. Their centuries-old vineyards and viticulture traditions thrive in the climate of sun,

Population of wider area: 6,000
Nearest international airports: Trieste Friuli Venezia Giulia, Venice Marco Polo, Treviso International, Ljubljana Jože Pučnik.
Key websites: www.slovenia.info; www.brda.si; www.vilavipolze.eu; www.greendestinations.org; www.simcic.si; www.sanmartin.si; www.klet-brda.si
Icons: the Isonzo (Soča) River, Dobrovo, Medana, Šmartno, the Simčič Family and Wine Estate, Vila Vipolže, Vinska Klet G.B., Alojz Gradnik, Klinec Homestead Art Colony, Eco-Hotel San Martin, Gonjače Lookout Tower, Sabotin Peace Park, Gredič Castle.

fresh sea air, cool Alpine winds and terroir of fertile opoka (or flysch) soils, making the Brda Hills Slovenia's foremost wine-producing area. World-class wines combined with exceptional local produce makes any visit a culinary adventure; indeed, it is recommended that every walking or cycling experience is accompanied by a slow, multi-course meal on a terrace overlooking a vineyard.

Commercial winemaking for local people is a relatively new phenomenon. Traditionally, the colonate system prevailed – a kind of feudalism where tenants were required to give their crops to their landlords. This meant the main wines from Brda were associated with the estates, castles and villas of European nobility, who were enjoying their so-called 'picnic in a foreign land' throughout the 19th and early 20th centuries. Today, local families are producing their own wines or are working with the Vinska Klet G.B. wine co-operative whilst a number of these historic villas and castles have been cleverly repurposed as community enterprises or family-run hotels.

The Renaissance Vila Vipolže in the village of the same name is now a centre for cultural tourism conferences, weddings and events. A short distance away in Dobrovo is the castle Grad Dobrovo, housing a fine restaurant, the Zoran Mušic Art Gallery and the area's museum. It is now the home of Rebula Wines, where guests can taste over 20 of its products, and the starting point for many of the themed walks and cycle trails in Brda. The destination's main tourist information centre is in Šmartno's Medieval Village.

The elegant Gredič Castle was formerly the residence of Count Silverio De Baguer, a Spanish diplomat and ambassador to the Vatican. He is widely regarded as taking the lead in reorganising wine production in Brda, planting his own vineyards

Above: Šmartno's Medieval Village.

in 1880 and introducing Brda wines to the Papal cellar. The castle was later acquired by the Simčič family. Renovated and remodelled in 2012, the castle, still known locally as Ceglo Villa, is now a boutique hotel with vinoteka, a Michelin-starred restaurant and art gallery. In 1957, Zvonimir Simčič founded the Vinska Klet G.B., a co-operative that has united over 400 family wine growers to elevate local wines into a global success story. In honour of Count Silverio De Baguers' legacy, the co-operative has named its high-end wines Klet Brda Bagueri.

In 1860, another Simčič – Anton – bought a small farm in the delightful hilltop border village of Medana, where wine meets art and poetry, home of the region's most prolific poet, Alojz Gradnik, and the Klinec Homestead Art Colony. Business success followed, with Anton opening a village shop, an inn and a wine store in Vienna. His four sons inherited the different enterprises and today a fifth-generation Simčič, Marjan, oversees the family's wine estate. Marjan expresses the Brda-wide philosophy of wine growing, acknowledging that great wines are born in the vineyard. He believes in the power of nature, saying, 'In Brda, nature has created the ideal climatic conditions for growing vines. The sun generously warms the air, and the warm wind caresses the curves of the Goriška Brda hills. Our vines are carefully selected and grown according to traditional methods. The soil was deposited on the surface of the hills by ancient oceans. Wind, rain, and sun have ground, washed, and heated it for thousands of years. The result is opoka, a soil rich in minerals from the Earth's ancient history, which enables us to produce unique wines with a recognizable terroir. Experience has taught us to apply only natural methods to vine cultivation and not to use irrigation, artificial fertilisers or insecticides. This all produces elegant and noble wines.'

The population of Brda is less than 6,000. The largest of the area's 45 villages (and its administrative centre) is Dobrovo, which has less than 500 residents. The crescent-shaped hilltop village of Šmartno, described by Gradnik as being like an 'eagle's nest', sits at the geographic centre of the region. With its medieval walls, anchored by five towers, this must be one of the prettiest villages in Slovenia and maybe the whole of Italy and Istria. Appropriately, its church, the largest in Brda, is dedicated to Saint Martin, the patron saint of wine, celebrated in November with Saint Martin's Wine Festival.

Šmartno is where you will find the family-run eco hotel San Martin. The marketing expertise of Vesna, together with her sommelier husband, Bogdan Valentinčič, has created the award-winning 14-room hotel with balconies overlooking the village from an abandoned former Yugoslav school. Vineyard running, walking in the Plešivo Forest, exploring the Krčnik Gorge or discovering classic wine estates (such as Movia, Klinec, Edi Šimčič, Erzetič, Ščurek and Ferdinand) are recommended activities.

The Brda tourism team (Brda Tourism, Culture, Youth and Sport Board) does a first-class job organising and promoting activities and events as well as creating imaginative trails for cycling and walking. There are almost 300 km along ten well-marked cycle routes named after local fruits, including cherry, fig, apricot and plum, eight hiking trails and three thematic routes, the highlights being Gradnik's Poetry Trail and the evocative Walk of Peace. Two stages of the Alpe Adria (Grossglockner to Trieste long-distance trail) and the Juliana Trail also navigate through Brda.

There are creative workshops with local lavender and olive oil producers, wine discovery tours and insights into beekeeping you can visit using Hop-on Brda, a region-wide electric cycle hire scheme. Traditional festivals, such as the annual Cherry Festival in May/June, combine with new events such as The Open Wine Cellar days in June, the Brda and Wine culinary feats in April, the Dreams of Medana: Festival of Books and Wine,

the Heroes of the Vineyards Marathon, the Brda Contemporary Music Festival and Days of Elemental Sounds to deliver a year-round programme to attract tourists. The efforts have been recognised nationally and internationally, most recently with an award for an innovative platform to promote Brda cherries during the pandemic lockdown. The 2021 initiative, Brda Cherries in Every Home, was recognised by the global Green Destination organisation as international best practice.

Although there are a limited number of hotel rooms, the accommodation stock is bolstered by farmsteads, with rooms allowing visitors a direct connection with nature, tradition and local produce. Interesting attractions touch each emotion, from the soaring 360° views from the Gonjače Lookout Tower (north to the Julian Alps, east over the Trnovo Forest, south over the karst to Trieste and west over the Fruilian Plains) to the heart-wrenching Sabotin Peace Park below the village of Podsabotin in Italy, which tells the shared story of the World War I Battles of the Isonzo Front.

Today's relative prosperity, driven by its fine wines, good local food and quality tourism experiences, belies the fact that during the late 20th century Brda was considered the cheapest area to buy property on the Yugoslavian Monopoly board. Slovenia is designated European Region of Gastronomy 2021 and Brda is now one of the most appealing destinations for food and wine lovers.

Above: Cycling in Brda.

ISLE OF ARRAN, NORTH AYRSHIRE, SCOTLAND

Arran the island: island time in no time

The journey to a destination should be entirely focused on raising expectations and enhancing levels of anticipation of great things to come. Whichever direction you start from, whatever route you take to get to the ferry terminal at Ardrossan harbour, the Isle of Arran seems to gradually unveil itself: giving enticing glimpses that hint of a special place the closer you get to boarding the Caledonian MacBrayne (CalMac) ferry for the hour-long crossing to Brodick Harbour and your arrival on the island. The big scenic reveal of Arran is especially sharp as you turn west off the M77 from Glasgow onto the A71 then onto the A78 when the drama of the Island's magnificent landscape, dominated by Goat Fell (874 m), appears directly in front of you as if floating on the horizon in the Firth of Clyde. This profile of the north Arran hills as seen from the Ayrshire coast is referred to as the 'Sleeping Warrior', due to its resemblance to a resting human figure. The island sits between the mainland and the Kintyre peninsula but having more in common both culturally and physically with the Hebrides.

There are two alternative routes from Glasgow and the north: the first is the attractive country roads passing Lochwinnoch and the town of Kilwinning; the other is the coast road which follows the southern shore of the Firth of Clyde wending its way through Greenock (former fishing village, port and now the main cruise ship terminal of Scotland's west coast) and Largs (a popular seaside resort with a strong Viking heritage) after which the traveller is introduced to the three most southerly of Scotland's 790 islands: first passing Greater

SCOTLAND

●ISLE OF ARRAN

Population of Lamlash: 1,000
Population of wider island: 5,000
Nearest international airports: Glasgow International, Edinburgh International, Prestwick.
Key websites: www.visitarran.com; www.visitscotland.com
Icons: Brodick Castle, Lochranza Castle, Taste of Arran, Arran Aromatics (Sense of Scotland), Isle of Arran Distillery, Isle of Arran Brewery, Goat Fell, The String, Auchrannie Resort, Caledonian MacBrayne, Visit Arran, the Arran Trust, Cold Water Island Tourism.

• •

Cumbrae then catching cameo appearances of the Isle of Bute, before getting a distant view of the hump in the ocean that is Ailsa Craig (a volcanic plug whose granite rocks have been the source of curling stones for over one hundred years) and, of course Arran.

As the ferry approaches Brodick Pier, the island gradually introduces itself to visitors – a

job it has done for well over a century. Early guidebooks published in the 1920s extolled the virtues of a holiday on Arran, however, it was not until the 1950s that tourism really developed with steamboats carrying thousands of day-trippers and holidaymakers from the industrial towns of Scotland's Central Belt. It was 1953 and the arrival of the first car ferry, the 'Arran' that heralded the start of Arran's real love affair with tourism – today it is worth almost £65 m a year to the island's economy up £30 m in less than a decade.

It is easy to be seduced by the charms of this compact (32 km-long, 16 km-wide) island, referred to by Visit Arran as 'the enchanting jewel in Scotland's scenic crown, a visual feast, boasting culinary delights, its own brewery and distillery, and stacks of accommodation'. Visit Arran pulls no punches in its promotion of the destination: 'a place where you can find a little bit of everything you'd ever want from a Scottish island; an ever-changing coastline, dramatic mountain peaks, sheltered beaches, verdant forests, diverse wildlife, great cultural festivals and a wealth of tasty local produce'. The island has the best ice cream in the world produced by the Isle of Arran Ice Cream Company. Its cheeses are second to none and Arran Aromatic cosmetics are regularly found on the shelves of leading beauty salons across Europe. All the praise it receives is valid and true and Arran always surprises and never lets you down. It is always a delight to visit. This has been endorsed by CNN who recently named Arran as one of the top seven islands in the world to visit along with Trivago naming it as the top European island to visit in 2016.

Arran is well known for its varied scenery, indeed, all the variations in Scotland's dramatic landscape can be experienced on this one island because it sits astride the Highland Boundary Fault dividing the island into the 'Highland' and 'Lowland' geology that has made Scotland famous. Arran is a geologist's paradise and means that it is best explored by pulling on the hiking boots or jumping on a bicycle. There are not many places

in the world where, in a three-kilometre walk, you can see evidence of changing environments that span more than 100 million years from Devonian to Permian times. The result is an amazing geology and landscape that was studied in the 1780s by the father of modern geology, James Hutton, who discovered a geological phenomenon that allowed him to demonstrate the great age of the Earth and the evidence of 'former worlds', some of which were explored and filmed by Sir David Attenborough for his TV series *Life on Earth*.

All of this led the renowned Scottish writer and comedian, Billy Connolly, a good friend of the island, to state that: 'The Isle of Arran is the true Gem of the Clyde. Loved by the residents, and adored by visitors, it is truly a miniature Scotland'. He was not the first to use this analogy. For many years the island had been promoted nationally and internationally as 'Scotland in miniature'. In 2006 the local community together with representatives from businesses and the tourism sector took a bold but very carefully considered and thought-through decision to ambitiously re-brand the island as 'Arran-The Island: Island Time in No Time'.

This was a clear statement of intent. It is unambiguous in claiming Arran to be the most accessible of the Scottish islands. A place that captures the essence of an island escape and, most significantly, whose 5,000 residents were sufficiently proud and confident to proclaim that their 432 sq. km island was as good as any other island destination for a holiday. Arran is a fine, year-round, short break destination and easy to navigate. The main road, the A841, circumnavigates the island, staying fairly close to the coast with 'The String Road' climb over the middle of the island from Brodick west to Blackwaterfoot. Almost all Arran's settlements and many of its visitor attractions lie on or close to the main road round the island and, idiosyncratically, tourists are recommended to do a clockwise tour of the island. Lamlash is Arran's 'capital' and its largest village over-looking Lamlash Bay and Holy Island. It is

home to the council offices, hospital and secondary school – where in 2012 the world's first-ever Cold Water Tourism Conference took place hosted by the some of the school's older pupils.

The north is the more mountainous northern half of the island. On the shores of Loch Ranza is is a village set in spectacular scenery where the mountains and the sea collide, attractions include Lochranza Castle and the Isle of Arran Distillery – the island's only distillery. Whisky has always been produced on Arran and the Distillery has been in production for over 160 years. It has recently opened the Rowan House, a new blending and tasting building in the grounds of the Lochranza Distillery and the development of a second distillery at Lagg, at the south end of the island. The slipway at Lochranza welcomes the Arran to Clonaig (Kintyre peninsula) summer-only ferry – Arran's little known 'back door'. Continuing clockwise on the road trip, south of the distillery the road takes you over the shoulder of the jagged mountains and the routes up Goat Fell en route to becoming reacquainted with the coast at Sannox then on to the National Trust's Brodick Castle and the award-winning Auchrannie Resort and spa complex.

It is hard to summarise the many attractions or to do justice to the overall the appeal of Arran – The Island. An ancient Irish poem, rather bucolic in style, called *Agalllamh na Senorach*, first recorded in the 13th century does, however, go some way to rectify this problem:

'Arran of the many stags
The sea strikes against her shoulders,
Companies of men can feed there,
Blue spears are reddened among her boulders
Merry hinds are on her hills,
Juicy berries are there for food,
Refreshing water in her streams,
Nuts in plenty in the wood'

As with all the destinations in this book Arran's tourism success is based upon a concerted, collaborative, effort by a dynamic group of community and business leaders who have formed

Visit Arran, the island's dynamic destination management organisation. It has over 140 partners representing 240 businesses and has developed the Arran Ambassadors programme and introduced the Golf Pass, the Arran Card and the Arran Passport all designed to help the visitor enjoy the island. This strong commitment to partnership working is to ensure a quality experience for all visitors and involves all sectors of the tourism industry as well as other businesses: the serviced and non-serviced accommodation, heritage attractions, the Taste of Arran food and drink cooperative, other island produce, activity providers, community groups and also taxis, car hire companies, haulage contractors, CalMac and public transport services as well as the local newspaper. Visit Arran has also spawned he Arran Trust. This is the island's innovative visitor gifting scheme where voluntary contributions from visitors, currently about £55,000 a year, are used to fund projects that look after the beautiful landscapes and environment of Arran.

Perhaps the most outstanding aspect of a visit to Arran is the immersion of tourists into the community and local ways. Visit Arran regularly gets comments from visitors saying how much they enjoy spending time in the community; that they are treated like temporary locals not paying guests. This is creating a strong emotional connection with the wellbeing of the guest and the resident at the centre of the work of Visit Arran and ensuring a sustainable experience for the benefit of all.

JYVÄSKYLÄ, FINLAND

The city of lakes, light, Alvar Aalto, movement, sport and wellbeing

FINLAND

●JYVÄSKYLÄ

Population of city: 132,000
Population of wider area: 170,000
Nearest international airports: Jyväskylä,
Tampere, Helsinki.
Key websites: www.visitjyvaskyla.fi;
valonkaupunki.jyvaskyla.fi; www.finavia.fi
Icons: Alvar Aalto (1898–1976), Alvar Aalto Museum,
Säynätsol Town Hall, Neste Rally of Finland,
Petäjävesi and Tajumäki Old Churches, Toivola
Old Courtyard, Sauna Culture, Lutakko Square,
Muurame Church,the University, Nokia.

● ●

Above: City and its lakeshore.

Jyväskylä, in central Finland, lays claim to a number of different synonyms: the city of lakes (there are 328 in the city); the city of theatres (there are 11); the city of museums (there are eight); the city of light; the city of movement, sport and wellbeing; the city of human technology; the capital of sauna culture; Finland's capital of sport and recreation; the city of Alvar Aalto... and, actually, all have a legitimate claim to be the reason to visit the fastest growing city in central Finland.

Jyväskylä, founded under Russian rule in 1837, is some 270 km directly north of the capital Helsinki, in Finland's Lakelands – hilly, forested countryside speckled with over a thousand lakes. As you descend into the city's airport, having flown over thousands of kilometres of forest, Jyväskylä appears as an oasis. The city sits on the crossroads of the country's major road, rail and waterway networks. It is built on the north shore of Lake Päijänne on a ridge overlooking two of the largest

of the three hundred lakes in the city: Jyväsjärvi and Tuomiojärvi. This is a city with long, cold, snow-filled winters, relatively mild but short summers with long days of up to 20 hours of daylight.

Jyväskylä has good accessibility, is strategically located in the centre of the country and offers a very high quality of life. It is no surprise, therefore, that it has become the home to world famous Finnish companies including Nokia, M-Real and Metso Paper as well as a young population attracted by the higher education institutions, the range of sporting activities and the environment. The city's rapid growth over the past 40 years has been due to a number of factors: a forward-thinking, ambitious City Council working with the communities in the wider region to create the networked Jyväskylä city region; the global reputation of its University and Polytechnic (indeed it has been called 'the Athens of the North' due to the quality of its educational facilities – over one-third of the population are students); the ability to attract new technology companies; and, establishing a world-class, convention centre (Jyväskylä Paviljonki) within a lakeshore area dedicated to the needs of business, conference and meetings tourism.

The city is regarded as the 'home' of one of the world's greatest architects and designers. Born in the small town of Kuortane in 1898, Hugo Alvar Henrik Aalto and his family moved to Jyväskylä where he joined the city's Lyceum before studying architecture at the University of Helsinki. He returned to Jyväskylä where he settled, started a family and began his illustrious career, referring to it as his home city. Indeed, the city in turn is home to some 30 of Aalto's creations representing each stage of his career from early classicism, through the phase of functionalism and experimentation, to the monumentalism of his final years. Key buildings including the University, the Town Hall, the 'Experimental House' and, of course, the building that now is the eponymous museum. Today Visit Jyväskylä, the city's tourist board, has organised a walking trail where tourists can tread in the master's footsteps – one of many imaginatively themed tours of the city. Aalto was more than an architect of over five hundred projects. His work included the design of textiles, furniture and glassware. He was a painter and a sculptor who regarded these talents as mere 'branches of the tree of architecture' helping to contribute to the idea of *'Gesamtkunstwerk'* where the finished building is created as a total work of art.

In recent years, the city has been rewriting the rules of successful development by placing tourism, sport, human kinetics, wellness and wellness technology at the heart of its, highly focused plan – hence it has become known as the 'Human Technology City', a rather clumsy title that describes the remarkable way this destination is harnessing its highly scenic, forest and lake land setting for a wide range of innovative outdoor activities together with its research in all aspects of the way the human body works. Jyväskylä has

focused on attracting expertise and developing specialisms in environmental, human and wellness technology opening, for example, the Agora Human Technology Centre, the Nanoscience Centre and the Viveca Wellness Centre. This idea of human technology in the city is based on the fact that human values, such as innovation, openness, trust, cooperation, partnership, environment and corporate and individual wellness are the basis of good quality of life, a strong business culture and a great place to visit.

At the heart of the city's tourism appeal is being '100% Finnish', which is firmly rooted in the local culture, its nature, the wonderful range of sport and recreational facilities, the unique sauna culture (there is a must-visit sauna museum and village at Jämas), of Aalto's architectural and design legacy and the many resources that contribute to wellbeing (safety, cleanliness, peace, tranquility, entertainment, local foods, clear air).

Until recently tourism was dominated by those visiting for conferences, meetings and business exhibitions. However, in recent years, leisure tourism has grown attracting increasing numbers of international visitors, especially from Germany, Russia, UK, Sweden and France. The accommodation stock has improved, the wellness products and services have developed and innovation, linking research about the functioning of the human body, is giving visitors the chance to take part in outdoor adventure activities that have far greater physical and psychological benefits than most other destinations. For example, extensive research at the city's Institute for Olympic Sports has demonstrated the links between over-exercising and stress, spawning new technologies that allow 'the heart to tell you more than just your pulse', and the creation of a range of consumer devices which help individuals monitor and interpret their own bodies to achieve optimum benefits.

Jyväskylä is the base of the Finnish Aquatic Institution, which has developed a range of technologies to test and monitor the healing and recuperative effects of swimming in natural, open, water. This builds on the strong regional tradition in this part of Finland of taking exercise in the lakes and rivers that are so plentiful in the area resulting in a revival of interest in fitness in nature and new equipment such as the water belt flotation aid which has stimulated interest in lake swimming and the new activity of water jogging (developed by the Finnish Central Association for Recreational Sports and Outdoor Activities, the body that successfully developed Nordic Walking).

There are two UNESCO World Heritage sites in the city: firstly, the Petäjävesi Old Church, built between 1763 and 1765, is a masterpiece of construction in wood which was inscribed on the World Heritage list as a prime example of northern wooden architecture in 1994. The church is representative of Scandinavian, Lutheran church architecture and the long tradition of log building; secondly, the Struve Geodetic Arc (inscribed by UNESCO in 2005) on the site of the Oravivuori Arc Point, which offers beautiful views of lake Päijänne. The Arc was created in 1816–1855 to determine the size and shape of the Earth using a chain of survey triangulation measurements stretching from the Arctic Sea to the Black Sea, through ten countries with six of these points in Finland.

Cleverly, Visit Jyväskylä has harnessed the UNESCO sites to provide the foundation for a series of creative new experiences involving sport and adventure activities. They have created the a UNESCO canoeing trail in nature. A company called Tavinsulka has developed a multi-stage walking trail through picturesque scenery stretching for almost 60 km from the Old Church at Petäjävesi to Jämsänkoski, through an area of lakes and river gorges ending at the Struve Geodetic Arc, and on to the Kärkistensalmi bridge with a visit to the Alvar Aalto Experimental house.

This is a city of events. There is an impressive, year-round programme of over five thousand

events; the undoubted highlights being the City of Light Festival, the Triennial Graphica Creativa, the winter Arctic and Fabulous Film Festival and, of course, Rally Finland. This was first held under the name Jyväskylän Suurajot (Jyväskylä Grand Prix) in 1951. Today it is formally known as the Neste Rally Finland, and, previously, the Rally of the Thousand Lakes. It is part of the World Rally Championship taking place in July each year in the Lakeland area and beginning and ending in Jyväskylä. It is recognised as the oldest and the fastest event in the multi-stage, global competition thereby gaining the prestigious reputation of the 'Grand Prix of Rallying'. The event has become one of the largest annually organised public events in the Nordic countries, attracting hundreds of thousands of spectators each year to the city.

Above: Old wooden church of Petäjävesi village.

KITZBÜHEL, AUSTRIA

Sophisticated luxury effortlessly rubbing shoulders with traditional Tirolean hospitality, contemporary wellness and legendary downhill skiing

Kitzbühel is a self-assured, confident, world-class destination that exudes the new alpine lifestyle of tradition and modernity: where mountains, nature and sport meet global luxury brands in a comfortable, unpretentious, symbiotic relationship in the heart of the Alps. This is where urban flair and international brands meets classic Tirolean tradition and sophisticated hospitality. As a tourism destination it enjoys its well-earned, legendary status. It is internationally known for its love of the finer things of life (exclusive shopping, gastronomy, fine accommodation and wonderful scenery) as well as its passion for summer and, especially, winter sports. The snow sports in particular have made Kitzbühel the place of legends, sporting heroes and epic victories. Put all these factors together and you have the 'Kitzbühel way of life'.

The destination is located at the easternmost corner of the Federal State of the Tyrol, east of Innsbruck, west of Salzburg and just over two hour's drive south of Munich. It is nestled in a basin between the imposing, majestic mountains of the Wilder Kaiser, the Kitzbüheler Horn and the Hahnenkamm. Kitzbühel, together with the neighbouring, unspoilt Tirolean villages of Jochberg, Reith and Aurach, for a powerful, highly, attractive four-season, destination which have been effortlessly welcoming guests for many years with the three outlying villages providing the perfect relaxed complement to the busy-ness of Kitzbühel.

Jochberg, just south of Kitzbühel on the road to the Thurn pass, was also a former 3,000 year-old copper mining community (the Kupferplatte

Population of town: 8,500
Population of wider area: 13,000
Nearest international airports: Salzburg, Innsbruck, Vienna, Munich (Germany).
Key websites: www.kitzbueheler-alpen.com; www.kitzbuhel.com
Icons: Hahnenkamm Race, The Strief, Alfons Walde, Kitzbüheler Horn, Wilder Kaiser, Franz Reisch, Schwarzer Adler, Tennerhof Gourmet and Spa de Charme, Grand Tirolia hotel, A-Rosa Schlosshotel Kitzbühel, Bio-Hotel Stanglwirt, Balthassar Hauser.

mine is now a tourist attraction). There is a fine, large, heated outdoor woodland swimming pool surrounded by good countryside for mountain-biking and walking. This village was also a place of pilgrimage as recorded in the so-called *'Mirakelbuch'* (miracle book) of 1505. It is still possible to take the purportedly healing waters in

the Saint Wolfgang chapel in the parish church. In winter Jochberg is part of the single KitzSki Kitzbühel-Kirchberg skiing area and the popular torchlight walks and horse-drawn sleigh rides. The village of Reith bei Kitzbühel sits at the base of the Wilder Kaiser north of the town. Dating back to 1190, when the first church was built, it is a good base for active holidays: golf at the Kitzbühel Schwarzsee-Reith golf course; hiking and cycling with the Gieringer Weiher and Lake Schwarzsee as beautiful lakes for wild swimming. Aurach Unteraurach, Oberaurach and several scattered settlements together form the municipality of Aurach bei Kitzbühel. Mining was also the main source of revenue for many centuries, with two crossed hammers on the village emblem serving as a reminder of this heritage, whilst a wildlife park is a major attraction today.

The star of the destination is the most legendary sports town in the Alps. A town that has fuelled the imagination about the alure and romance of winter sports, it has recently been at the vanguard of using new technology to promote summer walking and cycling trails. Throughout the past hundred years since becoming a hotspot for tourism it has consistently redefined the meaning of luxury service and hospitality. Kitzbühel is known as the 'Gamsstadt' (the town of the goat-like antelope, the Chamoix), receiving its official status as a town in 1271. The town in the 16th and 17th centuries was based on copper and silver mining. Kitzbühel's historic, charming and compact town centre – referred to by local people simply as the 'Stadt' – is based around two squares each characterised by a colourful ensemble of medieval merchants' houses (the town's museum, Heimatmuseum is housed in one of these historic buildings) and is framed by two, handsome main streets which are full of delightful, Tirolean vernacular houses, many of which are colourfully painted with typical Austrian scenes by the local artist and architect Alfons Walde.

The area first welcomed summer tourists in the mid-18th century attracted by the spectacular natural scenery. The arrival of the railway in 1875 further boosted the number of visitors. The area's development as a winter sports destination dates to the 1890s when Franz Reisch imported skis from Norway and made the first ski runs on the Kitzbüheler Horn with ski races starting in the winter of 1894/95. It is no surprise that Kitzbühel is regarded as being the birthplace of Austrian skiing and home to one of the first celebrity stars of the sport. The Hahnenkamm is the legend that underpins the legend. This mountain is part of the Ski-welt area which for three days in January each year fills the destination with over 100,000 tourists drawn to see the world's most prestigious downhill races, now into its 80th year, and the single most challenging race on the Strief run.

By the turn of the 20th Century the destination had established a reputation as a magnet for Europe's high society as well as celebrities of the film and music industries. These luxury-seeking markets continue to enjoy the elegant shopping in the flagship stores, the quality restaurants and the large cluster of five-star, wellness and spa hotels. Increasingly, however, the destination has broadened its appeal attracting new tourists drawn by the range of summer outdoor activities and evening entertainment together with a wider choice of smaller, family-run hotels, traditional inns and guesthouses. There is an extraordinary range of things to do with over 20 golf courses, hundreds of kilometres of themed walking routes and cycling trails, daily walking tours with trained guides and a network of quality sports facilities. The destination organises an impressive year-round programme of events, highlights of which are the signature events and vibrant local events involving local groups. The signature events include: the Austrian Open Tennis, BG Kitzbühel Triathlon, Kitzbühel Hahnenkamm Race, Kitzbüheler Horn Road Race and the Snow Arena Polo World Championships. The smaller

events programme includes over 40 folklore concerts and the Kitz Summer Nights.

The ease of access (there are regular high-speed trains to Munich and Vienna with good connecting local services) together with a main road network to Innsbruck, Salzburg and beyond to Venice) helps put this destination within easy reach of the key markets of middle Europe. The delivery of these consistently great tourist experiences is guaranteed by the finely tuned, very efficient hospitality industry. The marketing of the destination together with the co-ordination of the events and festivals, the provision of tourist information and the stewardship of the brand is the job of Kitzbühel Tourismus. This highly professional local tourism body has a clear vision for the destination led by a Board of Directors and a dynamic group of highly motivated executives.

The plans for tourism in the destination are regularly reviewed and curated by Kitzbühel Tourismus in close collaboration with regional bodies, commercial partners together with the community and the experienced leaders of businesses through the region. Public policies and the collective efforts are aligned to deliver for the common good. This is a community that knows which side its bread is buttered ensuring that tourism really is everyone's business; understanding that quality does not happen by chance and that customer care is at the heart of ensuring the continued success of the destination's much-prized reputation for quality. This includes having a streamlined approach to supporting innovative ideas and private sector investment in tourism development.

This refined way of working is best illustrated by the way in which the destination has positively responded to the demand for more superior hotels with the opening of the Schwarzer Adler, Tennerhof Gourmet and Spa de Charme, Kitzhof Mountian Design and the Grand Tirolia hotel in recent years. The efficiency of this approach was best illustrated when, on a visit to Kitzbühel in 2006, I was given a book by the manager of the A-Rosa Schlosshotel Kitzbühel entitled *380 Days* which tells the story of the creation of this magnificent 104 bed/ 45 suite hotel with spa and golf course from its conception in September 2003 to its opening just 380 days later.

One cannot leave this destination without reference to the completely unique, highly original, and super-fun, Bio-Hotel Stanglwirt which celebrated 400 hundred years of providing fine hospitality in 2009, and 150 of those years the welcome has been provided by the Hauser family. From the early days of the farm being a modest guesthouse to the extraordinary campus that is the Stanglwirt today, the Hauser's have constantly reinvented, expanded and innovated to create a model of Tirolean craftsmanship, gastronomy, hospitality and wellness. Over the past 40 years, throughout its incredible evolution into one of the most successful and spectacular family hotels in Europe, Balthassar and Magdalena Hauser and their young family have ensured that it remains a working farm and that the family traditions for exceptional hospitality are always maintained; and that the famous *Weisswurstparty*, held on the eve of the Hahnenkamm downhill run continues to be the most sought-after ticket in town.

• •

Above: The Hahnenkamm Downhill Race.

LAUSANNE, SWITZERLAND

Capital olympique, Belle Époque lake steamers, grand luxury hotels and the world's leading hotel management school

SWITZERLAND

● LAUSANNE

Population of city: 140,000
Population of wider area: 402,000
Nearest international airports: Geneva / Genève Aéroport.
Key websites: www.thelausanneguide.com; www.olympiccapital.ch; www.lausanne-tourisme.ch
Icons: La Flon, Beau-Rivage Palace Hotel, Ouchy, International Olympic Committee, Olympic Museum, AQUATIS, Plateform 10, Museums, Tour de Sauvabelin, Ecole hôtelière de Lausanne, Rolex Learning Centre, Lausanne Palace Hotel, Lavaux Vineyards.

In 1994, on the centenary of the Modern Olympiad, the International Olympic Committee (IOC) awarded Lausanne the unique title of 'Olympic Capital' in recognition of its contribution to sport in general and to the Olympic movement as a result of enjoying a long-established relationship with the IOC.

Lausanne tumbles down over the terraces of three hillsides, with hidden medieval squares and gothic Cathedral, down to the shores of Lac Léman (Lake Geneva) at Ouchy and Vidy. The city is the capital of the Canton of Vaud, less than an hour from Geneva. It is a city known for its discreet historic charm, exceptional sporting credentials, cultural vibrancy, world-class higher education and inherently high standards of hospitality all set within a wonderful natural environment. The city has breath-taking views southwards over Lake Geneva, with its fleet of Belle Époque steamers, to the Jura Mountains and the spa town of Evian-des-Bains in France.

It was these really appealing characteristics that led to Baron Pierre de Coubertin, the founder of the modern Olympic Movement deciding, in agreement with the City, to establish the headquarters of the IOC in Lausanne in 1915 when he declared: 'this is the most apt location imaginable for the establishment of the administrative headquarters of Olympism. The Olympic spirit will find the pledge of freedom that it needs to progress in the independent and proud atmosphere that one breathes in Lausanne.' This special relationship – and there is only one Olympic Capital in the world – was constantly reiterated by Juan Antonio Samaranch when I had the pleasure to interview him in 1990 and 1992. Catalan-born Samaranch was the second longest serving President of the IOC (after Coubertin). He loved the lifestyle of his adopted home and led the case to designate Lausanne with the Olympic Capital status and make this small Swiss city the envy of the world.

Lausanne takes this status very responsibly with the City Council creating an environment for hosting international organisations active in sport. This has allowed the continual expansion of the network of international sport federations, major players on the Olympic scene – more than 20 at this point in time – to which can be added around 20 different organisations, such as the Court of Arbitration for Sport (CAS), which now exist in the city. Lausanne is a city that takes sport seriously recognising it as a powerful economic force for growth and granting sport the same status as any other sector of the economy – and why not? A recent study shows that the IOC and the many international sports federations now based in the city contribute over €250 million each year to the economy of Lausanne. During the 100 years of common history the IOC and the City achieved many stand-out moments notably the opening of the International Olympic Museum and the announcements by the IOC in 2018 that a new HQ for the IOC would be built in Vidy in a modern, exciting building designed by the Danish architectural firm 3XN. The presence of the IOC and numerous other sporting bodies in Lausanne guarantees an impressive menu of highly varied, international sporting events in the city each year: from the annual marathon to Cyclotour du Léman.

The Olympic Museum sits like a summer palace in its own delightful, sculpture-filled garden on the shores of the Lake at Ouchy. This sleek, clean, sharp, modernist building was a key project of the Samaranch era. It moved from its very modest beginnings in the city centre to its present site in 1993. Twenty years later the interior was completely refurbished with new exhibits interpreting the origin of the Games and celebrating the Olympic spirit. It is the embodiment of the Olympic Movement, celebrating sport, art, and education, with this triumvirate of elements reflecting the make-up of the city itself.

Indeed, Lausanne's appeal is far from being entirely sports orientated. This is an expressive, vibrant, cosmopolitan city that was recently declared, by a world-renowned trend magazine, as the best small city in the world – an accolade that is hard to dispute. It is no surprise that Lausanne is the HQ city for a number of global companies including Tetra Lavas, Nestlé Nespresso, Logitech, SPORTACORD and, of course, the IOC.

Alongside its long-standing and close affinity with sports tourism, contemporary art and architecture are fast becoming a key feature of the city. In addition to the designs for the new IOC campus there is a necklace of powerful new architectural statements. The silver rings, with their shimmering exterior discs, make up La Cité de l'Eau AQUATIS Aquarium / Vivarium and hotel located in the city's Biopôle Science Park. Conceived almost 20 years ago, and funded by a specially created Foundation, this is a unique European concept focusing on all aspects of freshwater habitats and their conservation around the world.

Elsewhere, Plateforme 10 will unite three of Lausanne's museums and is set to be a major European arts hub as a new arts district in the city, on the site of the city's former train sheds. After a decade of planning and development, the first to open was Musée Cantonal des Beaux-Arts (MCBA) to be followed by Musée de l'Elysée (photography) and Mudac (contemporary design and applied arts). MCBA was designed by award-winning Estudio Barozzi/Veiga – the team behind The Art Institute of Chicago. The whole scheme is part of the transformation of Lausanne train station which is set to become a major transport hub for the region. On the campus of the École polytechnique fédérale de Lausanne is the Rolex Learning Centre. This is a highly idiosyncratic building, which looks like a slice of Emmental cheese, and was designed by Japanese architects Kazuyo Sejima and Ryue Nishizawa This is a must-see tourist attraction whether or not you are a fan of ultra-modern design.

Despite the multi-layered topography, Lausanne is a very walkable city. Explorers of the city are helped on their way by the recently refurbished funicular railway from the Ouchy waterfront and by massive public lifts from La Flon to the central railway station which connects with the city's exceptionally efficient, integrated, local transport system. However, exploring Lausanne on foot is the best way to experience the stair-cased Vielle Ville (The Old City), Place de la Palud or La Flon. La Flon is the heart of the city of Lausanne, pulsing with life, day and night, in a modern and innovative setting. It's another of the city's architectural success stories: a district of former warehouses that starts at the Place de l'Europe, a vibrant area of restaurants, bars, clubs, boutiques, cinemas, bowling and exhibition spaces. In the winter, it hosts an ice-rink and in the summer a sandy beach. From industrial wasteland to an alternative city centre. Undoubtedly the best 360° views of the city, the Lake and the Alps and Jura Mountains is from the 35-metre-high La Tour de Sauvabelen situated in the forest in La Bois De Sauvabelin, in the northern suburbs of the city. This wooden tower and viewing platform opened in 2003 and was funded by local businesses each funding each of the 302 steps to its summit.

This is also a city renowned for its collection of grand, luxury, lake-view hotels – the Lausanne Palace, the Royal Savoy and, of course, the Beau-Rivage Palace. These are the Grand Masters of the Belle Époque era where tradition, discretion and absolute adherence to the fine culture of the highest Swiss hotel traditions are maintained. These glorious statements of old-school luxury have hosted international celebrities, royal families and world-renowned artists and have witnessed the signing of international treaties. For over 150 years they have remained relevant to the demanding needs of their clientele and their historic architecture still dominates the Lausanne skyline.

A major ingredient of Lausanne's success as a world-class tourist destination is the team at Lausanne Tourisme. This organisation has matured over the past 30 years to become one of the most outstanding destination management and marketing organisations in the world. Throughout this period, it has been led by visionary individuals supported by highly professional specialists and fully supported by the City Council and its numerous industry partners. Lausanne Tourisme has served to present the city in the global tourism marketplace. It has embraced the adjacent destinations of Vevey-Montreux and is encouraging innovative tourist experiences (such as the Wine Train that shuttles back and forth from Lausanne through the UNESCO World Heritage Lavaux Vineyards and Tech Tours), constantly supporting the wide range of traditional and new sporting and cultural events, including the city's signature event: the unconventional Festival de la Cité. This unique cultural week-long event is full of unexpected delights in an annual programme that combines theatre performances with music, dance, circus and art installations which aim to build a bridge between the living performance arts and a creative, new, urban culture – admission free! Other regular events include all forms of international sporting competitions (from athletics to pétanque), the Swiss Dance Days, Prix de Lausanne and the Lausanne Art Fair.

Above: The Olympic Museum.

LINZ, AUSTRIA

Innovation and creativity driving constant change

This is a tourism destination that, given its 20th century history, really shouldn't be on anyone's bucket list; but have no hesitation – make a visit and make it soon – this is a vibrant, stimulating, easy to navigate, small city with year-round appeal.

Located astride the River Danube midway between Austria's world-famous cultural destination giants of Salzburg and Vienna, Linz is fast becoming one of the world's most exciting, dynamic and experiential cities. *'In Linz beginnts'* (it all begins in Linz) is a famous Austrian saying which reflects the city's newfound identity and confidence.

Not so long ago the city had a reputation, within Austria and beyond, as being 'Linz stinks!' – literally and metaphorically. From its Roman origins, Linz flourished as a trading point in the Middle Ages. Its status gradually diminished over the next 400 years reducing its influence to that of a modest provincial town.

In the 1930s, however, under Germany's emerging Third Reich, Linz became a patronage city of the Führer who had spent his early life in the city. It was singled out for special urban and industrial investment, especially for steel and armaments production with its future as Hitler's retirement city and the Third Reich's cultural centre.

For ten years immediately post-war Linz was a divided city, with the demarcation line dividing the Soviet-occupied northern zone from the United States-occupied zone to the south of the Danube. It was first a 'City of Barracks' and then declared a 'City of Peace' in 1986. War-time factories were

Population of city: 200,000
Population of wider area: 400,000
Nearest international airports: Linz, Salzburg, Vienna and Munich.
Key websites: www.ars.electronica.at; www.linztourismus.at
Icons: The Danube, Ludwig Wittgenstein, Ars Electronica Centre & Festival, The Lentos Contemporary Arts Centre, The Bruckner House Concert Hall, Mural Harbour, Höhenrausch, Schlossmuseum, the Old and the New Cathedrals, the Klanwolke Festival ('The Sound Cloud'), Tabacfabrik Innovation Centre, The Kepler Salon and the 'Linzer Torte'.

Left: The Flying Ship by Alexander Ponomarev, part of Höhenrausch.

turned to civilian use; the extensive bombing of the city necessitated bold new plans and a strong investment in culture and education. It remained a heavily industrialised city with none of the tourist appeal of other Austrian cities. Here there are no high mountains, few classical historic buildings and no snow sports; but there are exceptional things to do and see – including the Voestalpine Steelworks visitor centre, the wonderful Höhenrausch hybrid rooftop sculpture park-cum-observation tower-cum-theatre, and the Mural Harbour outdoor graffiti gallery.

Today, Linz is synonymous with progress, vitality and vision. This is founded on culture, new media, sustainable urban development and highly creative tourist experiences. Indeed, few post-industrial cities in the world have transformed their physical, perceptual and tourist image as radically and successfully as Linz. It has recently been voted as the city with the best quality of life and work-life balance in Austria.

The widely acknowledged catalyst for this transformation was being the 2009 European Capital of Culture. In 2017, Linz became a UNESCO City of New Media and was recently acknowledged as the city with the best quality of life and best work-life balance in Austria. 'This city was so unattractive it was free to reinvent itself and it is now impossible to stop the revolution', says Manfred Grubauer, the charismatic and wise chair of Linz Tourismus – the destination's managment and marketing company.

At the heart of this metamorphosis is the remarkable Ars Electronica. This is a unique phenomenon that began life in 1979 and still thrives today as an annual avant-garde festival that explores the confluence of art, technology and society – in 2019 it attracted over 110,000 people to the city including global innovators delivering mind-bending innovations to grandparents, nursery schoolchildren and the world's leading scientists. The Festival is accompanied by an annual competition – Prix Ars Electronica – which serves as a showcase of technology and arts excellence, attracting entrants ranging from Oscar winners such as John Lessop of PIXAR fame, global musicians such as Peter Gabriel to emerging young talent.

The Ars Electronica Centre is a permanent visitor attraction christened the 'Museum of the Future'. In daylight you could easily miss this unprepossessing hexahedron on the north bank of the Danube overlooking the cruise terminals, the historic city centre and the Nibelungen Bridge, (originally designed for Hitler's triumphant return to the city). The exhibitions on art, technology and society segue into laboratories and laboratories segue into exhibitions throughout the centre purposefully appealing to many different audiences from cruise ship passengers to local schoolchildren. The highlight of the Ars Eelctronica Centre is the unique 'Deep Space – the Theatre of the Future': an extra-ordinary 8D virtual reality experience. At night, the exterior of the building acts as a dynamic 'screen' allowing interaction with people as Bluetooth-connected pads along the banks of the Danube linked to mobile phones create a unique light show visible across the city

Another wonderful legacy from the Capital of Culture 2009 is the Höhenrausch Festival. This is a network of wooden bridges, walkways and regularly-changing immersive art installations that sits high above a school and shops, passing through a church tower in the city centre – unmissable and exhilarating in its boldness, simplicity and innovation.

Linz is a compact, walkable city. A city of short distances. Its charm rests firmly with the juxtaposition of the old city with new technology and architecture; with its dark past and brave vision for the future. It is a city of open conversations, a desire to experiment and a collective will to do things that are good for the community.

Add to this independently run hotels, great museums and concert halls, restaurants, bars, small family-run shops together with a fine public transport system, easy access to the Danube Valley (wine, cycling, walking and cruising) and you have

a great destination for a short break and unique location for conferences.

Linz is an exemplar of a post-industrial city which has successfully transformed itself and has placed tourism and culture at the heart of this transformational process. And, importantly, the process continues: the concept of 'Linz Changes' has to be ongoing by its very definition.

The success of the city as a tourism destination is driven by a well-organised tourism organisation with strong leadership and a clear vision for tourism development; the open, transparent and collaborative approach to communications involving politicians, businesses, culture operators and residents in planning all aspects of tourism; and, the constant desire for change involving innovation, creativity and experimentation, which is evident in all aspects of the tourism experiences in the city.

Above and right: Ars Electronica Centre.

LJUBLJANA, SLOVENIA

A compact, clever capital city with a green soul, a cultural heart and an innovative frame of mind

If you were going to set out to design a small city as the perfect tourist destination from scratch you would undoubtedly end up with somewhere looking like Ljubljana, the capital of Slovenia, the figurative and literal (almost) centre of the country. Your ideal design would have a fairy-tale castle perched on a wood-clad cliff overlooking a river winding through the historic allies and streets at the heart of a city dominated by signature architectural features – churches, old squares with markets, tree-lined avenues – and parklands sweeping into city.

This ideal destination would be compact and easy to get around. There will be a local airport, good public transport and it will be free of cars. The surrounding countryside will be within touching distance. There will be quality places to stay; lots of riverside restaurants and bars serving local produce; small shops selling artisan and designer crafts with a pleasant vibe. It will be safe, well-managed and loved. It will constantly innovate, creating new experiences for the visitor and the resident. More than anything else, local people will have great pride in sharing their culture and heritage with guests.

As the American architect, Hugh Newell Jacobsen, wrote: 'When you look at a city, it is like reading the hopes, aspirations and pride of everyone who has built it.' A city reflecting the energy of its residents; an engine for growth for the country; an incubator of ideas and innovation; a liveable, proud, citizen's city exhibiting tangible evidence of its rich past with a pleasant surprise at every corner.

Population of city: 280,000
Population of wider area: 500,000
Nearest international airports: Jože Pučnik Ljubljana Airport (Slovenia), Zagreb (Croatia), Venice Marco Polo, Trieste, Treviso (all Italy), Klagenfurt and Graz (Austria).
Key websites: www.visitljubljana.com; www.mgmi.si
Icons: Ljubljana Grad, Ljubljanica River, Tivoli Park, The Triple Bridge, The Dragon Bridge, Prešeren and Prešeren Square, Franciscan Church, The Celica Prison Hostel, Žala Cemetery, Ljubljanajam Gastronomy Tours, Gostilna AS, Nebotičnik Building, Grand Hotel Union, Vander Urbani Resort, Metelkova Mesto Artist Colony, National Gallery, Monument to the Victims of All Wars, Olympic Ljubljana, University of Ljubljana.

• •

This model could be Ljubljana, the fast-growing capital of the parliamentary Republic of Slovenia– the first State from the former Yugoslavia to gain independence in 1991 following the civil war and the first of the Balkans to become a member

of the European Union 2004. In 2014, the city celebrated its 2,000th anniversary of the founding of the original Roman settlement of Emona on the northern bank of the Ljubljanica River which threads it's way in a canalised form through the city separating the medieval old town sitting under Castle Hill from the more recent commercial centre of the city. It is delightfully youthful, both in terms of its time as a capital and in terms of its demographics, as more than 25% of the population are under 24 years old and there are over 40,000 students studying at the University.

Ljubljana is located on the main motorway network connecting the major cities of northern Italy, Austria and Germany with Croatia and the Adriatic Coast. There are good, integrated rail connections and Ljubljana's Jože Pučnik Airport is less than 30 minutes north west of the city.

The physical development of Ljubljana has been carefully planned over many centuries. The beginnings of modern city planning date back to the

period after the earthquake in 1895 when Ljubljana was a provincial centre in the Austro-Hungarian Empire. In 1940, the authorities applied policies to carefully control the growth of Ljubljana. Sixty years later, they adopted a plan that has seen the wise management of land, transportation and the protection of heritage and the natural environment. Strong, determined, civic leadership has been key to the sustainable approach to the growth of Ljubljana. The city's sustainable development credentials run deep: it is already listed in the top 20 most sustainable destinations in the world. Slovenia's most notable architect, Jože Plečnik (1872-1957) left an indelible legacy of fine buildings in Prague, Vienna and, especially, Ljubljana. The inventiveness of Plečnik found sustainable solutions to spaces, places and buildings long before the term became vogue.

The city's sustainable credentials were celebrated when, in 2016, it became the European 'Green' Capital. Achieving this status had been the result of a remarkable, visionary strategy introduced by the Mayor, Zoran Jankovic, who recognised that fundamental to the future of the city as a great place to live and a great place to visit was the iconic Tivoli Park; the fact that almost 50 per cent of the city is forested and that 90% of the population lives within 300 m of green, open space. His 'Vision 2025' set ambitious goals for sustainable transport – the Kavalir is a fleet of electric buggies that scuttle around the city centre giving rides for free – conserving green space, recycling, fully utilising public buildings, celebrating its most respected architect and elevating the role of art, culture and gastronomy. Such is the drive that Ljubljana, with its 26 local municipalities, is a candidate city to be European Capital of Culture 2025.

Slovenia in general, and Ljubljana in particular, has become a crossroads of ideas and innovative practices benefiting from the very positive relationship it has with its near neighbours of Italy, Austria, Hungary and Croatia. In 2019 the Slovenian and Croatian Tourist Boards launched the 'Feel Slovenia: Experience Croatia' tourism campaign recognising the synergies between these two young countries. The fresh, bold and confident new sustainable tourism plan for Slovenia clearly maps out a way forward to become a global, green, boutique destination which demands quality and fosters contemporary natural and cultural experiences.

This is clearly evidenced in Ljubljana where Tourism Ljubljana has established a fine reputation as an organisation delivering great products and experiences that are fully aligned with the national tourism strategy with many innovative, creative events now available. They are constantly pushing the boundaries with clever marketing and supporting 'out-of-the-box' ideas for new visitor experiences.

The 'Moustache Tour', for example, is a guided cycle tour of the city with three daring moustached creative 'giants' of the city – an architect, a writer and a painter – respectively: Jože Plečnik, Ivan Cankar and Rihard Jakopič who each leave their mark on Ljubljana as great artists. Defined as a tour that captures the atmosphere of an authentic retro-barbershop with visits to the visionary room of the architect, the favourite bar of the writer and the National Gallery of the painter. Elsewhere, on the 11th floor of Nebotičnik – Yugoslavia's first 'skyscraper' designed by Vladimir Šubic in 1993 – is a wine and cocktail bar providing 360° views of the Julian Alps and the city.

In the Metelkova district, between the main railway station and Prešeren Square, a 19th century Austro-Hungarian army barracks that is now the counter-culture centre of Ljubljana. It is both edgy and safe, complete with the legendary former prison turned hip-hostel, with each cell now a bedroom complete with bars on the door, designed by a different artist. From Metelkova graffiti artists commence their highly personalised tours, passing hotels with bee hives on their roof tops, explaining the cult figures behind as well as the meaning of the artworks that are found on buildings across this neighbourhood and inspired, perhaps, by the library of the wonderfully named *House of Dream Books* to be found on the narrow Bohemian infused Trubarjeva cesta.

This fresh, innovative approach is evident for tourists to enjoy in the dramatic fortress that is Ljubljana Grad (The Castle), which sits atop Castle Hill. It is one of the iconic buildings of the city and is the country's most visited tourist attraction. Over the past few years the Castle, owned by the City Council but managed by a special 'arms-length agency', has developed a range of innovative, imaginative and highly regarded of attractions, shows, events and restaurants within the Castle walls. The 'Time Machine' is a fusion of living history and time travel. Dating originally from the 12th century, much of what is seen today dates from the 16th century and a re-build that followed a major earthquake in 1511. This former prison and fortress, sits above lush woodland on Castle

Hill. Visitors can take one of many paths from the old city to the castle gate or arrive directly into the inner courtyard via a scenic funicular railway.

It is in the realm of gastronomy that the city, as with the country as a whole, is now witnessing extraordinary growth and shift in quality. In Autumn 2019, the world-renowned Michelin Guide announced that in 2020 it would be publishing a guide dedicated to Slovenian food and drink excellence. Michelin regards Slovenia as a unique destination with exceptional natural assets and a strong sustainable commitment that enables the production of the highest-quality ingredients. Talented Slovenian chefs transform these into unique culinary creations, which from a gastronomic perspective makes Slovenia (and Ljubljana) a must-visit destination.

For many Slovenes one restaurant changed Ljubljana's gastronomy, pre-dating the current trend by one hundred years. Tucked away in what looks like an ancient farmyard near Prešeren

Square is Gostilna AS, established in 1888. It is a Ljubljana institution with the traditions of Slovenian hospitality marrying the serving fine wines paired with the best of local recipes. Helping visitors explore the flavours of the city are tours organised by Okusi Ljubljana (Taste Ljubljana). The evening tour begins with street food, includes a traditional gostilna and a couple of contemporary restaurants. One of the highlights is the visit to Druga Violina, a special traditional restaurant run as a social enterprise employing young people with special needs serving simple Slovenian dishes before culminating on the 11th floor of Nebotičnik.

Above: The Monument to Victims of All Wars, Ljubljana.

Glen Affric.

LOCH NESS, THE HIGHLANDS OF SCOTLAND

Dramatic landscapes, captivating stories and the mystery continues

Loch Ness is a one of the world's most fascinating places. It has several features which give it iconic status, universal importance and global awareness. As a result, it is one of Scotland's top five most important brands (along with whisky, tartan, Edinburgh and the Isle of Skye). The dominant feature is the eponymous large, deep, freshwater loch extending for approximately 37 km southwest of Inverness – the capital of the Highlands – making it the second largest loch in Scotland after Loch Lomond. However, due to its great depth, it is the largest body of freshwater in the British Isles, containing more freshwater than all the lakes in England and Wales combined.

Loch Ness sits in an extraordinary landscape of the Great Glen (from the Scottish Gaelic *Gleann Albainn* meaning the Glen of Scotland). This is a National Scenic Area fashioned by glaciation that carved out the rocks along the Great Glen Fault line – an enormous geological fracture – that bisects the Scottish Highlands into the Grampian Mountains to the south-east and the north-west Highlands. This geology is highly significant for our understanding of the 'Earth's Heritage' due its underlying geological structure. It is a landscape of great beauty, variety and moods – an environment which provides a canvas for a rich biodiversity and many rare habitats. A high proportion of the area has international and national designations that recognise their importance and ensures their conservation.

The Glen's strategic importance in controlling the Highland Scottish clans, particularly around the time of the Jacobite risings of the 18th century, is recognised by the presence of the towns of Fort

● LOCH NESS

SCOTLAND

Population of city: 47,000
Population of wider area: 55,000
Nearest international airports: Inverness, Edinburgh, Aberdeen, Glasgow.
Key websites: www.visitinvernesslochness.com; www.visitscotland.com; www.jacobite.co.uk; www.scottishcanals.co.uk
Icons: Loch Ness and The Great Glen, Urquhart Castle, Fort Augustus, The Caledonian Canal, Jacobite Cruises, Culloden Battlefield, Good Highland Food, Willie Cameron, Adrian Shine, Aldourie Castle Estate, Castle Stuart Golf Course, Loch Ness Marathon, Loch Ness 360° Trail, Loch Ness KnitFest, Belladrum Tartan Heart Festival and the Monster.

William in the south, Fort Augustus in the middle of the glen, and Fort George, just to the north of Inverness. It has been a major route for many centuries from the Drovers to the needs of the military, and with the Caledonian Canal opening in 1822 as an important shipping route. This resulted in many man-made features (roads, hydro-electric schemes, castles and abbeys) which testify to the importance of this area as a transit route. The design and construction involved in creating these features harnessed the talents of famous British inventors and engineers, including James Watt and Thomas Telford, whilst the monks of Fort Augustus Abbey introduced hydro-electricity in 1890.

This destination is, undoubtedly, one of the best-known destinations in the world. This has, of course, been achieved through the popular recognition and mystery associated with the alleged sightings of 'Nessie' (a cryptozoological monster), which has been the subject of serious investigation and research for over one hundred years and which has captured the imagination of the world, all fuelled by a 1937 report in the Inverness Courier quoting the sighting of an enormous creature in the Loch. Importantly the story has touched a deep vein of interest present in all of us surrounding our interest in, myths and legends.

The history of tourism at Loch Ness is intrinsically tied to the development of cruising on the Loch, which pre-date sightings of Nessie, dating back to the early part of the 19th century with paddle steamers plying their trade on the Loch and through the Caledonian Canal in the 1840s and reaching their 'glory days' in the 1890s. However, in the period after World War I until the late 1940s the trade fell into decline. But in 1948 there were positive indications of the 're-birth' of cruising on the Loch as a result of publicity about the Monster, although passenger numbers were modest rarely rising above 10,000 per annum.

In the early part of this century it became clear that as a leading tourism destination of such importance, Loch Ness was facing a number of challenges. For far too long its tourism importance it has been overlooked by public agencies. This resulted in a lack of investment in its basic tourism infrastructure. Seasonality, the number of small-scale businesses and low tourism spending had compounded the issues. Many local businesses were operating at low margins making it difficult for them to re-invest.

As a result, Loch Ness had slipped down 'the tourism agenda'. Guidebooks and websites were reporting on the area in negative ways and the destination was underperforming in terms of the economic return to its visitors. As a result of this lack of investment, by both the public and private sector, the destination appeared rather 'tired'. Given its iconic status this situation could not be allowed to continue. Loch Ness needed a major injection of resources combined with renewed energy and interest to begin its regeneration. There was a realisation that Loch Ness could not wait for the mythic to turn up and lead its revival. It was clear that this destination was about more than a monster.

Local business owners took this challenge to heart by creating a dynamic new tourism partnership to drive change. This group was led by Freda Newton MBE, the new owner of the Jacobite cruising company – now rebranded as Loch Ness by Jacobite – and the charismatic Highland Ambassador, Willie Cameron. The Visit Loch Ness initiative was supported by Highlands and Islands Enterprise, the Highlands Council, Historic Scotland and Scottish Canals. Fifteen years on and Inverness is now part of the collaboration helping to continually improve the tourist experience.

Loch Ness is now a destination loaded with outdoor activities taking full advantage of the land and waterscape; new walking, cycling and canoe trails have been established – including a crowdfunded 360° trail around Loch Ness. Investment has taken place creating first-class attractions at Urquhart Castle, expanding the Jacobite fleet and building new visitor centres. High-quality lodges and restored castles provide luxury accommodation comparable with anywhere in the world with great local cuisine by Good Highland Food and Cobbs Bakery and the signature festivals and events (Belladrum, the Marathon and KnitFest) continue to flourish.

• •

Right top: Loch Ness by Jacobite.
Right below: Urquhart Castle.

MALI LOŠINJ, LOŠINJ, CROATIA

A sojourn for wellness and well-being

CROATIA

● MALI LOŠINJ

Population of Mali Lošinj: 7,200
Population of wider area: 8,600
Nearest international airports: Lošinj Airport;
Riejka International (Island of Krk).
Key websites: www.visitLošinj.hr;
www.visit-croatia.com; www.Lošinj-hotels.com;
www.jadranka.hr
Icons: Gallery Fritzi, Apoxyomenos, Dolphins,
Wellness and Well-being, Professor Haračić,
Gari Capelli, The Bellevue Hotel, aromatherapy,
Jadranka Hotels and Villas.

Lošinj – the Island of Vitality. **This is a big claim for a small Croatian island.**

This community has always been outward looking; a seafaring community with many renowned sea captains. As a result, it is no surprise that today's community is confident and ambitious. It understands global wellness trends and is positioning itself as a leading, competitive, sustainable Mediterranean destination. For Lošinj, 'vitality' goes beyond wellness and well-being. It is about the capacity to live, to grow and to develop with energy and vigour. It is about living life to the full in a vibrant, dynamic and authentic way.

It's a simple concept when applied in a pristine natural environment with clean air and sea, a year-round mild climate, nutritious local foods and drink, peace, tranquility, dark skies and air full of natural fragrances. The recognition of the island's health and wellness qualities were confirmed in 1892 when the towns of Mali Lošinj and Velie Lošinj were declared a 'climate and rehabilitation resorts' by the Austrian government.

Lošinj, in the Kvarner Gulf south of Rijeka, is the 11th largest Adriatic island. It is part of the Cres–Lošinj archipelago of 36 islands and islets. Cres and Lošinj have a shared history but are separated by an 11 m wide canal and are connected by a small bridge at the small town of Osor, itself considered to be a fine outdoor heritage museum and home to an annual Music Festival.

There is extraordinary plant diversity. Throughout the centuries the island's sailors returned from their travels with over 80 exotic species (including myrtle, magnolia, orange, eucalyptus and tamaris) enhancing the island's native 1,100 plant species. There is an abundance of herbs and indigenous flora – including Aloe Vera. These plants form the basis of natural health cosmetics and aromatherapy product manufacture on the Island.

In 1892, Professor Ambroz Haračić, a Croatian biologist, studied the island's specific microclimate. The island's climate is a critical feel-good factor. There are few extremes in the feel-good sensation graph of temperature – 'very hot never appears and very cold is very rare'. It averages 207 sunshine days – over 2,600 hours of sunshine a year. Sea temperatures range from 12 degrees in winter to 24 degrees in summer. This led to the island being proclaimed a 'climatic health resort' for bronchial diseases. Indeed, the latest research from the Croatian Meteorological and Hydrological Service confirms that the moderate climate, clean air and the natural, endemic, aerosol produces significant health benefits especially in improving lung function and reducing stress.

This led the Director of this Research, to state that, 'Lošinj is useful to persons with respiratory disorders. A sojourn in Lošinj, especially in the autumn and spring months, could lead to long-term, prolonged remission by improving expectoration and reducing coughs and chronic lung disease as well as reducing the need for medication.'

The key to the Island's approach to tourism development is based on the collective agreement, community and businesses. This includes an agreed target to grow the maximum volume of tourists to three million overnights per annum, with an agreed capacity that at any one time there will be no more than 30,000 people on the Island of Lošinj including both residents and tourists (who are mostly Germans, Slovenes and Austrians).

The Lošinj Tourist Organisation is a public–private partnership set up as a not-for-profit company. Its initial President was the Mayor, Gari Cappelli, who later became the Minister for Tourism in Croatia. He is a natural leader and an obvious visionary. The Island's tourism emphasises a sustainable, year-round, balanced approach that harnesses the vitality branding as the primary means of delivering this goal, stating: 'we want to have a health story for us not just the tourists. It is our story. We have now introduced aromatherapy sessions in our primary schools. Our local population must live it to "sell" it.'

In recent years a number of significant investments have been made to enhance the tourist experience: improving accessibility, notably completing the regional road connecting Lošinj to the main ferry ports linking to the mainland and the development of a new airport.

The recent opening of a new museum at the Kvarner Palace in Mali Lošinj to showcase the story of the APOXYOMENOS (a large antique bronze statue dating from 2nd–1st century BC discovered on the seabed off the coast of Lošinj in 1999. The bronze represents an athlete in the process of cleaning sweat, dust and oil from his torso using a scraping tool. In many ways it is a symbol for the Island's proposition as a centre of excellence in wellness and vitality) together with the Gallery Fritzi for Contemporary Art has enriched the cultural offer.

There have been over 250 kms of way-marked footpaths created in recent years including a route giving great views of the Island's famous dolphin pods and another designed as 'The Footpath of Vitality' with interpretive panels to inform users about posture and breathing techniques enabling them to maximise the health benefits of exercise with nature; there is also a year-round programme of wellness events reinforcing this message of vitality.

The most impressive development has been the 2014 re-design of the Bellevue Hotel, the island's first five-star hotel, and the opening of Villa Hortensia by the Jadranka Group, owners of 'Lošinj Hotels and Villas'. The Bellevue project and the enhancements to their four other hotels in Lošinj represents the first phase of the company's five year multi-million-euro investment programme investment on the Island.

The best example of the public–private partnership at work is the exemplary student support program, introduced by the Mayor and supported by the tourism industry, which is designed to ensure that Lošinj's young talent returns to the island once they have completed their studies. The hotel companies operating on Lošinj have established a fund, administered by a Trust, providing young people from the five islands of the Lošinj–Cres archipelago who go to the mainland to university with a regular monthly stipend to support them through their years of study plus a further two years when they return to the Islands.

This all adds up to an extraordinary story of a bold, ambitious, small island community harnessing its natural assets in a clever, innovative way to position itself as a leading wellness destination. It has the community's interests and quality of life at the heart of its tourism ambitions ensuring jobs, opportunities and tourist spending is re-invested in the Island. This is a great example of a well-managed sustainable destination.

· ·

Right above: Hotel Bellevue and the Čikat peninsula.
Right below: La Punta.

NANTES, FRANCE

Phantasmagorical monsters and breath-taking sculptures make the whole city a living contemporary art gallery

In 1839 a young lad from Feydeau, an island in the Loire, became obsessed by the daily traffic of sea-going boats plying their trade of sugar and spice on the River Loire, financing the city's dark history of slavery. He voraciously devoured stories from his teacher, the wife of a sea captain, who kept him enthralled with readings from *Robinson Crusoe* and other tales from the great age of exploration. So, that year, at the age of 11, he stowed away on a sailing ship heading downriver to the Atlantic. However, the ship was to dock before leaving the Loire Estuary where the boy's father reclaimed him, imploring that the best travels he should make would be 'in his imagination'.

Before that young stowaway, Jules Verne, had reached his 50th birthday he had published a series of meticulously researched, adventure novels destined to fire the imagination of anyone interested in geography and travel. The 'voyages extraordinaires' series: *Journey to the Centre of the Earth* (1864), *Twenty Thousand Leagues Under the Sea* (1870) and *Around the World in Eighty Days* (1873), which were catalysts for the growth of interest in contemporary travel (maybe we are all descendants of Phileas Fogg). Nantes was Verne's home city: a former shipbuilding centre that fell on hard times and eventually closed in the late 1980s, but which is now brimming with creative talent, extravagant artworks and oozing with the spirit of adventure – all so much part of the legacy of the great poet and novelist. Nantes Tourisme, know as Le Voyage de Nantes, is the city's impressive, highly-imaginative, tourist organisation. It leads a

Population of city: 305,000
Population of wider area: 630,000
Nearest international airports: Nantes Atlantique, Rennes, St. Nazaire Montoir, La Rochelle
Key websites: www.nantes-tourisme.com; www.lesmachines-nantes.fr; www.levoyageanantes.fr
Icons: Jules Verne, Loire, Festival des Allumées, Estuaire project, behind Les Machines de L' île -Nantes, Cathedral of St. Peter and St. Paul, Musée d'Historie de Nantes, Passage Pommeraye, Mètre à Ruban, Le Grand Elephant.

Right: Les Machines de L'ile, Nantes.

highly-original approach to tourism development, tourism marketing and promotions using language that echoes that of Jules Verne. As tourists we are invited to participate in *Le Voyage de Nantes*. Nantes and the Loire-Atlantique département were once part of the historic province of Brittany. In the mid-20th century, the French government created a new level of local government by combining départements into larger regions. However, Nantes and the Loire-Atlantique département were not included in the new region of Brittany; instead it was designated Pays de la Loire and later given the status as the Nantes Metropole in 2015 in order to drive economic growth. Located on the Loire at the confluence of two of its tributaries, the Erdre and the Sèvre Nantais, it has its own island – the île de Nantes, which is surrounded by two branches of the river – the *'bras de la Madeleine'* at the north and the *'bras de Pirmil'* at the south.

This is a hard-working, blue-collar, estuarine town; very different from the vineyards and châteaux of the upper Loire valley, which makes its outrageously brave transformation even more impressive. Indeed, if ever there was a prize for the most successful, radical and canny imaginative transformation of a post-industrial port city then Nantes would be on top of the podium. Leading the bold turnaround have been four innovative, highly-skilled, determined personalities, fully supported by an army of creative talent, enlightened political leaders and an open-minded community. The four visionary cultural activists behind the re-invention of Nantes are: Jean Luc Courcoult, Jean Blaise, François Delaroziere and Pierre Orefice.

Jean Luc Courcoult and Jean Blaise were the first of these originators to arrive on the scene, preparing the ground that would support an epidemic of art and creativity which would flourish over the next 30 years right across the city, eventually flowing down the Loire Estuary to embrace Saint-Nazaire. Blaise, an Algerian-born artistic director, arrived in Nantes as part of

Jean Luc Courcoult's Royal de Luxe mechanical marionette street theatre company who made Nantes their base in 1989.

For Blaise great art must be performed in public places. Royal de Luxe's giant puppets were soon stomping around the streets of the city.

In 1989 Blaise outlined a radical recovery plan for the city. It began with the founding of the Maison de la Culture whose first action was creating the Festival des Allumées which, for each annual edition, ran from 1990 to 1995, highlighting art and culture from six global cities (including Barcelona, St Petersburg and Havana) with the works visible from 6 pm to 6 am cropping up in in unlikely places, industrial wasteland. From the first year, the image of Nantes changed, suddenly appearing younger, more innovative and vibrant. This adventure continued with other transformational events and festivals. It began with, *Fin de siècle* ending with the opening of the *Lieu unique* (Unique place), a former Lu biscuit factory in Nantes to be a space for artistic exploration, which gave birth to the Nantes metropolis concept of creating an event that would strengthen the links with the Loire, the estuary and its little known landscape. In 2007 the remarkable *Estuaire* project began resulting in 30 major on-site art works all of which remain. These include a giant sea snake, the chimney house, the submerged house and *Misconceivable* – a soft, stranded boat.

By 2011 it had become very apparent that art and tourism were intimately linked. As a result, the *Voyage à Nantes* structure was created to merge cultural bodies and the tourism office. The first initiative of this new body took the city by surprise. One morning residents woke to find a 15 km pink line (converted to green in 2013 when the city became the European Green Capital) painted on the city streets. Reactions were mixed. The line was a simple tool for people to follow to explore the cultural and historic sites in the city (the Cathedral of St Peter and St Paul, Musée d'Historie de Nantes and the 19th century shopping arcade – Passage

Pommeraye). Importantly the trail included many site-specific, often outrageous and provocative, permanent art installations designed to enliven the city such as *Mètre à Ruban* (an outsize tape measure); *L'arbre à basket* (a tree covered in basketball hoops); and Daniel Buren's *Moon Rings* (18 large rings on the banks of the Loire acting like a giant telescope looking at the city with the rings turning red, green and blue at night).

The path also includes the Nantes slavery memorial: Two thousand spaced glass inserts commemorating the names of slave ships that sailed from Nantes and the names of the other 290 slave ports in Africa, the Americas, and the Indian Ocean. Upon entering the memorial visitors are greeted with The Universal Declaration of Human Rights and the word 'freedom' written in 47 different languages from areas affected by the slave trade.

Delaroziere (former machine designer with Royal de Luxe) and Orefice are the force behind *Les Machines de L' île -Nantes*. This project, initiated in 2003, is amazing in every sense and fundamental to the experiment of change that has been happening. It is the most novel response to the desire to alter the perceptions of the city. It works by harnessing the collective imagination of the citizens with the audience playing an active role in each project that emerges from the ideas factory that has been established on the site of a former shipyard on île de Nantes. The team describe their development of complex, large-scale, machines as being 'part theatre, part architecture that explores movement which is the expression of life. The fantastical mechanical monsters evoke dreams and dreams are what fuels the greatest human adventures. And, the building of each machine is, in itself, an adventure for both the company and the audience'

Les Machines' first bold statement of intent was *Le Grand Elephant*. Inaugurated in 2007 this great 15-metre-high 50 tonne mechanical beast strides around the L' île de Nantes roaring and spraying

water. This daily spectacle is an event in itself but visitors can also ride the beast, climbing aboard the pachyderm's wooden body. The 'Elephant' was followed by *Le Carrousel des Mondes Marins* – interactive carousel with craft to ride in that look like mythical sea creatures. 'The Heron Tree' (*L'arbre aux herons* is a massive artificial tree encircled by flying herons whilst the *Three Buffalos* and other startlingly out-of-this-world rides delight all ages.

None of this creative endeavour should come as a surprise. There has long been a streak of anarchic art and culture in the city. Nantes has been described as the birthplace of surrealism, since André Breton (leader of the movement) met Jacques Vaché there in 1916 and a few years later Breton called Nantes 'perhaps with Paris the only city in France where I have the impression that something worthwhile may happen to me'. The city inspired a number of surrealists over the years including Flaubert, Henry James and Julien Gracq who wrote *The Shape of a City*, published in 1985, about Nantes. It was also the hometown of French New Wave film director Jacques Demy. British painter J. M. W. Turner visited Nantes in 1826 as part of a journey in the Loire Valley, painting a view of Nantes from Jules Verne's Feydeau Island.

The creative drive continues and in 2018 the circle was completed with Voyage de Nantes inviting Royal de Luxe to return to lead a new program of art-inspired activity for the next five years. According to Courcoult he aims to create a series of four or five cultural interventions in that part of the city each year. This time around, apparently, there will be no giant puppet on the horizon. He states, 'the emphasis will be on "images", "imaginary situations" and "amazing stories" with the aim to give people the chance to dream, with humour, poetry and, above all, emotion' – a great reason to visit Nantes.

NORTH PEMBROKESHIRE AND MYNYDDOEDD Y PRESELI, WALES

Ancient land of poets, writers and artists

WALES

● NORTH PEMBROKESHIRE

Population of city: 1,600
Population of wider area: 50,000
Nearest international airports: Cardiff, Bristol, Birmingham.
Key websites: www.visitwales.com; www.visitpembrokeshire.com; www.theretreatsgroup.com; www.melintregwynt.co.uk; www.coldatnight.co.uk; www.tyf.com; www.pembrokeshirecoast.wales
Icons: Foel Cwmcerwyn, Fishguard, St. Davids, bluestones, Carn Ingli, Pentre Ifan, Skokholm, Ynys Dewi, St. David, Landsker, St Davids Cathedral, Cwm Gwaun, Waldo Williams, Tafarn Sinc, Rosebush, Pembrokeshire slate, the Retreats Group, Joe Allen.

Organisations that exist to market and manage tourist destinations are, just like tourists, transient things, coming and going in different guises and all too often politically contrived and controlled bodies. The common feature of all the destinations in this book is that they break with this traditional approach and use hybrid ways and means to create better places to live that are better places to visit as a result. In these destinations, people and place are centre stage, for, at the end of the day, great tourism destinations are made by the inventiveness and hospitality of local people and the close relationship they have with the place they call home.

Nowhere is the focus on local people – their talent, creativeness and sheer, slightly rebellious, zest for life – better exhibited than in North Pembrokeshire, West Wales. This is the part of Pembrokeshire that sits north of the Landsker, south of Afon Teifi and west of Carmarthenshire.

For centuries, the Landsker Line, extending from St Brides Bay in the west to Carmarthen Bay in the east, has been a divide separating the Welsh and English-speaking people of rural West Wales, especially in Pembrokeshire. It was originally the product of a frontier of 50 castles established in the 12th century by English and Flemish immigrants trying to protect themselves from the indigenous Welsh, evolving into a contested cultural space and earning South Pembrokeshire the title of 'Little England Beyond Wales' by the 17th-century antiquarian George Owen. The debate about the relevance of the Landsker as a borderline continues today.

Pembrokeshire north of the Landsker is the subject of this essay, an area that has an independence of spirit, with communities proud to be distinctive and different when delivering *croeso* – a special welcome to guests.

As a place, North Pembrokeshire's landlocked mountain range and wild, rugged Irish Sea coastline is splintered by the Gwaun, Nevern and Teifi rivers and pockmarked with bays, cliff-framed coves, craggy headlands and sandy beaches. Hugging the edge of the coast is the Pembrokeshire Coast Path, established in 1970 following a survey of its potential by the Welsh naturalist Ronald Lockley and now part of the All-Wales Coast Path, and both the coastline and the mountains form part of the Pembrokeshire Coast National Park.

There is a modest archipelago of offshore island nature reserves: Ynys Dewi (Ramsey), Grassholm, Skomer, and Skokholm. For over 200 years from 1324 Skokholm was a rabbit farm, like many islands. In 1927 the then young Ronald Lockley took on the lease, going on to write many books about island life, setting up an early conservation society and the first British bird observatory. Lockley was forced to leave Skokholm at the start of World War II, but his ornithological legacy survives. The island is now owned by the Wildlife Trust of South and West

Left: Preseli Hills, Pembrokeshire.

Wales. His son Martin, inspired by the geology of the area – a key factor for the designation of the National Park – became Emeritus Professor of Palaeontology at the University of Colorado.

The geological highlight is the Preseli Hills, known locally and historically as Mynyddoedd y Preseli. The mountain range stretches 20 km from Newport in the west, with its ancient harbour (the Parrog), to the village of Crymych in the east, the self-proclaimed capital of area. At 536 m, the highest point of the range is Foel Cwmcerwyn, with Cwm Gwaun, a glacial meltwater valley, dividing the Mynydd Carningli and the northern uplands from the rest of these unenclosed, sheep-grazed moorlands.

This treeless, open, ancient ridge of igneous rock rises from the plateau of south Pembrokeshire and the rolling countryside of Ceredigion to the north as a majestic figure would arise from their chair – enigmatic, brooding, yet beguiling at the same time, it is a landscape known in Welsh as *gwlad hud ac lledrith* (land of myth and enchantment). The Preselis never fail to deliver on this promise. There are legends associated with King Arthur, Bedd Arthur being one of the many alleged sites of Arthur's grave and St Non, the mother of St. David, offered as Arthur's niece. A rocky outcrop is known as Bwrdd y Brenin (the King's Table) and Cerrig Marchogion (the rocks of the knights) high on the Preseli ridge is said to mark the spot where the mythical boar Twrch Trwyth killed several of Arthur's knights and turned them into stone.

Foel Cwmcerwyn presides over 14 other peaks, the sacred sites, ancient hillforts, standing stones and the encircling, essentially Welsh, communities of Eglwyswrw, Brynberian, Blaenffos, Mynachlog-ddu and Maenclochog. From this summit one experiences the most expansive and maybe the best views in the whole of Wales: from Snowdonia (Yr Wyddfa) and the Llŷn Peninsula across Cardigan Bay to the north-west, the Brecon Beacons to the east and Gower and the Bristol Channel to the south. Uninterrupted wonderment, bar for those days when low clouds with mystical qualities envelope the mountains.

Archaeological research revealed in 2020 not only confirmed that the bluestones used in the building of Stonehenge were categorically sourced from Carn Meini but that, dramatically, a much earlier version of Stonehenge existed on the slopes of the Preselis before being 'stolen' and re-located to Wiltshire. Local place names such as Cerrig Lladron (stones of the thieves) may well have given clues to this being the case long before the 21st-century academics arrived.

This all makes these mountains a special place, full of surprises. At its base, just north of Maenclochog, is Rosebush, a very English punctuation mark in a very Welsh environment. The slate quarries at Rosebush flourished in the 19th century and roofed the Houses of Parliament. The Maenclochog Railway (1876) terminated in the village, allowing it to develop as a tourist resort 'for those seeking nature and repost' as well as a source of slate. The former resort hotel of Tafarn Sinc, built in 1872 and closed to passengers 1937, is today a thriving community-owned pub.

The charismatic and engaging local geologist Dr Dyfed Elis-Gruffydd sees the Preselis as *'gwlad beirdd, llenorion ac artistiad'* – a land of poets, writers and artists. The mountains, once desired by the UK Government to be used as a permanent military training ground, were the inspiration for poems by Thomas Parry-Williams, E. Llwyd Williams and Waldo Williams. Waldo, a pacifist and nationalist, was headmaster at Mynachlog-ddu, the school sitting in the lee of the mountains. His writings focus upon feelings of belonging, of the harmonious living he witnessed in the local communities and expressed in his 1936 poem 'Cofio', from which a quotation is fittingly inscribed onto a standing stone erected in his memory that looks towards his beloved mountains.

Close to Waldo's stone is an old farm embedded in the landscape that serves as the studio of local artist Elizabeth Haines, for whom the Preselis are a constant muse. She describes her work, influenced by the St Ives painters, as being about reading and interpreting nature, having 'evolved over the years into a style which occupies a precarious hinterland between topography and abstraction, frequently described as surreal and dreamlike.'

John Knapp-Fisher shared the desire to paint every day. His Croesgoch studio housed a prodigious collection of evocative sketches and paintings depicting the North Pembrokeshire coastline, farmsteads and villages. For the English artist Graham Sutherland, a visit to Pembrokeshire in 1967 led to a creative renewal that helped restore his reputation as a leading British artist – his works can be seen in the National Park's Oriel y Parc in St Davids.

St Davids itself is the smallest city in Britain, its cathedral dedicated to the patron saint of Wales.

The cathedral, with its bishop's palace, sits in a sheltered valley surrounded by a windswept sacred headland of ancient saints: St Non, St Justinian, St Caradog, St Patrick and, of course, St. David, making it a place of pilgrimage for centuries. In 1123, St Davids was granted a privilege from Pope Callixtus II, who declared that two pilgrimages to the cathedral were equal to one journey to Rome.

This place was also where Keith Griffiths spent his formative years. The Welsh architect founded and chairs Aedas, one of the largest global architecture and design practices. Born in Merthyr Tydfil but brought up in the city, he attended the local school, Ysgol Dewi Sant, before reading architecture at the University of Cambridge. In 2009, Griffiths established the Griffiths-Roch Foundation to purchase and restore historic buildings on the peninsula as elegant, luxury boutique hotels.

Above: Carreg Samson.

The Foundation has completed restoration of the 12th-century Grade 1 listed Roch Castle, which is both spectacular and dramatic, with panoramic views over the Preseli Hills and St Brides Bay, the Grade 2* listed former Tudorbethan vicarage of Penrhiw, a tranquil sanctuary nestled in acres of gardens, enveloped by woodland, the river and meadows, and the 18th-century Grade 2 listed former windmill

Twr y Felin. They now form the Retreats Group of hotels. Twr y Felin is Wales' first contemporary art hotel, its permanent collection including contemporary urban and Welsh artists who were commissioned to create work inspired by the Pembrokeshire landscape.

Pebidiog is a stunning trilogy exploring ideas of beginning, being, and belonging. The book is a collection of photographs taken by world-class photographer Marcus Oleniuk, who spent two years exploring and documenting the landscape and its inhabitants to capture the true reflection of the area. Once complete, the prose was added by Mererid Hopwood, who, in 2001, became the first woman to win the bardic chair at the National Eisteddfod of Wales. Published by the Retreats Group, Hopwood reminds us that the ancient name of this north area was Pebidiog, stating that the pages are 'a journey to give the traveller a sense of how the story of Pebidiog unfolded from the days of giant tombs to the surfing afternoons of 21st-century summers.' Wonderful stuff.

An old-school chum of Griffiths' is Eifion Griffiths, who, with his partner Amanda, are the third generation of the family to own and operate Melin Tregwynt, a small whitewashed stone rubble woollen mill, founded in 1912 when Henry Griffiths, the present owner's grandfather, bought the property. There has been a mill on this site since the 17th century, when local farmers would bring their fleeces to be washed, carded, combed, spun into yarn and woven into sturdy blankets. The old-fashioned hand looms have all been replaced by more modern machines, but Tregwynt's signature double cloth, Cartheni Cymraeg (Welsh blankets) in patterns and colours inspired by tradition and the landscape are still produced. They are timeless in design, contemporary in appeal and keep the tradition of Welsh weaving alive.

This North Pembrokeshire creative cluster has many of the characteristics of the art colony in Cornwall: talent attracted by the area's landscape, liminality, rurality and sense of place. The same factors help create an environment where creative and innovative tourism pioneers can flourish. This tourism roster of pioneers is headed by Leonard Rees, who 60 years ago offered tourists exceptional self-catering through his Quality Cottages company; his son, Tim, has evolved the concept into fresh, sustainable, community-friendly forms of accommodation with Quality Unearthed.

James Lynch, better known as the fforestchief, is based near Cilgerran and created Fforest Farm. Overlooking the Afon Teifi gorge and Teifi Marshes nature reserve – a place to enjoy the simplicity, pleasures and beauty of outdoor living in an outstanding natural environment complete with the communal Lodge, Y Bwthyn (their own little pub) and the cedar barrel sauna tucked into the woods for what James calls the après-sea treatment. Nearby, the owners of the Rhosygilwen Mansion have created a culture centre of excellence for visitors showcasing the best of Welsh music.

The original engineer of environmentally atuned outdoor activities is, undoubtedly, Andy Middleton of TYF Adventure, who introduced the world to the sport of coasteering and started the world freestyle kayaking championships, with TYF at the forefront of low-impact adventures in the outdoors and high-impact sustainability innovation and strategy with business and government. TYF's self-styled mission is to 'help people fall so deeply in love with nature that it changes the way that they live, drawing inspiration from wildlife and wild places on the St Davids peninsula.'

Living in Maenclochog in the early 1970s was an honour. Becoming part of the community was humbling. Working in North Pembrokeshire was uplifting. My first task was to lead the conservation of what remained of the 500-year-old Melin Trefin, a corn mill abandoned in 1918, in the historic village of Trefin, close to Porthgain, Abereiddy, Abercastle and Mathry between St Davids and the port of Fishguard. Trefin was the birthplace of Edgar Phillips, a poet who became Archdruid of Wales, and Cerys Matthews, former lead singer with the band Catatonia. The mill was immortalised by William Williams (1875-1968), known by his bardic name Crwys, in his poem 'Melin Trefin'. The work laments the closing of the mill and symbolises the dying heritage of rural village life in this part of West Wales. Its powerful opening line, '...*Nid yw'r Felin heno'n malu yn Nhrefin ym min y mor...*' ('The mill is not grinding tonight in Trefin at the edge of the sea') says it all.

Above: Whitesands beach.

Snowdon from Capel Curig.

NORTH WALES, ERYRI, YR WYDDFA AND THE CONWY VALLEY, WALES

Re-imagining and re-inventing an ancient landscape as the adventure capital of Europe

Many destinations around the world have successfully harnessed the idea of holding dedicated 'themed years' as a means of successfully generating tourist interest as well as stimulating new, highly-focused, product development. Visit Wales has led the way in using this idea, delivering a sequence of themed years which has generated high levels of interest by the global media, pulling in new tourists from around the world and stimulating famously innovative new

experiences for visitors. This, all-Wales, themed years programme kicked off in 2016 with the Year of Adventure. It was followed, in subsequent years, by themes of Legends, The Sea, Discovery and, in 2020, The Outdoors. The destination in Wales that has taken full advantage of this fresh themed approach, especially in terms of the years of adventure and the outdoors, is Snowdonia, which, along with other areas of North Wales, has now been recognised as one of the adventure tourism

WALES

Population of Gwynedd: 128,000
Population of wider area: 680,000
Nearest international airports: Liverpool John
Lennon, Manchester International, Birmingham
International (England), Dublin International
(Ireland).
Key websites: www.visitwales.com;
www.businesswales.gov.wales;
www.visitsnowdonia.info; www.gonorthwales.co.uk;
www.anturstiniog.com
Icons: Yr Wyddfa (Snowdon), Eryri (Snowdonia),
Bounce Below, Zip World, Adventure Parc
Snowdonia, Antur Stiniog, National Slate Museum,
Plas y Brenin, Conwy Valley, Llechwedd, Snowdon
Mountain Railway, UNESCO World Heritage Sites,
Castles of the Welsh Princes, Wales Rally GB,
Blaenau Ffestiniog, Betws-y-Coed, Portmeirion,
Clough Williams-Elis and Eric Jones.

capitals of Europe.

Re-invention and re-imagining is a common
feature of the success of many of the destinations
in this book and the success of adventure tourism
in North Wales has very clearly involved the creative
re-imagining of this epic landscape – especially
within the post-industrial slate lands as a result
of the boom in new, innovative, adventure tourism
experiences created by serial entrepreneurs
collaborating with motivated, highly-committed
community groups.

However, the re-invention of Snowdonia is not
necessarily a new phenomenon. From the end
of the 18th century, Wales became a hotspot for
visiting artists seeking out wild nature and the
country of ancient peoples. They were inspired
by the Romantic movement's fascination with
the re-casting of the landscape of North Wales to
convey the effect, described in Edmund Burke's
1757 treatise on aesthetics, as the idea of 'sublime
beauty', rejecting our historical fear of the wild

nature of these mountains. For young artists,
including J.M.W. Turner, Snowdonia became part
of their apprenticeship seeking out the 'sublime'
mountains, waterfalls, old mines, slate quarries
and the ruined castles of North Wales to inspire
their work and, as an unintended consequence,
initiating an early tourism boom.

The foundations for this current phase of the
contemporary re-invention of this part of North
Wales for tourism were set down in the early

years of this century by the members of the Wales Tourist Board (the forerunner of Visit Wales). The Board identified the early signs of trends that were moving tourists towards taking part in outdoor adventure activities and taking advantage of what is known as 'the biophilia effect', whereby physical exercise and relaxation in a wonderful countryside setting dramatically improves physical and mental well-being. This resulted in a series of plans for Wales encouraging activity tourism: creating an environment where walking, cycling, water sports and other outdoor activities could flourish. Against this backdrop, it was the tourism businesses in Snowdonia that fully embraced this opportunity in ways that few of the former Wales Tourist Board could have anticipated.

Ancient; strong; rugged; proud: overseeing the coast and river valleys of Snowdonia and seemingly the whole of Wales is Yr Wyddfa – Snowdon. At 3,560 ft this is one of the highest mountains in Britain. It has an alpine topography. Ordovician volcanic rock has been sculpted by glaciers to create the distinctive peak, the sharp arêtes of Yr Lliwedd and Crib Goch, the rock faces and scree slopes of fragmented rock with the scooped-out cup-shaped cwms (such as Glaslyn and Llyn Llydaw). Yr Wyddfa is the sentinel of North Wales. From its summit, on a clear day, there are the most extensive 360° views over Wales, north-west England across the Irish Sea to Ireland and beyond to the Lake District and the Scottish Borders – a prospect encompassing an estimated 24 counties, 27 lakes and 17 islands. Today, Snowdon is a busy place. It is often described as 'Britain's busiest mountain' with, each year, over a quarter of a million making their way either on foot or by train to its summit. It is one of the locations of the UK's Three Peaks Challenge and it is at the heart of the route of the Snowdonia Marathon – twice voted as Britain's best marathon.

Writing in *A Prospect of Wales*, first published in 1948, Gwyn Jones stated that: 'Through the defile of Aberglaslyn into the heart of Eryri. This famous district, like everything good in Wales, is neither vast nor pretentious. The scale may be small, but the proportions are perfect. Snowdonia is a grand illusion. The same mountains which can beguile the walker can challenge the climbers of Everest.'

The first recorded ascent of the mountain was in 1639 by botanist Thomas Johnson. Other mountaineers followed to scale Snowdon and the other peaks in the range (Tryfan and Cnicht). One of these was Frank Smythe, from whom comes a very poignant story. In December 1940, Smythe, already a veteran of climbs in the Himalayas, escaped the blitzed city of Liverpool for the mountains of Snowdonia. One day whilst walking above the Ogwen valley a Spitfire 'whirled through the pass' at his feet and, a few days later, on Yr Wyddfa, Smythe reflected that 'there was a silence reminiscent, not of a British countryside, but of the plateaux of Central Asia'. 'Was it possible', he asked, 'that the greatest war of all time was raging? Never had war seemed more insane'. In a similar vein, when walking Yr Wyddfa with two of my grandsons in Summer 2019, the scream of a Hawk fighter jet from RAF Valley on a low-flying training mission racing beneath our feet provoked important questions about the way we use wild places.

In the 1950s Snowdon was used by Sir Edmund Hillary and members of his team in practice for their successful attempt on scaling Mount Everest in 1953. Today it is possible to reach the summit of Yr Wyddfa with ease using the 1896 Snowdon Mountain Railway – a 4.6 mile-long narrow-gauge rack and pinion railway that departs the village of Llanberis (at the base of the mountain). Alternatively, there is a choice of a number of well-established, engineered and managed footpaths. The main routes to climb Snowdon are: The Watkin Path from Nant Gwynant; the Pyg and Miners' tracks from Pen-y-Pass; The Snowdon Ranger

· ·

Right: Adventure Parc Snowdonia.

and Llanberis Paths; and, the Rhyd Ddu Path. Crib Goch is one of the finest ridge walks in Britain, but this is a climb that is tourists are discouraged from attempting because of the severity of the route. At Snowdon's summit is Hafod Eryri, an award-winning visitor centre, designed by the architect Ray Hole, which opened in 2009, replacing the previous railway station terminus and café built in 1934 and designed by the local architect and creator of the Italianate village of Portmeirion, Sir Clough Williams-Ellis.

The mountains of Snowdonia (Yr Eryri) offer a stunningly varied and attractive landscape deserving of its designation as a National Park in 1951. This remains an inherently wild place, however, man's impact over the centuries has been profound. Forestry and agriculture together with the mining for gold and copper and, especially, the extensive quarrying for slate has made a lasting impact on the landscape and culture of the area. It is within the forests and the former slate quarries that the new generation of 'made in Wales' ideas for original outdoor adventure experiences have rapidly appeared. Within the forests and the wonderfully unusual habitats of slate-scarred landscapes there is now a myriad of unique opportunities for all-action adventure activities.

Snowdonia, stretching from the Conwy Valley in the east to Porthmadog in the west, has now become the must-visit destination for year-round outdoor adventure, upstaging previous claims by some other destinations in the United Kingdom. The range of activities to set the adrenalin running is

extraordinary: from white water kayaking and the world's longest and fastest ziplines to trampolining in the underground chambers of the abandoned slate quarries around Blaenau Ffestiniog, several world-class mountain biking parks and Europe's largest inland surfing centre and indoor adventure park built on the site of a former aluminium factory at Dolgarrog in the Conwy Valley – a very real example of re-invention. All these new things to do in the outdoors build upon the heritage of the area for hosting internationally-renowned events such as the Wales Rally GB and the presence of centres of excellence in mountaineering (Plas y Brenin), the national centres for water sports (Plas Menai), the The Olympic Sailing Centre, Pwllheli and the white-water canoeing and rafting centre near Bala.

As a result, of these developments Wales, and especially North Wales, is winning numerous international tourism awards. Fresh ideas for enjoying and respecting the outdoors continue to emerge making this a destination to watch with interest and to visit over the next ten years or so. The slate landscape is to be considered for inclusion on the UNESCO World Heritage list. The bid – *Llechi Cymru* – celebrates the heritage and culture of the slate industry but sees inscription on the World Heritage list as another dimension of re-imagining the area and further enhancing the area's appeal to tourists.

Left and above: Zip World.

NORWAY'S NATIONAL TOURISM ROUTES

Eighteen carefully selected highways passing through the most beautiful parts of Norway

NORWAY

Nearest international airports: Oslo Gardermoen, Bergen Friesland, Tromso, Bodo, Ålesund Vigra, Sandnessjoen.

Key websites: www.najonaleturistvege.com; www.visitbergen.com; www.visitAlesund.com; www.juvet.com

Icons: Trollstigen (Geiranger-Trollstigen), Vøringfossen (Hardangervidda), Stegastein (Aurlandsfjellet), Steilneset (Varanger), Peter Zumthor, Louise Bourgeois, Jan Olav Jensen and Carl-Vigge Hølmebakk, Juvet Landscape Hotel, Bergen.

This is one of three selections in this book that breaks with my own convention of choosing tourism destinations that are small, compact and are, very definitely, focused on a specific place. The National Tourist Routes of Norway is included because not only is it a marvellous concept but also because it has been executed with all the panache, meticulous planning and creativity that are the hallmarks of all the other destinations in this book. This is an inspirational new interpretation of the great driving routes of the world such as The Garden Route in South Africa, the Great Ocean Road in Australia, the Pacific Coast Highway and, of course, Route 66 (USA).

There are 18 motoring routes, with over 250 specially designed viewpoints, rest areas and art installations, now making up the National Tourist Routes of Norway. They are to be found along the western, indented seaboard of Norway – from Jaeren and Ryfylke in the south to Havøsund and Varanger in the north high above the Arctic Circle.

The routes closely follow the coast and fjords; then they dive inland to cross the grand landscapes of the high mountains before flowing through the fields and woodlands of the valleys and plains of central Norway. They are threads that connect destinations, giving travellers more than using a road simply to get to somewhere else. This is a transformational scheme that has positively impacted on all the communities along their routes. It has prompted imaginative tourism developments – such as the family-run Juvet Landscape Hotel (at Valldal Trollstein–Geranger Route) – and has also changed the world's perception of Norway as a country. The approach taken by the Norwegian Public Road Administration, together with the Norwegian Tourist Board, is a benchmark of innovation and creativity which is now inspiring

• •

Above: Trollstigen Viewpoint, Geirvanger-Trollstigen.

other similar projects such as The Wales Way – three new national tourist routes in Wales.

This has been a long-term project over a quarter of a century in the making and, there is still another five years to completion. Back in 1993 representatives from the National Public Roads Administration (NPRA) looked at famous touring routes around the world. The Romantische Strasse in Germany and La Route du Vin in France, along with Route 66 fuelled their imagination as they realised that that roads and tourism go together. Four years later they initiated two pilot projects before inviting applications from all over the country to bring forward proposals to 'let the roads become the attraction'. Clear and strict criteria were devised and applied with 60 proposals evaluated before the 18, best of the best, covering nearly 1,650 km were eventually selected.

In Norway, there is a long tradition for adapting buildings and structures to meet the harsh climatic conditions and the arduous terrain. Clearly, Norwegian architects and designers have drawn on this tradition in their efforts to enhance and elevate the tourist experience along these routes. The goal is that the architectural and artistic interventions should not only help to facilitate and enhance the visitor's experience of nature, but also become an attraction in their own right. One author has commented on the role of these installations rhetorically asking: 'How can you improve a view that's already sublime? Norway's untouched coasts, fjords and mountain valleys offer some of the most dramatic vistas in Europe, but by their nature they are pretty difficult to get to. How do you help people appreciate a wilderness without it ceasing to be one?' The suitably apt Norwegian response to this challenge can be traced back to the country's great modernist architect, Sverre Fehn. His philosophy was that architecture, if carefully considered as an incision on the landscape, can easily serve to elevate nature without competing with it and, in so doing, it becomes an experience in itself.

The tone for the project was set in the two pilot projects with the bold work of two young architects: Jan Olav Jensen and Carl-Vigge Hølmebakk in designing the routes at Sognefjellet and Gamle Strynefjellsvegen combining extraordinary architecture inspired by the raw landscape with thought-provoking art. These two routes remain amongst the most popular of them all. As a result, the decision was made to invite over 40 Norwegian architects and artists along with a small number of internationally-renowned personalities, such as the Swiss architect Peter Zumthor and the American–French artist, Louise Bourgeois, to design amenities and the 'pauses' along each of the tourist routes. The artworks are there to reinforce the character of the route and to encourage the tourist to think deeply about what they are experiencing.

To date, more than 50 architects, landscape architects, designers and artists — some of whom are young while others are well-established – have set to work. The emphasis has been placed on innovation and creativity, and with this focus Norway has managed to unleash an extraordinary creative force; many young architects have earned wide acclaim for their innovative tourist route projects. The whole scheme is overseen by an independent Architecture Council to ensure quality and impartiality. The results are often jaw-dropping be they clever, witty, designs for simple viewpoints and toilet blocks as at Akkarvikodden (Lofoten) or Jektvik (Helgelandskysten), or outrageous suspended viewpoints as at Trollstigen (Geiranger-Trollstigen), Vøringfossen (Hardangervidda) or at Stegastein (Aurlandsfjellet). In some locations a very profound story is told through contemporary architecture combining with art. This is very definitely the case at Steilneset (Varanger) with a haunting memorial in memory of the 91 victims of witch trials in Finnmak designed by Zumthor in collaboration with Bourgeois.

Good starting points for an initial exploration of some of the southern routes are Bergen and

Ålesund. Bergen is Norway's second city straddling the confluence of a number fjordsand hemmed in by steep, forested slopes. It is photogenic for both the contemporary neighbourhoods (its commercial streets, parks and civic buildings), and the older, historic areas of Bryggen, the famous historic timber wharf with UNESCO World Heritage Site status and nearby cobbled street with their white-painted wooden houses. The city centre and northern neighbourhoods are on Byfjorden, 'the city fjord', and the city is surrounded by mountains; indeed, Bergen is known as the 'city of seven mountains'. According to tradition, the city was founded in 1070 by King Olav Kyrre and was named Bjørgvin, 'the green meadow among the mountains'. It served as Norway's capital in the 13th century, and from the end of the 13th century became a bureau city of the Hanseatic League.

The port of Bergen is Norway's busiest in terms of both freight and passengers, with over 300 cruise ship calls a year bringing nearly a half a million passengers to the city. Ålesund is situated on the coast at the end of the E136, 240 kilometres (150 miles) north-east of Bergen, and is adjacent to the Hjørund and Geiranger fjords – a UNESCO World Heritage Site. This is a sea port noted for its concentration of Art Nouveau architecture and occupies seven of the islands with the town centre located on islands Aspøya and Nørvøya. The town has a rapidly developing culinary scene with a wealth of new innovative restaurants and bars and artisan producers accessing the best seafood and local produce.

• •

Above: Steilneset memorial, Varanger

PODČETRTEK (TERME OLIMIA), ROGAŠKA SLATINA, SLOVENIA

Modern wellness, traditional healing and contemporary architecture

PODČETRTEK

SLOVENIA

Population: Rogaška Slatina 5,000 and Podčetrtek 4,000

Population of wider area: 12,000

Nearest international airports: Jože Pučnik Airport Ljubljana, Franjo Tuđman Airport Zagreb, Vienna International, Flughafen Graz.

Key websites: www.slovenia.info; www.terme-olimia.com; www.visitpodcetrtek.com: www.visit-rogaska-slatina.si; www.atlantida-rogaska.si

Icons: Rogaška Slatina, Podčetrtek, Terme Olimia, Vonarsko Jezero Lake, Virštanj wines, Rudnica Observation Tower of Health and Joy, Donat Mg, Rogaška Crystal.

Sustainable, smart, green Slovenia. The Slovenian Tourist Board (STB) has a brave strategy with sustainable development and quality as its *raison d'être*. It is a boutique destination that did many things right before COVID and will now excel in the years to come. The plan encourages year-round tourism and the exploration of lesser-known parts of this delightfully varied, compact country, encouraging higher added-value experiences unique to Slovenia that will delight residents and enchant international tourists.

Something special is happening in every dimension of tourism there. Innovation thrives in this environment and family businesses have stepped up to the mark, especially in the world of gastronomy, with charismatic, strong women having led the drive for this new approach. They include the inspired team in the national tourist board to the influential thinkers in sustainable development, hospitality education, gastronomy and outdoor adventure. Maja Dimnik, for example, the founder of World of Glamping, could be the mother of this phenomenon. Novel forms of glamping abound in Slovenia: the Forest Glamping Resort Blaguš on the shores of Lake Blaguš (east of Maribor in the north-east of the country); the Chocolate Village on the international Drava cycling route west of Maribor in the picturesque grounds of a chocolate factory, Ortenia in Podčetrtek and the Garden Village in Bled.

Gastronomy and wellness are two cornerstones of the way forward. Slovenia is a proven culinary destination, having its own Michelin Guide and being the European Region of Gastronomy 2021. This, according to Maja Pak, Director of the STB, 'is as a result of our pristine nature, high-quality raw materials and renowned master chefs creating the right conditions to develop our gastronomy as part of the drive for Slovenian Unique Experiences and pursuit of wellness tourism.'

There are 15 recognised spa, health and wellness centres in Slovenia and a dedicated Slovenian Spas Association, established over 60 years ago. These centres meet the strict conditions required for obtaining the status of state-verified spas and are a major driver of tourism in Slovenia, accounting for one-third of all overnight stays. A flagship product of Slovenian tourism for years, they are more relevant today than ever before.

Rogaška Slatina and Podčetrtek (Terme Olimia) combine in the same valley to create a successful, multi-layered wellness destination. Located in the north-east of Slovenia in the region of Savinjska, literally touching the border with Croatia, it is an attractive 90-minute drive from the Slovenian capital, Ljubljana, an easy route of a similar distance north-west of Zagreb, the capital of Croatia, or three hours south of Vienna, Austria's capital. Savinjska is Slovenia's third most significant tourist region, with 30 per cent of all the country's spas.

Terme Olimia is the dominant driver of family wellness tourism in the municipality of Podčetrtek. This is a landscape of highly attractive countryside and steep, wooded hills, each topped by a distinctive church or castle, the fertile valley of the River Sotla and its tributaries brimming with vineyards, orchards, flowering meadows and small, neatly maintained villages and farms. Much of the area is designated as the Kozjansko Regional Nature Park, one of the oldest and most extensive protected regions in Slovenia.

Wellness and health-seeking visitors have been attracted by the thermal springs of this area for more than four centuries. It was in 1935, however, that the natural hot springs attracted the attention of local priest Frederik Strnad, who, together with experts, proved the therapeutic effects of the Terme Olimia natural thermal springs: the thermal water acts as a natural remedy, successfully treating rheumatic and skin diseases, arterial circulation

· ·

Left: Rogaška Slatina Thermal Spa.

disorders and injuries of bones, muscles and the peripheral nervous system. In 2021, the minister with responsibility for the economy and tourism is Zdravko Počivalšek, the former manager and director of Terme Olimia; indeed, Terme Olimia is a company owned by the Government of Slovenia.

It has its origins in 1966, when the spa Atomske Toplice opened with a basic wooden swimming pool using thermal spring water and a small hotel. In 2000 it was renamed Terme Olimia after the nearby monastery of Olimje, and today, after 50 years of development and diversification, Terme Olimia is an extremely appealing wellness resort offering a wide choice of accommodation, from the 5* Glamping Olimia Adria Village to 4* apartments and a 5* hotel. There is an extraordinary range of family and adult-only swimming pools, a modern sauna complex, excellent gastronomy, beauty services and adrenaline adventures together with the Thermal Park Aqualuna. This rural resort is defined by its highly innovative, bold, sustainable architecture.

The management team at Terme Olimia believes that tourism can have a positive impact on the local community and that businesses should work with the community and Tourism Podčetrtek, a community interest economic development association which involves the villages of Podčetrtek, Bistrica ob Sotli and Kozje and Terme Olimia. Together they have established the sports hall Podčetrtek, Sports Park Gaj, cycling and walking trails and the reopening of the Vonarsko Jezero Lake connecting Terme Olimia and Rogaska Slatina.

This has stimulated investment in wineries, such as Virštanj wines, innovative family-run guesthouses and restaurants, such as Homestead Amon, combining wine production with a golf course and pension, the Haler family's micro-brewery with restaurant and pension, the Ortenia apartments in nature, several small farm attractions, each with restaurants and/or apartments (such as the Jelenov Greben deer

farm, homestead Stiplošek Jožetov grič and tourist farms Štraus Kramer and Volavšek and one of the oldest pharmacies in Europe in Olimje Monastery. New experiences include the Witch's Hut – land of fairy tales and fantasies – and the museum of the Korenček family from 100 years ago, the tourist road train from Olimje to Rogaška Slatina, a wine tourist road and the Syncerus Chocolate Boutique.

In July 2019, the remarkably beautiful and simple Rudnica Observation Tower of Health and Joy opened to the public. Rudnica is a cluster of hills just north of Terme Olimia. Rudnica or rudnik, means 'mine', reflecting the mining once prominent here. The highest peak is Plešivec, at 686 metres. The other peaks are Olimska gora, Mala Rudnica and Silavec. The 36-metre-high wooden Tower of Health and Joy, which sits on this latter hill, was entirely funded from the local tourism tax and gives a panoramic view this bucolic borderland.

Just 15 km north of Terme Olimia is the classic heritage spa resort town of Rogaška Slatina, surrounded by hills and nestling at the confluence of a number of delightful wooded valleys of beech, boxwood and ginkgo on the slopes of the Boč uplands. This small community of some 5,000 people has secured global fame for the curative qualities of its legendary magnesium-rich mineral water (branded Donat Mg) and crystal glassworks. This is a town where mythology and legend meet research-based evidence to shape its wellness tourism offer.

According to legend, everywhere Pegasus, the winged horse of Greek mythology, stamped his hoof to the earth, an inspiring water spring burst forth, and Rogaška claims to be one of these stamping grounds. The Donat Mg uses an image of Apollo on its branding, as it is claimed that the Greek god instructed Pegasus to drink from the Rogaška spring rather than the spring on the holy mountain of Helicon – a profound heritage indeed, and a source for over 400 years of the spa being recognised as a centre for medical tourism.

Architecturally, Rogaška Slatina reflects and respects the fine traditions of Europe's classic spas (such as Marienbad, Karlovy Vary and Baden-Baden) with its central park, landscape gardens and promenades completed with a statue of Pegasus by Vasilij Četkovic Vasko. Dominating Rogaška is the central park in an avenue of grand Secession buildings – a forward-thinking artistic and design movement started in Vienna in 1897 by Gustav Klimt – including the Grand Hotel with its Crystal Hall, the focal point for many cultural events.

In the 16th century the alchemist Leonhard Thurneysser was the first to describe the mineral spring in the town. It was later praised by the imperial physician Paul de Sorbait in 1679 and by Joseph Karl Kindermann in his 1798 history of Styria. The chemist Adolf Režek set up a small laboratory in Rogaška Slatina in 1931 and published various material about the town and its special waters.

The Rogaška Medical Centre is a well-established, highly professional and modern facility sitting at the apex of the classically designed central promenade and park of the town. The multi-storey building is a centre of excellence for the diagnostics, prevention and treatment of a wide range of ailments, harnessing the powers of the Donat Mg waters.

There are half a dozen luxury hotels in the destination. Without doubt, however, the one stand-out hotel and one of Rogaška's flagship products is the strikingly designed up-scale 5* Atlantida Boutique Hotel, which sits on the lower south-west-facing slopes of Cvetlični hrib, surrounded by woods and overlooking the town. The hotel pursues the mythology theme, being named after Plato's imagined Atlantis and its claim to be a source of magical energy and wisdom. This first-class wellness and spa centre successfully combines quality design with exceptional fine cuisine using all local products.

It is the vision of a former visitor to Rogaška, the retired Croatian banker Jzidoi Sucić. When asked about his reason for this bold investment, he replied that the town had been his escape from the stress of the financial world when working in Zagreb, so when he retired it was a natural progression to invest in a project that would be fun, enjoyable and to which he could also use as a guest. In many ways it has become the contemporary heart and soul of Rogaška Slatina, reflecting everything good about the town and its traditions with a contemporary twist.

• •

Above left: Podčetrtek.
Above right: The Podčetrtek Valley.

ROVINJ AND THE ISTRIAN PENINSULA, CROATIA

Re-inventing quality Istrian experiences, harnessing the power of local produce and creative talent

ISTRIA
●ROVINJ

CROATIA

Population of city: 15,000
Population of wider area: 208,000
Nearest international airports: Pula, Zagreb, Venice Marco Polo and Trieste.
Key websites: www.istria.hr; www.rovinj.co; www.visit-croatia.co.uk; www.croatia.hr
Icons: Kravata oko Arene, Rovinj, Motovun, Lim Fjord, Pula Amphitheatre, Lighting Cranes, Maistra Hotels and Resorts, truffle hunting, Zigante, olive oil, Malvasia wine, Giants of Motovun Forest, St Euphemia, Rovinj Nights.

Despite its obvious historical appeal to mass tourism, Croatia is steering a different course shaped by a clever, strong and focused tourism Master Plan and political leaders who understand the needs of the industry. And, within Croatia, the most appealing destination must be Istria – a 3,600 sq. km heart-shaped peninsula in the north abutting Slovenia some 50 km south of Trieste, the oft-contested, now Italian port city.

The coast has traditionally been the focus of tourist activity with its historic towns such as Vrsar, Pula, Porec and Rovinj and the resorts of Umag and Novigrad. The Istrian interior is characterised by medieval hilltop villages (including the smallest towns in Croatia – Hum, Motovun, Grožjan and Oprtalj) set amongst rolling country and forests – a countryside that lost almost 90% of its population, who exited during the four years of civil war from 1991–1995. This is a countryside of legends – giants and štrigas, a mischievous band of witches. It was Istria where, in the 'Legend of the Argonauts'

search for the Golden Fleece, the people of Colchis, who had pursued Jason in the north Adriatic decided Pula was a place of refuge. This Roman infused port city would later inspire Dante's *Divine Comedy* and today is leading with innovation in tourism in the way it uses the Roman Amphitheatre for contemporary events such as ice hockey and the largest red tie art installation as well as 'Lighting Giants' illuminations of the large cranes in the docks.

Istria is now leading the re-invention, and has become the epitome of a successful transformation, in Croatian tourism. It is driven by an enlightened and inspired Istrian Tourist Board. The Istrian approach closely follows the themes of the national strategy with the key 'actors' realising that quality and unique visitor experiences are the keys to competitive advantage. The momentum leading to the rapid transformation of the tourism industry is the result of three key factors: highly focused leadership in the public and private sectors; innovation and creativity in the delivery of tourist experiences and the realisation that a collaborative approach involving the community is essential.

Croatia is a small country with beautiful nature, interesting traditions and history, rich cultural heritage and diverse gastronomy. It has a favorable geographic position situated in the southeast of Europe, where the Adriatic, the Mediterranean, Middle Europe and Southeast Europe (the Balkans) meet. With its 1,200 islands, islets and rocks and numerous bays, coves and beaches, Croatia has one of the most indented coasts in Europe. There are eight national parks and the country has the largest number of protected non-material cultural phenomena in Europe – Festa Sv. Vlaha (St Blaise Celebration Day), lacemaking in Lepoglava and islands of Hvar and Pag, zvoncari (bellmen) from

Above: Hilltop towns and Istria's wine, olive oil and truffle interior.

the Kastav area, the cross procession, overtone singing, the spring procession of Ljelje (queens) and traditional manufacturing of wooden toys from Hrvatsko zagorje. There are seven UNESCO World Heritage Sites. In 2019 Croatia was ranked by the World Economic Forum's 'Travel and Tourism Global Competitiveness Index' as the 27th most competitive country for tourism out of 141 in the world and has pursued a quality-driven approach to tourism over the past ten years.

The current Minister for Tourism, Gari Capppelli, clearly understands these principles: 'Our mission is to ensure a good business environment and guidelines for development for everybody in the tourism sector. Our job is to create the right environment for enterprise together with the infrastructure to allow investors to stand a better chance to be successful. Sustainable tourism means that the community works hand-in-hand with the investors.' The Croatian Tourism Strategy emphasises various tourism products such as culture, health, business, sports, cycling, gastronomy as priorities in terms of diversifying away from sea and sand and growing a year-round tourism industry.

The Istrian peninsula is located at the head of the Adriatic between the Gulf of Trieste and the Kvarner Gulf. It is shared by three countries: Croatia, Slovenia, and Italy. The largest part of the peninsula belongs to the Republic of Croatia. Most of the Croatian part of the peninsula belongs to the Istrian County. The name is derived from the Histri tribes, who are credited as being the builders of the hillfort settlements (castellieri). The Romans described the Histri as a fierce tribe of pirates, protected by the difficult navigation of their rocky coasts. It took two military campaigns for the Romans to finally subdue them in 177 BC. The region was then, together with the Venetian part, called the Roman Region of 'Venetia et Histria'.

Following the Austrian defeat by Napoleon, Istria became part of the Napoleonic Kingdom of Italy (1806–1810) and then part of the Illyrian provinces of the French Empire (1810–1813) after the Treaty of Paris. After World War I and the dissolution of Austria-Hungary, there was a strong local movement toward Istrian independence, but in the end Istria was partitioned to Italy in 1920 – when its political and economic importance declined. In 1926, use of Slavic languages was banned, to the extent that Slavic family names were ordered to be changed. In World War Two, Istria became a battleground of competing ethnic and political groups. Pro-fascist, pro-Allied, Istrian nationalist, and Yugoslav-supported pro-communist groups fought with each other and the Italian army. After the end of World War Two, Istria was ceded to Yugoslavia. The division of Istria between Croatia and Slovenia became an international boundary with the independence of both countries from Yugoslavia in 1991.

Today, Istria is the most important holiday destination in Croatia. At the heart of this success lies a multi-cultural appreciation and a unique model for destination development founded upon deeply-rooted stakeholder involvement, exceptional levels of innovation and collaboration based upon synergistic enhancements across all sectors – tourism, food and drink, infrastructure development, unique village hotels and farmhouse restaurants, konobas and an intense focus upon the quality of local products and services in order to deliver guests with unique, unforgettable, Istrian experiences charged with positive and warm emotions. From the outset the tourism plans identified a value not a volume approach. Every product created in Istria is imagined in terms of what it would look like of its quality when benchmarked against its competitors.

This is best evidenced in the comprehensive story of positioning the local gastronomy product and experiences. It would be impossible to deliver a credible, quality, tourist gourmet experience unless there was an investment in creating unprecedented levels of quality in the production of the autochthonous products and contemporary design

Adriatic Hotel in Rovinj.

in their presentation, promotion and marketing. As a result, tourism development had to commence with a program of support for those producing the local wines (the liquid gold that is Malvasia and the Muscat of Momjam), olive oils, vegetables and those harvesting the forest for truffles (white and black) and mushrooms and the seas and rivers for fish.

Today the Istrian gourmet product includes: internationally award-winning wines and wine tourism, extra-virgin olive oil tourism, prosciutto tourism, agro-tourism and truffle tourism together with a whole programme of year round activities and events packaged together with appropriate accommodation (farmhouses, village hotels) now drives tourism – and it helps that Denis Ivoševic (Director of Tourism) is a sommelier in wines, olive oil and truffles. Istrian hoteliers, small-scale producers, chefs and truffle hunters all feature in the key world tourism guidebooks and magazines.

So, Istria is now leading the re-invention and is the epitome of a successful transformation in Croatian tourism. It is driven by an ambitious masterplan, with the key 'actors' realising that quality and unique visitor experiences are the keys to competitive advantage. One of the industry leaders, Maistra Ltd – the foremost tourism and hospitality company in the region – is critical to this success story, changing the face of tourism in the area with a series of design-led hotels. Maistra Ltd is the hospitality arm of the Adris Group and was

formed in 2005. Today Maistra owns and manages a portfolio of hotels and resort complexes in Istria in the towns of Rovinj and the nearby fishing village of Vrsar, north of the Lim Fjord.

Over recent years Maistra has invested millions of euros to create premium hotels focused on the gloriously picturesque historic town on Rovinj. The elegant five-star Monte Mulini and the design-focused Lone Hotel allowed Maistra to introduce two global brands to Istria – Leading Hotels of the World and Design Hotels. Other investments have followed with the rennovation of the environment at Lone Bay; they refurbished and re-invented the Adriatic Hotel and created the much-celebrated Family Hotel Amarin. In 2019 Maistra opened the Grand Park Hotel Rovinj representing the single biggest tourist investment by Maistra so far, and one of the largest investments in tourism since Croatian independence. Facing the marina, the six-level hotel has been built into the natural slope, offering views of the sea and of the town. For the re-invention of the Adriatic Hotel in the centre of Rovinj, Tomislav Popovic, president of the Management Board of Maistra explains: 'Our intention is to create a hotel that would make guests aware of the vibrant arts history of the town.' The result is extraordinary. This is more than a hotel with an outstanding art collection; it's a hotel where the art fashioned the whole experience. 'It was the rebirth of the hotel that gave birth to the art.'

SAALFELDEN-LEOGANG, SALZBURGERLAND, AUSTRIA

Genuine, healthy and good — a drive-through destination successfully re-invents itself

Saalfelden and Leogang are two communities located in west-central Austria in in the Pinzgau region of the Province of Salzburg in Austria.
Saalfelden sits astride the A10 main road between Salzburg and the Italian border at Villach some 180 km south of Munich, 70 km south of Salzburg and 370 km south-west of Vienna. The communities sit on the valley floor of the Saalbach river and its tributaries and is encircled by high mountains of the Steinmeer Plateau, the Hochkönig Massif and the Leogang / Biberg ranges.

Saalfelden, also called Saalfelden Am Steinernen Meer is situated at the south-west foot of the Steinernes Meer (Sea of Stones) Mountains, near the Saalach River. It is an old market town, which has developed over the past 20 years as a winter and summer tourism resort specialising in biking, conferences and culture – especially jazz music. Leogang is a small historic village some 10 km west of Saalfelden that for the past 600 years has been a centre for copper and silver mining. It is now becoming a major centre for skiing and biking. A number of other smaller villages make up the destination known as Saalfelden-Leogang.

Despite having access to high mountains offering good skiing opportunities in the winter, Saalfelden Leogang has been a *Cinderella* snow sports destination relative to the internationally-renowned, traditional winter sports centres of Zell-am-See, Kaprun and Kitzbühel. Indeed, Saalfelden Leogang has historically been regarded as a transit, drive-through place for tourists en route to these other destinations. In Austria it has been

AUSTRIA

● SAALFELDEN-
LEOGANG

Population of Saalfelden: 16,000
Population of wider area: 20,000
Nearest international airports: Klangenfurt, Innsbruck, Salzburg (Austria), Munich (Germany).
Key websites: www.salzburgerland.com; www.saalfelden-leogang.com
Icons: The Ritzensee, Saalach River, The Flying Fox, Pinzgau cuisine, Saalfelden Sommerodeln, Leoganger Bergbahnen, the Ski Marathon, the Jazz Festival, Ski Circus, The Biking Centre, Schloss Ritzen Museum.

Left: Leogang Mountains.

regarded as a 'second generation', or second level, destination but is now one of a new cohort of places 'in growth' characterised by a strong, hard-working, cooperative approach amongst the community and tourism businesses. Two fine examples of this working together are: a 'hotel' specifically for staff working in the hospitality industry to solve the problem of the lack of available housing and to tackle concerns that accommodation for local people was being lost to the rented market for hotel workers; and building a bio-mass power station to provide cheap energy for the industry and the community.

Over the past 20 years, however, Saalfelden Leogang has transformed this perception and has been successfully developed as a year-round destination with a particular emphasis upon becoming Europe's Number One Biking destination by 2020 as well as a recognised centre for alpine skiing, Nordic sports and year-round cultural activities, the highlight of which is the annual Saalfelden Jazz Festival which has now been running for more than 40 years. The local tourism association has set its goal to be 'the leading example of a contemporary, dynamic destination in terms of driving sustainable development and 'digital futures' with five clear aims: to be one of the leading year-round destinations in the European Alps based on quality experiences 365 days a year; providing premium quality on all service levels capable of driving higher-value experiences for the guest and higher levels of income for the community; to be Europe's No.1 bike destination; to be Salzburg's alpine destination and to create an attractive living and recreational environment for residents and guests.

The Chair of the tourism association, local hotelier, Hannes Reidesberger, says 'we must take care to get the balance right so we don't simply count volume growth. It has to be all about value – added value for the guest and the host – and how the benefits from tourism can be shared and secured for everyone in our community.

This means it all depends on the experience we give to our guests and the value they place upon that experience. It's about knowing our capacity, growing the potential of our people and building relationships. It is about people and how they can be creative and innovate.'

As a result, there is a clear vision for the destination supporting interesting new sustainable developments. The result is an accessible, compact, easy to understand destination with an impressive selection of family-run, high-quality, hotels and other hospitality services providing a wide range of year-round activities and cultural experiences that make the most of the natural heritage and cultural assets as well as the established facilities such as: the Saalfelden Congress Centre; the Schloss Ritzen Museum in Saalfelden; the Mining Museum in Leogang and the Felsenfest Climbing Centre in Saalfelden.

A good example of the community's successful approach to tourism is the Bike Park and the ambitious objective of becoming Europe's number one biking destination. In 2001 the idea to create a centre of excellence in biking took root with modest beginnings but was boosted by the Flying Fox ziplines. Within five years local hotels were seeing benefits and by 2011 it had become a success story and the decision was taken to establish a community company working with international partners (such as Volvo, MAXXIS, Red Bull, Fox, Scott and GoPro) and the local Cable Car Company to create a new, state-of-the-art bike park in Hutten near Leogang. With a cluster of supporting facilities driving year-round winter sports and summer downhill biking and mountain biking with a wider cycling offer throughout the destination, including: Freeride, Enduro, e-Bike, Road bike and cross country as well as developing new trails and routes, a bike school with camps for children, men and ladies and families. The area now regularly hosts world cups and other international championships and will host the 2020 UCI World Cup (Downhill).

As a result, a raft of new hotels has been developed which are taking design and hospitality standards to a new level. Most are offering amenities and services specifically designed to meet the needs of the new activity and adventure-seeking tourists, including specialised spa treatments and massages, highly-trained guides and experts, and the provision of specialist bicycle repair, hire and insurance facilities. The accommodation stock in the destination is very impressive particularly in terms of the hotels which are setting new standards, which are capturing the attention of global media and winning international awards. These include: The Ritzensee Hotel and Spa, the Holzhotel Forsthofalm, the Naturhotel Forsthofgut, Mama Thresl, the Design Hotel Die Hindenberg and the Salzburgerhof 'Hotel of Sports'.

Holding the marketing and presentation of the destination together is a uniquely created brand for the destination which has been agreed by the entire community and all local businesses. Impressively local residents, including school children, are asked to keep a little booklet with them at all times describing how they should communicate the destination to visitors and friends. This even identifies how best to take personal photographs of the place for use on social media. The idea is simple: Saalfelden-Leogang celebrates the rich contrasts between the two communities and the setting – the village with the city; grass and forests; old and young; stone and wood; active and relaxation; new sports and old sports; traditional and contemporary. This means that everything that happens in tourism flows from emphasising these contrasts. So, for example, wood and stone are core underlying themes which are carried through into architecture and design in new build hotels and in the Congress centre; new sports are created to sit alongside traditional activities such as Nordic walking; and the traditional Pinzgau regional recipes are now infused with a modern twist and promoted as 'echt, gsund, guad' – meaning 'genuine, healthy and good' – great metaphor for this destination as a whole.

Above: Bikepark Leogang.

SOČA VALLEY, THE JULIAN ALPS, SLOVENIA

From the Julian Alps to the Gulf of Trieste the emerald beauty zigzags through the one of the most beautiful landscapes in Europe

The valley of the River Soča (known as the Emerald Beauty), with its various tributaries, must be considered one of the most stunningly beautiful, exceptional landscapes in the whole of Europe. The river rises as pure clear alpine water from a spring in a dark crevice in the limestone rocks at the head of the Trenta Valley, high in the Julian Alps. It then zigzags south through mountains and forests, connecting a string of small towns and villages. It flows through deep white-walled rock gorges and cascades over waterfalls and rapids before entering the Adriatic in the Gulf of Trieste, midway between Grado and Trieste, on the north-Italian coast. Throughout its 140 km journey it maintains its a distinctive emerald colour, which is so bright and consistent that you are always asking, 'are the colours real?' It is the result of small particles of the bedrock – called rock flour – suspended in the water and reflecting blue and green as it captures sunlight.

With this bucolic, Alpine landscape it is impossible to imagine that this place was the setting of one of the largest battles in the history of the First World War. After Italy declared war on Austria-Hungary in 1915, the Isonzo (Soča) Front was to become the bloodiest of frontlines for the next two years: almost 1.7 million soldiers died or were mutilated fighting in the mountains above the valley, with many losing their lives escaping on the steep slopes in freezing conditions and unchartered screes and canyons. Many of the valley's 300,000 residents were displaced – thousands destined never to return. In October 1917 at the Battle of

● SOČA VALLEY

SLOVENIA

Population of Tolmin: 3,000
Population of wider area: 20,000
Nearest international airports: Ljubljana Jože Pučnik Airport, Klagenfurt (Austria), Trieste, Treviso and Venice Marco Polo (Italy).
Key websites: www.slovenia.info; www.soca-valley.com
Icons: The Soča River, the Great Soča Gorge, the Memorial Church of the Holy Spirit, Ana Roš, Ernest Hemingway, Simon Gregorčič, the Soča Trout, the Mangart Saddle, Triglav National Park, the Miracle of Kobarid, Nebesa Chalets, fly fishing.

· ·

Kobarid (known as the Miracle of Kobarid) was the twelfth and final major battle of the Isonzo Front, where it is estimated that 40,000 troops were killed and 280,000 captured in the total rout of the invading Italian forces.

When Ernest Hemingway, who was later to become a war correspondent, reached this part of the border with Italy a year later, it was as a volunteer ambulance driver with the Italian

Kayaking in the Soča Valley

army. The absolute horror he witnessed amid the immense beauty of the Soča Valley moved him enough to make it the opening scene of *A Farewell to Arms* published in 1929: 'There was fighting for that mountain too, but it was not successful, and in the fall when the rains came the leaves all fell from the chestnut trees and the branches were bare and the trunks black with rain. The vineyards were thin and bare-branched too and all the country wet and brown and dead with autumn.'

Simon Gregorčič, along with Préseren, is one of Slovenia's best-loved poets, and a significant figure in the 19th-century struggle for national rights. He was born in 1844 to a farming family in the Soča village of Vrsno at the base of Mount Krn. The surrounding landscape and valley culture and lifestyle greatly influenced his writing. He studied to become a priest but did not stray far from his much-loved Valley, settling as a chaplain in Kobarid where he began to publish poems about social injustice, Slovene rights and the environment that embraced him. Gregorčič's most famous poem is 'Soči' – 'To the Soča'– describing the river from its mountain source to the coastal plains. In its headwater the river flows fast and unchecked in spring and is fuelled by the melting snows on Triglav, which he describes as being 'like the walk of the highland girls'. In the poem Gregorčič foresaw a day when the river would be filled with blood, and would need to burst its banks to 'draw the foreigners ravenous for lands to the bottom of your foaming waves.' What provoked the poet to write such a beautiful poem burdened with such a powerful, prophetic foretelling of the killing fields along the River Soča a decade before the beginning of the atrocities? Soči:

A clear arch will stretch above you,
Around you a hail of lead,
Rain of blood and streams of tears,
Lightning and thunder – oh, stifling battle!
Bitter steel will strike upon these lands,
And you will flow full of blood

In the years following the termination of warfare the battle sites, cemeteries and former barracks fell into decay. The absorption of the area into Italy in the immediate post-war years then became occupied by the Nazis during the conflict before becoming part of Yugoslavia upon the cessation of World War Two. In 1991, with the arrival of Slovene independence, the residents of the Soča Valley, as in Bled and Ljubljana, were finally able to look to creating a new, progressive future for their communities, putting tourism at the heart of this regeneration. In the Soča Valley this included a very definite, positive role for the presentation of the valley's dark heritage using it as a powerful tool to promote peace through tourism.

One hundred years on, in 2018, the one hundredth anniversary of the end of World War One coincided with the European Year of Cultural Heritage, the inspirational 'Pot Miru', or Walk of Peace, is a 90 km trail in five sections, established in 2017 by a Slovene Foundation (the Ustanova Fundacija Poti Miru v Posočju) working with the national Institute for the Protection of Cultural Heritage to connect all the war sites in the Soča Valley. It starts at Log Pod Margarton and ends at Mengore Hill near Most na Soči close to the confluence of the Soča and Idrijca rivers. The sites included are the narrow, restored Ravelnik trenches, Fort Merman, military cemeteries and local museums. The outstanding, most poignant yet beautiful of all the memorials is the Church of the Holy Spirit at Javorca. This wooden shrine stands high above the Tolmin River as a symbol of reconciliation. Above the entrance is the single word 'PAX' alongside the symbols from 20 countries. This trail is now on the tentative list for possible future UNESCO World Heritage status. Inscription would be a fitting tribute to the legacy and memory of those who died in the conflicts that have afflicted this oft-contested part of Europe, complementing the national monument in Ljubljana to the 'Victims of All Wars and Conflicts Connected to Slovenia' which was unveiled in 2015.

Clearly the Valley has not discarded its past in stepping into the future. Ironically one of the most dramatic routes into the Valley is from the north over the Mangart Saddle on a road originally constructed by the Italian army for military purposes. When relationships between Italy and Yugoslavia improved the road opened for public use in 1958 attracting international mountaineers to climb Mount Mangart. It is now the highest tourist road in Slovenia.

Sitting alongside this potent and profound backstory of conflict is the creative re-imagining of the mountains, the valley and the rivers to become as a renowned destination for a broad menu of outdoor discovery and activities – in the air, on land and in the water – with fly fishing, waist deep in the aquamarine waters on the 'queen of rivers' for the Soča trout and grayling, being a highly sought after experience.

Overseeing the successful development of these tourism experiences is the highly-regarded, award-winning Soča Valley Tourist Board. This is a not-for-profit company, led by the determined CEO Janko Humar, and consists of local businesses driving forward with a new vision for sustainable tourism with the involvement and support of all the local communities and businesses including over 60 specialist outdoor activity providers. The Tourist Board's exemplary approach to managing and marketing the Valley has rightly earned them the European Union accolade of being a European Destinations of Excellence (EDEN), a scheme launched in 2006 to celebrate best practice in sustainable tourism development. The key feature of the selected destinations is their commitment to social, cultural and environmental tourism.

As well as the multitude of outdoor activities the destination excels in the celebration of its local cuisine, notably Kobariški struklji (sweet dumplings with walnuts and raisins), the Tolmin and Bovec cheeses, and fine wines from local cellars. It also boasts having the 'Hiša Franko',

the family-run restaurant where, self-taught and local produce-reliant chef, Ana Rös has emerged to be voted the world's best chef in 2017. Having initially trained to become an alpine skier before becoming a member of the Yugoslavian national youth squad, Ana studied diplomacy in Goriza (at the southern end of the Soča Valley) where she met her artist partner, Valter Kramar, whose parents owned the Hiša Franko Restaurant in Kopbarid. Kramer took over the restaurant and Ana started as a waitress. She later qualified as a sommelier and then took over the kitchen, experimenting with the innovative remaking of traditional recipes from the upper Soča valley region, all prepared with local ingredients. Kobarid is now the home of the 'Gastronomic Circle', a group of restaurants pursuing excellence in local gastronomy.

Festivals are used to highlight the strengths of the destination's appeal. In June the Soča Outdoor Festival is a duathlon and series of trail runs whilst the autumn the Hiking Festival is for novices, families and expert mountaineers. It is a fusion of lectures, films and over 30 organised walks. Jestival, held in October, is a hybrid where food meets local and global art and crafts. Local restaurants and tourist farms are instructed to make sure that 'beers, local wines and homemade liquors are all poured from jugs.'

SOUTH SOMERSET, ENGLAND

Local legends and heroes rub shoulders with global nomads

GREAT
BRITAIN

● SOUTH
SOMERSET

For millions of tourists over the past 50 years this was a place to pass through as quickly as possible on the A303 (part of the Fosse Way Roman Road linking Exeter with Bath and, eventually, to Lincoln) en-route to Devon and Cornwall, or on the A37 heading to Dorset's UNESCO World Heritage Jurassic coast or, maybe by train, taking advantage of Yeovil's once famous status as a rail hub with a complex of five railway stations. Today, this corner of Somerset has become a much sought-after destination with a sophisticated array of contemporary cultural experiences sitting comfortably with unexpectedly rich and internationally significant cultural attractions.

There could be some concern that this destination has made this 'top' 50 due to my personal bias. I was born and bred in East Coker (once voted the 'Prettiest Village in Britain'), the eponymous second of T S Eliot's *Four Quartets* and former home of his forefathers before their emigration to the States. Indeed, my father, as the village carpenter, doubled as the undertaker, and was tasked with the interment of the ashes of the poet in the village church of St Michael and All Angels.

Put this confession and any ideas of bias to one side. South Somerset fully deserves its inclusion as a great destination. It remains relatively undiscovered by domestic and international tourists, but a new breed of discerning travellers is recognising the breath-taking opportunities, provided by the emergence of world-class experiences that now exist in this delicious countryside consisting of rolling lowlands broken by scarps and ridges forming a number of very distinctive landscapes – from the fen-like Levels to

Population of Yeovil: 45,000
Population of wider area: 170,000
Nearest international airports: Bristol International, Bournemouth, Southampton, Exeter, London Heathrow.
Key websites: www.visitsouthsomerset.com; www.visitsomerset.co.uk; www.discoversouthsomerset.com
Icons: Somerset Cider Brandy, Ham Stone, The Glovers, Coker Canvas, T S Eliot, John Steinbeck, Cadbury Castle, The Levels, Hauser & Wirth, Koos Bekker, Karen Roos and The Newt, Julian and Alice Temperley, Ian Botham, Roger Bastable, sculptor Gordon Young, explorer and buccaneer William Dampier, Westland Helicopters, The School of Lifemanship, Pittard's Gloves, Clarks, Roger Saul and Mulberry.

the pastures and parklands of the valleys of the Yeo, Isle, Brue and the Od, riddled with charming mellow Ham-stone market towns (Somerton – the former capital of Wessex), Castle Cary, Martock, Wincanton,

Hadspen House, The Newt, Somerset.

picturesque villages (East Coker, West Coker, Long Sutton, Curry Rival, Muchelney, Haselbury Plucknett) each with their staunch, looming church towers and orchards growing traditional evocatively named varieties such as Cap of Liberty, Coker Seedling, Hagloe Pippin, Muriel and The Squire's Codlin!

Sixty years ago, in a promotional guidebook published by The Great Western Railway, this area was described as a romantic and historic corner of ideal England: a land of soft hills, peace, stillness, blossom in springtime and deep thatch. The guide began by stating 'This is Home'. It certainly was for Eliot whose opening to 'East Coker' is: 'In my beginning is my end, in my end is my beginning.'

The guidebook went on to eulogise that: 'here one finds an oldness, a kindness and a wisdom: things in part of the countryside and the dwellers within it. A place full of fragrant legends' (from King Arthur to the Odcombe 'leg stretcher'). Although much has altered, little has changed. There is still an underlying independence about the place that comes from being side-lined and by-passed for centuries. The recent tourism developments have been led by a quirky mix of slightly anarchic, interestingly eccentric, local heroes and, recently, the arrival of an inspirational group of global nomads and visionaries. There is now a deep sense of the ancient sitting, very comfortably, with the modern – especially in terms of the often extravagant but never out-of-place new generation of tourism investments.

Nowhere is this better exhibited than in the medieval market town of Bruton (between Yeovil and Frome), whose wealth was founded on wool and silk producing a legacy of fine historic buildings, many of which house highly-renowned, long-established, public schools of which Bruton has three. The oldest, Kings, was founded in 1519. CNN recently described Bruton high street as being 'skinny'. That is a fair assessment of its physical state, but underplays a thriving centre for stylish art, design and craft galleries, family enterprises selling local produce, a slew of antique shops and a place where even the local shops have recognised the power of curated content to match the interests of high-value visitors.

'Inquissima haec bellorum condicio est: prospera omnes sibi indicant, aduersa uni imputantur' – success has many fathers; failure is an orphan. This old proverb could apply to the transformation of South Somerset from being 'a drive-through to must-visit destination'. And this change didn't happen overnight or by chance. Certainly, serendipity played a role, as did alchemy, but there was always more to the story involving local heroes, global nomads and an enlightened local authority.

For many observers, Hauser & Wirth's arrival in Bruton was the catalyst for this change in perception of the destination; for others it was the cherry on the cake: an endorsement of 20 years of hard work, selfless investment and visionary projects across a number of villages by a cohort of local heroes. In the case of Bruton, The Mill on The Brue Adventure Centre, which opened in 1982, pioneered activity tourism in Britain whilst the remarkable conversion and re-modelling of a Grade II Listed 18th-century house and 19th-century congregational chapel into At the Chapel is a clever hybrid (comprising a restaurant, bedrooms, wine shop, bakery, terrace and clubroom) that challenges all tourist board definitions of what it is.

Following a chance visit to Bruton, Durslade Farm was chosen as the location for the globally-renowned art dealership Hauser & Wirth (owned by Iwan and Manuela Wirth) to create a new type of art gallery which opened in 2015. The Swiss-born couple saw the potential to bring the medieval derelict buildings to life, conserving these historic buildings for future generations by creating a world-class gallery and arts centre complete with The Roth Bar & Grill, which is regarded as being one of the finest and most unusual cocktail bars outside of London.

Today, Bruton's story of transformation continues

• •

Right above: The Tithe Barn at Haselbury Mill.
Right below: Diana and Julian Temperley, Burrow Hill Cider and the Somerset Cider Brandy Company.

apace. There is a very tangible and palpable positive vibe throughout the community. There is a new sense of civic pride and confidence with the positive impacts recognised by local people and this chemistry now attracting other global players who know a special place when they see it. These are a kind of new generation of pirates – driven by creativity and a desire to make a difference with investments formulated by philanthropy and personal interest, such as David Roberts and his artist wife, Indré Šerptyté, who have bought a farm in the village of Charlton Musgrove 'as a great space to show our art collection'.

The most prominent of these 'new pirates' arrived in 2013 and have now curated the extraordinary conversion of the Emily Estate and Hadspen House just a few miles from Bruton. Behind this project are the visionary South African couple Koos Bekker and Karen Roos – the creators of the wonderfully re-imagined Western Cape garden estate, Babylonestoren, which has turned heads in the Franschhoek Valley for over ten years. Created

Above: Hauser & Wirth Somerset.

in the 1680s, the Emily Estate has been home to seven generations of the Liberal Hobhouse family, including Arthur Hobhouse, a founder of the national parks system in England and Wales and Emily Hobhouse (1850–1926) – the pacifist, feminist and welfare campaigner who is revered in South Africa where she worked courageously to save the lives of thousands of women and children interned in camps set up by British forces during the Anglo–Boer War. This suggests a more profound interest in Hadspen by Bekker and Roos that is more than a chance encounter.

Opened in 2019, The Newt, as they have renamed the property, brings together, as Roos says, 'the most beautiful parts of what we found – ancient woodlands, a walled garden, the pretty gardener's cottage – with new designs that will hopefully allow visitors to explore different eras of gardening history. And, of course, celebrate the apple, which is what Somerset is all about. People in South Somerset have been so positive about it. It helps that this instantly felt like home, So, moving here and creating this has been a wonderful, and very natural, progression.'

These are sentiments closely reflected by comments made by Iwan and Manuela Wirth: 'Somerset changed our lives profoundly and I think it's fair to say that we found a home away from our original home. We knew that in South Somerset we had found a place where we could bring all of our interests together: art, architecture, landscape, conservation, garden, food, education, community and family. We were inspired by the enthusiasm and encouraged by the support of the local community as we embarked upon this ambitious project.'

But it is not, and never was, just about Bruton. Local heroes in villages across the destination have been leading the change with a wealth of interesting, community-centric projects for the past 15 years. These include the visionary Ross Aitken at the working restoration of the Victorian Dawes Twine Works in West Coker as part of the village's celebration of the world famous 'Coker Canvas' sail cloth industry; Michael Haynes, founder of eponymous Motor Manuals and the Haynes International Motor Museum in Sparkford; Kingsbury Episcopi's Burrow Hill Cider Farm with its Somerset Cider Brandy by Diana and Julian Temperley with their world-famous fashion-designer daughter, Alice; John Leach and his pottery in Muchelney; and the irrepressible Roger Bastable's Haselbury Mill and his highly crafted but faux Medieval Tithe Barn. And, on the border to the north of the destination, but being close enough to claim, there is also Michael Eavis and his Glastonbury Festival.

This intriguing, very non-typical approach to destination development has been supported and encouraged by a soft-leather glove, hands-off, dispersed tourism strategy adopted by a tuned-in South Somerset District Council. Their own signature project, The River Parrett Trail, started in the late 1990s and began this whole village-centric, locally-focused process. The Parrett Trail, follows this quintessential Somerset river for fifty miles from source to the Severn, tying together a string of attractive villages whose residents animate the trail with sculptures, bike hire shops, cidermaking, a community choir and local events.

Above: Parabola, The Newt, Somerset.

TRENTINO, ALTO ADIGE, ITALY

The art of nature, culture, the courteous welcome and the reinvention of hospitality in Italy's land of the butterfly

● TRENTINO AND RIVA

ITALY

Population of Riva del Garda: 17,000
Population of wider area: 538,000
Nearest international airports: Venice Marco Polo, Treviso, Verona, Brescia, Orio a Serio Bergamo.
Key websites: www.gardatrentino.it; www.visittrentino.info
Icons: Trento, Riva del Garda, Rovereto, MART, Trentodoc spumante wine, Vino Santo, Tour dei Forti, Monumento dei Dante, Lake Ledro, Earth Pyramids of Segonzano, 'enrosadira', Maria Dolens: The Bell of Peace, River Adige.

Any destination whose main tourism promotion begins with a quote from William Blake before setting out its philosophy to life and to tourism is going to grab anyone's attention! Trentino's opening shot is 'Great things are done when men and mountains meet' from Blake's 1810 *Gnomic Verses* inspired by local legends about gnomes in the mountains. The philosophy is inspiring: 'a land which has proudly preserved its traditional values: hospitality, finding an understated, silent happiness in small everyday things as much as in the great mountain landscapes. An ancient philosophy which has fused with modernity to achieve a very high quality of life, with attention paid to environmental and sustainable energy issues. Harmony springs to mind: friendliness, relaxed and a place where the old coexists with the new, and beauty with depth.'

The autonomous Province of Trentino, together with the Province of Bolzano, make up the Region of Trentino-Alto Adige/Süd Tirol situated in the north of Italy bordering Austria and Switzerland.

It is one of the loveliest, most interesting parts of the country yet, for many tourists, once through the Brenner Pass this is a place merely to travel through to get to the resorts of southern Lake Garda or those of the Adriatic. Trentino is beautiful with its snow-capped peaks stretching from the Adamello-Brenta range to the most striking mountains in Europe: the Dolomites – mountains that were inscribed as a UNESCO World Heritage Site in 2009 for the spectacle created by the phenomenon of 'enrosadira' – when the dusk sunlight creates an extraordinary veil of pale pink later becoming a vivid hue bathing the peaks in a remarkable afterglow.

Trentino is the 'land of the butterfly' so called because, when viewed from above, the area looks like a butterfly with open wings. It owes its name to the city of Trento (the Provincial capital), which in Roman times was called *'Tridentum'* (Latin for 'trident'), because the city is surrounded by three hills with pointed peaks like the tines of a trident.

No surprise then that the fountain in Piazza Duomo depicts the god Neptune, famous for his trident. This statue is one of the icons of the city together with the 1896 Monumento a Dante in Giardini Pubblici and the Duomo – the cathedral which, in 2015, was severely damaged by spontaneous combustion, its clock ominously stopping at 10.50 am a few minutes before the fire began.

Trentino has a remarkably varied landscape. The area is sliced open north-south by the valley of the River Adige – at 420 Km it is the second longest river in Italy after the River Po. There are impressive mountains splintered by high, scenic, passes overseen by castles; green, wooded valleys dotted with hundreds of small glacial lakes (including the picturesque Lake Ledro where, in 1929, a huge group of Bronze Age pile dwellings was discovered and is now protected as a UNESCO World Heritage Site); to the south is the deep blue fjord of Lake Garda; in the north are the remarkably, beautiful earth pyramids of Segonzano – one of the most well-known geological phenomena in the world comprising the remains of moraine deposits from the last Ice Age consisting of towers, crests and pinnacles arranged like organ pipes and tall columns topped with rock.

It is a landscape of culture, nature, Italian lifestyle, charming villages and opportunities for a myriad of winter and summer sports. Some of the infrastructure of sport has a delightful backstory: be it the early 20th-century design competition for the Riva diving tower or the desire by King Augustus III of Saxony, a keen mountaineer, to create 5,000 km of walking trails in the Vale di Fasse at the turn of the 19th century.

This is classic border country with all the challenges of a contested land of frontiers and dual identities. From 1363, to the fall of the Austro-Hungarian Empire in 1918, the Region was part of Austria. In the north of the Region, Bolzano (the capital of the Province of Alto Adige) is very Austrian in character and appearance whilst Trento is markedly Italian. The region is bilingual with German prevailing in many areas, despite the former Fascist Italian Government's attempts to eradicate the language post-1918. The area witnessed some of the fiercest battles on the Italian / Austrian-Hungarian front in World War One resulting, today, in some profound experiences to commemorate this dark history, including: a network of 19 war museums and the Tour dei Forti, a 170 km trail that follows the forts along the frontline of the 1914–1918 conflict.

Less than 30 km south of Trento, on the A22–E45 motorway connecting Munich and Innsbruck to Venice and Trieste, is the former silk centre of Rovereto – Trentino's second town but the centre of the Province's remarkable dedication to contemporary art and culture. Here is located Casa d'Arte Futurista Depero and the MART (Museum of Contemporary Art Trento and Rovereto), one of the most important contemporary art galleries in Italy with its high street location and sculpture garden. It is the celebrated hub of a dispersed collection of galleries across the Trentino.

Just outside the town is, without doubt, one of the most powerful of statements about war and the importance of peace: the Campana dei Caduti, the Peace Bell, the 'Bell of the Fallen'. The Maria Dolens Bell, the biggest swinging bell in the world, was conceived by local priest, Don Antonio Rosaro. It was originally cast in Trento in 1924 from the bronze of cannons from the 19 nations involved in World War One to honour the Fallen of all wars and to invoke peace and brotherhood between the peoples of the whole world. It was baptised in Rovereto with the name 'Maria Dolens' in 1925 and placed in Rovereto Castle. Then, in 1960, due to a serious, crack the Bell ceased ringing. In 1964 it was once again recast before being blessed in Rome by Pope Paul VI and, in November 1965, returned to Rovereto and placed on the Colle di Miravalle overlooking the town. On it's hood the bell is engraved with the words of Pope Pius XII: 'Nothing is lost in Peace. All may be lost in War', and John XXIII: 'In pace hominum ordinata concordia et tranquilla libertas'. For over 50 years the Bell of the Fallen has sounded 100 chimes every evening to commemorate the fallen of the entire world, without distinction of faith or nationality, acting as a grave warning to the living: 'No more war.'

Riva del Garda is nestled at the north-western end of Lake Garda in the most dramatic of settings framed by Monte Rocchetta to the west and Monte Brione to the east, beyond which sits the attractive lakeshore village of Trabone. For many, Riva is the jewel of Lake Garda, the unchallenged tourism centre for Trentino. It enjoys a delightfully agreeable, year-round, micro-climate with luxurious vegetation including lemon trees, palm trees and olives. This former fortress town (the fort now houses MAG – the Museo Alto Garda), with its winding medieval, stepped-streets, delightful waterfront squares and gardens and the imposing 13th-century Torre Apponale Clock Tower, is a centre for water sports and outdoor activities and a bustling ferry terminal with elegant Belle Époque ships plying the lake and linking Riva with Limone and Malcesine.

What is especially impressive about the way tourism is managed and marketed in Trentino is the Province-wide strategy with a local level implementation involving 20 community-focused tourism organisations charged with delivering the overall strategy within their towns and villages. Overseeing this clearly structured and effective approach is Trentino Marketing, a company that focuses on creating, implementing and promoting initiatives and projects aimed at developing tourism for the greater good. Created in June 2015 by Trentino Sviluppo SpA, this company was formed by the Provincial Government to foster sustainable development. Each of the local tourism consorzio, such as Garda Trentino SpA for Riva del Garda, is structured to mirror that of the Provincial body.

Trentino Marketing's strategy is based on knowing how to grasp the challenges of a rapidly transforming market; cultivating the ambition locally to improve the reputation and image of Trentino and its ability to welcome and

accommodate tourists from all over the world; generating benefits for local businesses; and, communicating its philosophy. The company describes its job as being like a film director – ensuring that everyone involved in the community sees themselves as being indispensable actors to achieve the same ambitious objectives for the Province and for every town and village. The Trentino Guest Card is a neat tool bringing everything together, offering tourists free transport on all 'Open Move' transport services plus a host of discounted deals and free admissions.

The commitment to tourism is clearly reflected in this promise to deliver 'A courteous holiday offering efficiency, reliability and organisation plus a warmer element that makes a difference: simple courtesy derived from people who love and have managed to reinvent hospitality.' And it works! It is palpable. The Dalai Lama, the spiritual leader of Tibet and frequent visitor, has referred to Trentino as having 'an extraordinary spiritual energy'. Today, it is one of the most prosperous parts of Europe recognised by the national newspaper Il Sole 24 Ore as having the best quality of life in Italy and realising the positive contribution that tourism can make to its economy and lifestyle.

Above: The Bell of the Fallen, Rovereto.

TRIESTE, ITALY

A frontier city belonging to everyone and to no one, the sea-gate city of Vienna

Cities can never escape their history or their geography. This is particularly true of Trieste, described as being seemingly in 'a condition of partially suspended animation', a crossroads of the Latin, Slavic and Germanic worlds.

The city is vertically squeezed between the limestone ridge of the harsh, wild Karst plateau to the north and the cobalt blue of the eponymous Bay of Trieste at the tip of the Adriatic Sea, appearing to tumble down a hillside that becomes a mountain. In this way it is reminiscent of its near neighbour, the deep-water port of Rijeka, Croatia's third largest city, located just 75 km to the east on the Bay of Kvarner.

This is far from being a typical Italian city. As a border city, throughout its 2,000 years Trieste has always been a melting pot of cultures, always on the edge of somewhere, often traded as a commodity as a gesture of appeasement or convenience and always international in its outlook, maintaining and celebrating its cultural and ethnic diversity.

Today, it teeters on the edge of Italy, the country's eastern outpost. It has been the capital of the autonomous Friuli Venezia Giulia (FVG) for 60 years, a region which spans a wide variety of climates and landscapes, from the mild and temperate coastal and central plains to Alpine conditions in the mountains that border Austria and Slovenia to the north and east. In the west the coast is shallow and sandy, with numerous tourist resorts on the lagoons of Lignano Sabbiadoro (Italy's 'little Florida' according to Ernest Hemingway) and Grado.

Grado is a small historic seaside resort and

Population of city: 207,800
Population of wider area: 232,000
Nearest international airports: Trieste Airport (Ronchi dei Legionari), Venice Marco Polo, Treviso International, Ljubljana Jože Pučnik Airport.
Key websites: www.promoturismo.fvg.it; www.tastefvg.it; unicaffe.illy.com; www.illy.com
Icons: the Isonzo (Soča) River, Grado, the Carso, Illy Caffè, Francesco Illy, Trieste – Opicina Hill Climb, Trieste Folding Chairs by Aldo Jacober, the Elettra Sincrotrone Trieste Research Centre, the Savoia Excelsior Palace Hotel, the Urban Hotel Design, Bagno Alla Lanterna, Faro della Vittoria Lighthouse, Maximilian's Miramare Castle, the Opicina Obelisk and the electric railway, the Cathedral of San Giusto, Teatro Verdi and Teatro Rossetti.

working fishing port on a lagoon island accessed by a long, dramatic causeway across a wide expanse of the shallow, wildfowl-festooned waters of the lagoon, its flotilla of islets and the white-towered church-island of Barbana. This compact, delightfully serene thalassotherapy centre, much appreciated by Austro-Hungarian emperors, still retains its heritage core, an Instagramable harbour and Grado's cathedral, Duomo di Sant'eufemia. Grado was once more important than Venice, but after the 6th-century fall of the nearby Roman city of Aquileia (an important early centre of Christianity) Grado became the seat of the archbishops responsible for the Adriatic lagoon islands and for Istria.

Beyond Grado is the estuary of the Isonzo River. The coastline arcs eastwards as it rises into white cliffs, where the Karst plateau (the carso) meets the Adriatic. This is the riviera of the region, flowing all the way to the polyglot seaport that is the mysterious and puzzling Trieste.

Today the city is almost surrounded by Slovenia, physically and psychologically isolated from the rest of the Italian peninsula, which has helped to preserve its unique border town culture and its Triestino dialect, described as 'a strange melange of Italian, Austrian-German, Croatian and Greek'. The city has a convoluted history, being the subject of a tug-of-war between Italy and Austria and of serial conquests. However, this is a story with a happy ending.

Trieste is both modest yet grand, creatively resilient and always surprising. For centuries, Trieste was the great port of Vienna and the gateway to Zion for thousands of Jews fleeing from persecution. It was recently described by writer Umberto Saba as 'having unsociable grace. She is a city that does not like to show off, although she conquers her visitors at first sight.' In *Trieste*

Above: Canal Grande of Trieste.

and the Meaning of Nowhere (2001), the fine Welsh travel writer Jan Morris describes this Italian city dressed in Hapsburg clothes: 'the hallucinatory city ... the sea-gate of one of Europe's supreme political entities, the Hapsburg Empire ... that still offers echoes of old Austria.' Morris' poignant meditation on this unusual city makes it one of the finest travel books ever written.

The city flourished as part of Austria from 1382 and became a key asset of the Austro-Hungarian Empire from 1867 until 1918. During this time Trieste was one of the most prosperous Mediterranean seaports, particularly famed for coffee imports that once fuelled the coffee culture of Vienna and now reaches cafes around the world.

Founded in 1933 by Francesco Illy, a former World War I army officer and a Romanian émigré, Illy Caffè S.p.A is today a true global influencer in the art of coffee – both literally and metaphorically. A highly respected producer of quality coffee, the company's unique art collection often provides

inspiration for their brands and since 1999 they have run the only University of Coffee (Università del Caffé), located at their plant in Trieste.

At the time Illy established his company the city was undergoing an economic revival but then suffered from a complex history of annexation, territorial claims and counterclaims and unprecedented torment throughout World War II. In 1947, Trieste was declared an independent city state under the protection of the United Nations known as the Free Territory of Trieste, destined to become a focus of the struggle between the Eastern and Western blocs after the Second World War.

The territory was divided into two zones, A and B. From 1947 to 1954, Zone A was occupied and governed by the Allied military and covered the same area as the current Italian Province of Trieste, except for four small villages south of Muggia, which were given to Yugoslavia. This was part of Zone B, composed of the north-westernmost portion of the Istrian peninsula and under the

administration of the Yugoslav People's Army. In 1954, in accordance with the Memorandum of London, the vast majority of Zone A – including the city of Trieste – joined Italy, whereas Zone B and four villages from Zone A became part of Tito's Yugoslavia, divided between Slovenia and Croatia. The final border line and the status of the ethnic minorities in the areas was settled bilaterally in 1975 with the Treaty of Osimo. This line is now the border between Italy and Slovenia.

Summer 1972 was my first encounter with Trieste, arriving by train from Venice. In the outer suburbs of the city then, as now, the track hugged the high limestone ridge before a steep descent to the Centrale Station, located close to the quayside on the Piazza della Libertà. This is a statement building in a neo-Renaissance style, opened in the presence of Austrian Emperor Franz Joseph I in 1857 and a point of arrival and departure fitting of a great port city. Eight hours later, as the sun was setting, looking back on the city from the deck of the ferry departing for the Croatian islands, the vibrancy of the quays in the Old Port (Porto Vecchio), the hefty busyness of the harbour and the grand architecture of the Governor's Palace together with the equally majestic palaces of great shipping companies made it clear Trieste was a city to be reckoned with. She had conquered this first-time visitor.

Today, Trieste's deep-water port is still regarded as a maritime gateway for northern Italy, Germany, Austria and Central Europe. It also has one of the highest living standards among Italian cities, listed as one of the 25 best small towns in the world for quality of life and one of the ten safest cities in the world in 2021.

Left: More than 2000 sailboats take part in the 51st edition of the Barcolana regatta in the gulf of Trieste.
Top: Palmanova aerial view with Aquileia door.

Its streetscape is extraordinary, a cocktail of the very rational, especially along the waterfront, with the iconic Piazza Unità d'Italia, the Molo Audace stone pier stepping out into the Bay and the Canal Grande alongside crooked historic lanes and alleys and the pedestrianised Borgo Teresiano. This is the stage for the daily evening *passeggiate*, when the locals take to strolling the city and, as observed by Jan Morris, the habit of loitering – both highly recommended for tourists.

This a city of appropriated traditions and cultures. It is also about great food and drink, scientific innovation, music and literature.

At the end of World War I, a brief, unrepeatable period of what Bob Dylan would call the 'winds of change' emerged in Trieste that made a formidable impact on Italian poetry (with Umberto Saba's *Canzoniere* (Songbook), released in 1921), English prose (with James Joyce's *Ulysses*, published in 1922) and Italian prose. This was Richard Burton's 'favourite retreat', the consular office of Charles Lever, Stendhal and Ivo Andrić and the inspiration behind the works of Vladimir Bartol, Srečko Kosovel, Fulvio Tomizza and many other important writers and poets who wrote in Italian, Slovenian, German and other languages.

James Joyce, after arriving penniless in the city in 1904, spent 15 highly creative years in Trieste. It was here, especially at 4 via Bramante, that he wrote most of *Dubliners*, all of *Portrait of an Artist as a Young Man* and parts of *Ulysses*. In Caffè San Marco he struck up a creative dialogue with the native writer Italo Svevo, whose *Zeno's Conscience* is regarded as one of the great 21st-century comic novels. Zeno Cosini, the novel's hero, states that 'Life is neither ugly nor beautiful. It is original.' Trieste is certainly original, and it is also beautiful.

Today, the region's tourist board has created a very walkable literary trail including the bronze statutes of Svevo in Piazza Hortis and of Joyce on the bridge over Canal Grande as well as the plaque on the wall of 4 via Bramante with a quote by Joyce

from 16 June 1915: *'Ho scritto qualcosa'* (I wrote something).

Since the 1960s, Trieste has developed a formidable pedigree as a city of knowledge and enjoyed a longstanding tradition as a hub for scientific research and innovation, especially in the fields of sustainable growth and development. There are 30 national and international centres hosting over 5,000 permanent and 13,000 visiting researchers each year, making it one of the most important research locations in Europe. Indeed, in 2020, Trieste was designated the European City of Science. The theme selected for the year's celebrations – 'Freedom for Science, Science for Freedom' – became a metaphor for the hopes of society in the year of COVID-19 as the pandemic meant that the year-long festival had to be a hybrid affair of virtual and real-time activities.

Trieste is a city full of symbols and expressions of freedom in all its forms. Fifty years ago, it was the first Italian city to end the forced incarceration of the mentally ill. Today the former psychiatric hospital houses art exhibitions, cafes and a university in the Liberty Building alongside Parco di San Giovanni, while the Bagno Alla Lanterna public bathing area made a special contribution to the concept of freedom.

It is a city free of a major museum or art gallery, though, in fact, it does not need one. The whole city functions as a gallery of shared memories, from the iconic symbol of freedom that is Faro della Vittoria Lighthouse to Maximilian's Miramare Castle, the Opicina Obelisk and the electric railway, the cathedral of San Giusto, the Roman theatre with Teatro Verdi and Teatro Rosseti, and Micheze and Jacheze, the statutes of page boys that strike the bell every hour in the Municipal Tower.

The region's 'Made in FVG' and 'Live Like a Local' are highly imaginative tourist experiences that are represented in Trieste with, for example, 'Among the Artisan Workshops', a tour available in either Italian or English, led by the delightful Chiara

Marchi. Together you explore the creative spaces of some of the city's most innovative jewellers, print designers, carpenters and paper engineers.

In 2019, the Regional Government's dynamic PromoTurismoFVG initiated a much-heralded contemporary art project curated by the Italian art critic and author Demetrio Paparoni. The project involves 17 large-scale installations, including works by Antony Gormley, Anish Kapoor, Jeff Koons and Jaume Plensa together with 13 other world-famous artists, celebrating the United Nation's 17 Sustainable Development Goals.

Trieste is an enigma. The Italian philosopher and writer Mauro Covacich explained the conundrum of his place of birth by stating that 'Trieste is a southern city. The most southern city in Northern Europe.'

Above: Town of Grado.

TURKU AND THE SOUTHWEST FINLAND ARCHIPELAGO, FINLAND

The Christmas city and exuberant, contemporary, urban culture cradled in the arms of nature

Turku (derived from early Slavic language 'türgú', meaning 'the market place'), one of the original Hanseatic ports, is located on the south-west coast of Finland at the mouth of, and then straddling, the Aura River as it weaves its way intimately under ten bridges through the centre of Turku unlike any other river city. This region was originally called Suomi, which later became the name for the whole country, and is made up of 53 municipalities in the communities of Salo, Uusikaupunki, Åboland and Naantali. Turku acts as the gateway for the Southwest Finland Archipelago comprising over 40,000 islands and skerries, sometimes known as the 'Scandinavian Islands', sitting between Finland and Sweden. It is often referred to as 'urban culture cradled in the arms of nature'.

Although never officially founded, it is first referenced as a settlement in 1229 and the year is now used as the foundation year of the city. As a result, it is regarded as the oldest town in the country. It has all the main features of a medieval centre of power and trade: a cathedral, a castle, a river with waterways, a port and a marketplace. For over 500 years, from its establishment to the early 19th century, Turku was the most important city in Finland, a status it retained for hundreds of years when the area was under the rule the Kingdom of Sweden from 1323 until 1808 when Russia invaded Sweden. After this war when Finland became an autonomous grand duchy of the Russian Empire (1809) and fell under the direct rule of the Czar who moved the capital to Helsinki (1812), a number of the key government institutions did remain until the

FINLAND

TURKU & ARCHIPELAGO

Population of city: 190,000
Population of wider area: 430,000
Nearest international airports: Helsinki Vantaa, Tampere, Mariehamn, Pori.
Key websites: www.kissmyturku.com; www.visitturku.fi; www.visitfinland.com; www.moominworld.fi; www.lanaturku.fi
Icons: Aura River, Sibelius, Alvar Aalto, Tove Jansson, Goerz, Moomins and Moominworld, Meyer Shipyards, Wäinö Aaltonen Museum of Art, Luostarinmäki handicrafts museum, Christmas City, Island of Ruisalo, Föri Ferry, Kiss My Turku!

Great Fire of Turku in 1827.

During this period of Russian rule, the Finns did retain a considerable amount of autonomy; they kept their own legal system, language and religion, and were exempt from Russian military service. However, from 1899 Russian Tsar Nicholas

II inaugurated a policy of Russification of Finland, resulting in protests and a campaign of civil disobedience. In 1906, Finland passed a Parliament Act, which established universal suffrage, including the right for women to stand for elected office for the first time in Europe. This important legislation that would set the tone for the country's liberal and radical approach to civic society in the years following its independence from the Soviet Union in 1917.

For a time in the 20th century, Turku was the most populous city in Finland and, today, remains the regional capital, the sixth largest city in Finland, and an important business, high-tech, cultural and tourism centre. Its strategic location makes it an important commercial and passenger seaport (with over three million passengers travelling through the Port of Turku each year to Stockholm and Mariehamn) as well as an international centre for shipbuilding, especially for ocean-going cruise ships and their fit-out.

Along with Tallinn, the capital city of Estonia, Turku was designated the European Capital of Culture for 2011. This international accolade, in the same way that it was a catalyst for transforming the Austrian city of Linz (one of the other destinations in this book), had a profound effect on Turku, raising awareness of the city, stimulating civic pride and enhancing the cultural infrastructure of the city. Much of this investment has been linked with the conservation of, and the re-use of, old industrial buildings especially in the former Wärtsilä Shipyards and along the River Aura, which had traditionally been the focus of the city's industrialisation. Today the docks host the Conservatory with a number of concert halls and the maritime heritage centre 'Forum Marinum'; the Meccanno Hall is a contemporary apartment block with bars and restaurants; 1885 Brewery hosts the

Above: Restaurant Nooa, Turku marina.

Restaurant Rocca; and the former ironworks is now ARKEN – the University's Faculty of Arts.

The city's cultural centre organises a number of regular events, most notably the Medieval Market in July each year. The Turku music festival and the rock festival Ruisrock (held on the island of Ruissalo) are among the oldest of its kind in Scandinavia. The city also hosts another rock festival, Down by the Laituri, and one of the largest electronic music festivals in Northern Europe, UMF (Uuden Musiikin Festivaali, 'New Music Festival'). This is also a city of sculpture. Major works in key public spaces include: *The Theatre Bridge* by Jan Erik Andersson; *Network* by Outi Sarjakoski; *Harmony* by Achim Kühn and Kain Tapper's *Flowing of Time*.

There are also a dozen museums, such as the Turku Art Museum and the Wäinö Aaltonen Museum of Art. The Åbo Akademi University maintains the Sibelius Museum, which is the only museum in Finland specialising in the field of music. There are also several historical museums which tell the story of the city's medieval period such as the Turku Castle and the Aboa Vetus museum, built in the late 1990s over a 14th century archaeological site in the Old City. The Luostarinmäki handicrafts museum is housed in converted residential buildings that survived the Great Fire of Turku. The Föri Ferry commenced its free service across the Aura in 1904 and remains one of the icons of the city transferring passengers 'täl puol jokke; tois puol jokke' (on this side of the river, on the other side of the river') throughout the day, every day, ice permitting.

The Declaration of Christmas Peace, a tradition in Finland from the Middle Ages, takes place in the Great Square of Turku every year at noon on Christmas Eve every and, in 1996, Turku was designated Finland's official 'Christmas City'. The declaration ceremony begins with the hymn 'Jumala ompi linnamme' (*Martin Luther's Ein feste Burg ist unser Gott*) and continues with the Declaration of Christmas Peace read from a parchment roll in Finnish and Swedish.

The development and marketing of tourism in the city and for the wider Region is undertaken by Turku Touring Oy, a not-for-profit limited company, led by the company's inspirational Director, Anne-Marget Hellén. This former fashion journalist has provided the leadership and vision for tourism over the past fifteen years or so. She introduced the brave, edgy, marketing concept: 'Kiss my Turku!' and recently invited residents to express how they feel about Turku and the region to help promote the destination. For her Turku is 'like style, fashion and design' highlighting the small distinctive boutiques now peppering the city and the May 'Boutique Week'. For others Turku feels like: 'a big pop-up club in the Summer and a small fair in the winter'; 'it is my Paris, Tallinn and Stockholm rolled into one'; I love Turku and pretty strange as I am from Helsinki'; and, 'it is like entering Narnia through the wardrobe.'

Turku Touring excels at innovation and encouraging others to be increasingly creative. It widely regarded as a centre of excellence in tourism and experience management. There is a multitude of highly creative tourist experiences thriving in this destination: from the behind the scenes Meyer Shipyard tour, to the life of the 'Flying Finn' (Paavo Nurmi who took part in three Olympics), an evening in the spirit of Dali to various design and culinary walks – sampling delights such as the raisin sausage the Archipelago new potatoes and the Bishop's Doughnut. The land as seen from the water is a fundamentally important experience either by kayak, on Låna an electric picnic boat, maybe on an archipelago cruise ship or having a dining experience sailing at night through the islands on the on the Steamship S/S Ukkopekka.

Bringing many of these opportunities to the tourist is the group, Doerz, which helps travellers find real-life, authentic, unique, experiences with, and involving, local people. There is the experience of berry picking with Marjatta, vintage and flea market shopping with Ida or beer tasting

with Tapani – a chance to see their everyday life by getting to know over 50 real locals who are willing to share their culture and insights with tourists based on five themes: urban culture, food, outdoor, traditional and active. Individuals offering experiences at Doerz is freelance work that they do in their own time. They are not the usual type of traditionally-trained, professional tour guide. These are ordinary people who are passionate about what they do and love sharing that with other people.

The Doerz mantra is simple: 'perfect is boring; tourism as we have known it is dead. Long live the new way of travelling! Where the tourist is regarded as a temporary local and where they want to experience the city through the eyes of a genuine local and do the things that locals do. No one wants to be a tourist anymore'. Doerz is a platform to make this happen. It is a community that is building the bridge between travellers and locals. The Doerz Local is a service for our customers looking to tap into the live like a local trend and start offering locals experiences for their own customers. The guides are regarded as hidden heroes and are at the core of the Doerz community.

Less than 10 km north of the city centre is the old medieval, seaside town of Naantali – a spa town resort, which has long been regarded the summer capital of Finland, and is home to 'Moomin World' – the theme park, which opened in 1993, sitting on Naantali's delightful, tree-covered, Kailo island – dedicated to the stories of Tove Jansson (1914–2001), a Swedish speaking Finn, whose first story was about these fantasy characters (titled *The Moomins and the Great Flood* published in 1945). The Moomin stories became a very popular Swedish TV series some 25 years later followed by the opening of Moomin Valley in the Tampere Art Museum prior to creating Moomin World and in 1991 launching a concept for a new theme park in Japan.

Above: Turku Cathedral.

VADEHAVSKYSTEN, THE WADDEN SEA, DENMARK

All along the watchtowers: big skies, long vistas, a flotilla of islands and nature-inspired gastronomy

The Wadden Sea (Vadehavskysten) is one of the world's largest and most important unbroken inter-tidal sand and mudflat wetland ecosystems, its 500 km of coastline internationally recognised as an area of major ecological, economic and social importance. The Wadden Sea is designated a national park, incorporating the Dutch Wadden Sea Conservation Area, the German Wadden Sea national parks of Lower Saxony and Schleswig-Holstein and most of the Danish Wadden Sea Conservation Area. A trilateral agreement has been formulated between the German, Dutch and Danish governments with the objectives of developing a unified vision for the future of the sea, supported by a Joint Declaration on the Protection of the Wadden Sea (1982). In 2009, the Dutch and German areas of the Wadden Sea were designated as a UNESCO World Heritage Site, with the Danish areas being added five years later.

Its ecological importance is based on the great biological productivity and diversity of the complex mosaic of coastal ecosystems, comprising mud flats, sand banks, seagrass beds, salt marshes, mussel beds, islands, estuaries and river systems. These systems provide some of the most important habitats for coastal waterfowl and shorebirds and form a major staging area on the East Atlantic Flyway for migrating birds. Renewable resources derived from the Wadden Sea ecosystem also sustain a wide range of economic activities, from fisheries to energy production. The natural and cultural landscape is unique in Europe, making it one of the key tourism and recreation destinations

DENMARK

● THE WADDEN SEA (VADEHAVSKYSTEN)

Population of main city: 72,000
Population of wider area: 116,000
Nearest international airports: Esbjerg, Billund, Hamburg International.
Key websites: www.vadehavskysten.dk; www.nationalparkvadehavet.dk; (app for Apple and Android) Vestkysten
Icons: UNESCO World Heritage Wadden Sea, Ribe, the Cathedral of Our Lady Maria, Esbjerg, Fanø, Rømø and Mandø Islands, Marsk Tower, founder of Maersk Shipping, Hans Brorson, *Man meets the Sea*, Svend Wiig Hansen, Dorte Mandrup.

for Northern Europeans.

This extensive and relatively flat coastal wetland environment was created around 12,000 years ago at the end of the Ice Age. The tides ebbed and flowed over millions of years, creating this huge expanse of ancient natural scenery with its many

habitats, home to numerous plant and animal species, including marine mammals such as the harbour seal, grey seal and harbour porpoise. It is a dynamic, quickly changing environment of fast tides, big skies with scudding clouds and long vistas. The air is clean and the winds can be powerful, as the constant reshaping of the murmuration of countless starlings will testify.

Early in 2020, the communities that make up the Danish Vadehavet established a unique collaboration to promote and manage tourism. This includes historic Ribe, Denmark's oldest town, and Esbjerg, the country's west-coast capital, centre of alternative energy and the youngest urban centre in Denmark at just 150 years old. Attractive, characterful towns and villages pepper the lowlands and the coast backed by sand dunes that run to the border with Germany, while a flotilla of small islands adds to the sense of place. The most intriguing island, Fanø, has its own chapter in this book.

The starting point for a visit should be the heritage tour de force that is the well-preserved medieval Ribe and its recently reinvented Wadden Sea Centre nearby – gateway to the UNESCO World Heritage site and winner of the 2020 Meyvaert Museum Prize for Sustainability. The Danish architectural practice Dorte Mandrup, inspired by this landscape, pays homage to the traditional Danish farmstead in the design of the new centre through the use of traditional, resilient, local materials, such as timber and thatch and the original brick walls. It is a neat, highly contemporary antidote to the historic authenticity of the town's narrow cobbled streets and well-preserved houses, some dating back to 710 AD, when the town first made its mark as a trading centre between Scandinavia and the rest of Europe.

Above: Ribe.

It is no surprise that Denmark's oldest town is home to the country's oldest cathedral. Ribe's Church of Our Lady Maria dates from 1150 and is not just an icon of the town but also its distinctive square, Borgertårnet, or Commoner's Storm Watch Tower, rising out of the surrounding marshes, is visible for miles and a landmark for the Wadden Sea. Built to give citizens a 'big view' of impending attack or inclement weather, the walk-in tower gives the visitor a fine understanding of this environment, the vastness of the sky and the sheer extent of the wetlands.

The cathedral's carillion bells chime four times a day, twice with a folk song about Queen Dagmar of Denmark and twice playing the eighteenth-century Bishop of Ribe Hans Brorson's hymn 'Den Yndigste Rose er Funden' ('Now Found the Fairest Rose') and contributing to Ribe's own in-built symphony: the sound of rushing water through the old mills, the cry of wildfowl, the voice of the Night Watchman's tours and footsteps on cobbles.

Next to the cathedral is the wonderful Kannikegården, a contemporary take on a community hall and proof that modern architecture can give the past a future and the future a past. A similar theme is developed in the Jacob A. Riis Museum, which tells the story of the boy from Ribe who emigrated to America in 1870, emerging as the journalist whose hard-hitting articles exposed New York's wretched slums and earned praise from President Roosevelt, who called him 'the ideal American'.

Now protected as part of the national park is the intriguing Meadow of the Heads (Hovedengen) leading down to the River Ribe. In the 1500s, the town was much troubled by pirates, and legend has it that it was customary to put the pirates' decapitated heads on stakes at the entrance to the harbour as a deterrent and warning to others, hence Hovedengen. A similar story of foreboding ('Thou shalt not suffer a witch to live', Exodus 22:18) is explained in HEX!, the museum of the 1624 Ribe Witch Hunt.

Not far away is a new meadow of welcome. In Spring 2022, the 25-metre-high MARSK Tower, designed by the innovative Danish architectural firm Bjarke Ingels, will open. Its unique placement in Hjemsted by Skærbæk allows for uninterrupted 360° views as far as Esbjerg, Sild and Rømø from the lookout platform, while at its base is Marsk Camp (a campsite for motorhomes), a restaurant and other amenities.

Continuing the shift from the old to the new, Esbjerg was only established as a town in 1868 but has grown to become Denmark's most important North Sea harbour. In addition to its fishing and shipping activities, it also became a centre for agricultural exports and today is a specialist cluster of wind turbine and alternative energy activities, part of the World Energy Cities partnership. In summer 2022 the city will turn to wind power of a different genre when, for the fifth time, it hosts the start of Sail Training International's Tall Ships Regatta. The series will see the majestic ships sailing south from Esbjerg through the North Sea to Harlingen, Netherlands, as part of an exhilarating Race One. There will then be the Cruise-in-Company, a coastal sailing leg south to Antwerp, Belgium, culminating in Race Two, which will take the fleet from Antwerp back north through the North Sea to Aalborg, Denmark, for the final celebrations.

Esbjerg is brimming with good, relevant museums that narrate the history of the place and its fine cultural venues. The most striking physical icons of the city are its water tower (another high-level vantage point overseeing the Wadden Sea) and the dramatic sculpture *Man Meets the Sea*. Unveiled in 1995, the quartet of alabaster sculptured titans is a timeless tribute to man's contemplative nature. This installation, designed by Svend Wiig Hansen, is said by *Atlas Obscura* to have 'universal appeal representing all of man as opposed to any one ethnicity. The stark white statues are completely devoid of decoration, allowing visitors to map their own contemplative thoughts onto the figures. Although the figures may look alike, keen observers will find subtle differences among them.'

A patchwork of small islands also includes Rømø and Mandø (designated a Dark Skies site in 2021), both linked to the Danish mainland by causeways. Rømø is the larger of these two, with a population of about 700 compared to Mandø's 40 residents. In Røndø's square-towered whitewashed church of St Clement there is a pew with the 19th-century nameplate of H.P.P. Møller, grandfather of Arnold Peter Møller, the founder of the famous Danish Maersk shipping company. The island's Naturcenter Tønnisgård is housed in a captain's farmstead, and includes a small exhibition about the Wadden Sea.

In 2020, a new organisation was established to bring all the communities of the area together to grow tourism in a sustainable way. Visit Vadehavskysten is nurturing innovative ideas by local people to create authentic Wadden Sea experiences for visitors. Horizontal alpinism, the challenge of mud walking, demands stamina and local knowledge to navigate the tidal flows. The oyster safaris also depend on local experts, where waist-deep explorers, often wearing army-green waders and carrying an underwater viewer, splash out in search of the European flat oyster (*Ostrea edulis*). More sedate but nonetheless intriguing experiences abound: take a trip on the Mandøpigen tour ferry or the island's beach tractor bus, or maybe spend a day with one of the specialist bird guides watching the flight of the starlings or visiting the Sneum Digesø Bird Sanctuary. Alternatively, several historic lighthouses are open to visit (at Blåvand, for example) and there are over 1,200 km of marked cycle route.

One of the instigators of the new destination body is Lars Olsen, long-time sage of the Danish tourism industry, who enthusiastically relishes the opportunities of the Wadden Sea communities

working together. He sees this as a landscape/ seascape to taste in particular, where nature and gastronomy create a unique fusion. He eulogises about the salt marsh lamb, local beers and, of course, the oysters.

Olsen and his colleagues have cleverly juxtaposed imagery and words in their promotional materials that illustrate the uniqueness of the Vadehavskysten experiences, challenging our everyday perceptions: *Just another lazy day* features a seal sunbathing, *Just another highway* features a photo of the unpaved causeway to Mandø Island, whilst *Just another infinity pool* shows the limitless horizon of the sea. Clever, tantalising stuff.

Above: The Night Watchman, Ribe.

VALLETTA AND THE MALTESE ISLANDS, REPUBLIC OF MALTA

Ancient of days, a sense of wonder and Città' Umilissima

When starting the job of helping destinations to prepare plans for growing tourism, they are asked to list their tourism assets together with what they see as their strengths and weaknesses. Without exception, every destination says that the friendliness of local people is one of their key strengths. This is hardly a differentiator and tourists expect the natives to be friendly and welcoming, however, the friendliness and genuine warmth of welcome for tourists in Malta is, very definitely, part of its appeal, despite this small group of islands that constitutes the Republic of Malta having been invaded and subjected to overlords throughout its history.

The Maltese are a resilient, proud people, maintaining their language, culture and national identity against all the odds. Maltese and English are the official languages, coexisting yet so totally different, Maltese being a hybrid fusion of Arabic with Italian-Sicilian dialect. The population of Malta is mainly ethnic Maltese, descendants of Sicilian-Muslim colonisers from the last big repopulation of a thousand years ago. According to Brian Blouet in *The Story of Malta* (1967), 'The people, together with the physical environment have played an important role in the affairs of the overlords, especially the Knights of St. John and the British. In their turn the Maltese have adapted to the social and economic pressures which these overlords imposed on the islands.' Following 150 years as a British colony, Malta gained state independency in 1964, became a republic in 1974 and joined the European Union in 2004.

REPUBLIC OF MALTA

VALLETTA

Population of the city: 6,000
Population of wider area: 514,000
Nearest international airports: Malta International Airport.
Key websites: www.visitmalta.com; www.cityofvalletta.org; www.mta.com.mt
Icons: Valletta, Jean Parisot de Valette, Strait Street, the Grand Harbour, Gozo, Comino, Fort St. Elmo, the Mediterranean Conference Centre, Mdina, Ta' Qali Crafts Village, Popeye Village, Cittadella Victoria, Floriana Lines, Cottonera Lines, the Megalithic Temples, Knights of Malta, the Great Siege of Malta, the Three Cities.

• •

Malta is not one island but an archipelago of five islands that includes Malta, with Gozo to the north and the twin islands of Comino and Cominotto in between. None of them are large, and only the two largest, Malta and Gozo, are inhabited, with over

half a million people living on just 316 km². Flying into Malta International Airport (the former British RAF Luqa airfield), the view suggests that most of the main island is in continuous development as towns and villages merge. Yes, Malta is undeniably densely developed, but areas of conserved wild scrub, informal parks, well-designed and restored public gardens, fascinating, well-maintained historic cemeteries and swathes of cultivated land all provide welcome peace for wildlife and quiet contemplation.

Malta's climate makes it an ideal year-round destination, typically Mediterranean with hot, dry summers and endless days of unbroken sunshine accompanied by the warm sirocco wind. Autumn may see some rain, and the cool winters sometimes see strong northerly majjistral, grigal and tramontana winds. Streams appear during the rains then disappear just as quickly, leaving dry riverbeds and canyons. It is remarkable how green and fertile Malta can appear in spring given these

conditions. Much of the coastline consists of steep, often vertical, limestone cliffs reaching up to 200 metres, especially on the harbourless south/south-west coast of both Malta and Gozo. The rest of the coastline is indented with small bays, harbours and coves.

For a comparatively small island country, Malta has consistently punched above its weight in terms of its political and strategic importance. Its location, 95 km south of Sicily and 290 km north of Libya in a squeezed part of the eastern Mediterranean, has been the key factor shaping its history and making it historically attractive to bigger powers. Malta was big enough to hold a large garrison, with Valletta's Grand Harbour and Marsamxett deep-water ports being able to accommodate the largest of naval and merchant fleets. Today, these harbours comfortably handle the monster cruise ships.

Above: In Guardia Parade.

Gozo, the more fertile, green and less densely populated of the islands, lacks harbours, which limited its commercial development.

The Order of Knights of the Hospital of Saint John of Jerusalem, commonly known as the Knights Hospitaller or the Knights of Malta (sometimes Knights of St. John by the Maltese people), were a medieval military order. Originally headquartered in Jerusalem, Spanish Emperor Charles V granted the Knights a permanent base in Malta, where they stayed for 268 years from 1530 to 1798, in exchange for an annual fee of a single Maltese falcon (the Tribute of the Maltese Falcon). During this time, the Hospitallers continued their maritime actions against the Muslims. In 1565, this led Suleiman the Magnificent, the Ottoman Sultan, to despatch an invasion force of about 40,000 men to besiege the islands and gain a base to launch a possible assault on Europe in an event known as the Great Siege of Malta.

At first the battle went badly for the Hospitallers, but Grand Master Jean Parisot de Valette refused to surrender to the Turkish forces. Reinforcements arrived from across Europe and Malta survived the assault in what was to be the last epic battle involving crusader knights. Over their 250 years the Knights set about transforming 'merely a rock of soft sandstone' into a flourishing maritime power, a fortress with mighty defences and a capital city (Valletta, named after Grand Master de Valette).

Valletta, a grid-patterned city with narrow streets, was designed by Francesco Laparelli, a military engineer, and completed in just 15 years. It is the Fortress City, Città' Umilissima, 'A city built by gentlemen for gentlemen', 2018 European Capital of Culture and a UNESCO World Heritage Site. It has been reinvigorated and reborn over the last ten years to become a vibrant, lived-in,

working city and the administrative and commercial heartbeat of Malta. Its historic bastions, churches and palaces are heralded by traditional balconies in vivid colours, statues, fountains and coats of arms. Trendy restaurants, cafés and bars spill onto the pedestrianised streets, granting al fresco dining surrounded by grand architecture old and new.

There is a new city gate (Porta di terra) for Valletta together with a new Parliament building, Royal Opera House, piazza and outdoor performing space. Writing for the Air Malta magazine, Adam Claffey describes: 'The only constant in life is change. This new gate will be the fifth city gate Valletta has had in about 450 years. Piano's radical design caused some controversy, but these new developments just form part of a new phase for Valletta – a city dearly loved, by both those who live in Malta and by those who visit.'

Valletta is one of the smallest capital cities (the entire city is just 1 km long by 600 m wide) and the first planned city in Europe. It occupies a tongue of high ground known as Mount Sciberras separating the Grand Harbour and Marsamxett Harbour. There are breathtaking views within the city and from its encircling ramparts. It is picturesque in so many ways. It is compact. It is walkable, but be prepared for surprisingly undulating, rolling roads within the encircling walls and steep climbs on what Lord Byron referred to in his 1811 poem 'Farewell to Malta' as 'ye cursed streets of stairs' rising from the Harbourside. To help the visitor, the Barrakka Lift links Lascaris Wharf on the harbourside with the St. Peter and Paul Bastion and the restored Upper Barrakka Gardens.

Above: Valletta, Malta.

Malta is, however, first and foremost an ancient place. These islands have an extraordinary richness of heritage. There is evidence to suggest that civilisations have been living here since the early Neolithic period of 5000 BC, and in total there are 11 major megalithic monuments of Malta. Much of the heritage is inscribed on the list of UNESCO World Heritage Sites: the Ħal Saflieni Hypogeum, and the collection of temples (Ġgantija, Ħaġar Qim, Mnajdra, Ta' Ħaġrat, Skorba, and Tarxien) form the Megalithic Temples of Malta World Heritage Site.

The Maltese Government has a further seven features of its natural, cultural and built heritage on UNESCO's tentative list for possible inclusion as World Heritage, including Qawra/Dwejra, Gozo with its interesting geological features of the Fungus Rock and the Inland Sea; Cittadella, the small fortified town in Victoria, the main town on Gozo; the Knights' Fortifications around the harbours of Malta embracing the fortifications of Birgu and Senglea, the Floriana Lines, the Santa Margherita Lines, the Cottonera Lines, Fort Ricasoli and Fort Tigné and the walled city of Mdina (Città Vecchia), the former capital of medieval character in the centre of Malta with its Baroque buildings and St. Paul's Cathedral.

It was the late 1980s when the opportunity arose to be part of an international team, sponsored by the UN World Tourism Organisation, to prepare the Islands' first tourism plan. This was followed by numerous return visits for work (on heritage plans, museums, and visitor attractions), to teach (at the University of Malta, the Institute for Tourism Studies and the Institute for Small Islands and States) and for holidays – including a fine New Year's short-break in the renewed city of Valletta.

Over the past 40 years, as Claffey observed, much has changed and nothing has changed – Malta remains an enigma, full of surprises yet full of familiarity. Cars still drive on the left. Traffic congestion and pressures for development remain constant challenges whilst high-quality hotels sit cheek-by-jowl with poorer quality accommodation. Traditional village festivals take place close to locations with exuberant modern nightlife. Classic religious, military and civic architectural features still stand out amongst new urban developments. But that's Malta.

What has changed, and dramatically for the better, has been the renaissance of Valletta and the way Malta has upped its game with the quality, presentation and availability of fine traditional cuisine, often a fusion of its various cultural influences. There is an eclectic mix of Mediterranean cooking dominated by traditional, rustic, Maltese food: great local dishes include lampuki pie, rabbit stew, bragioli (beef olives) and kapunata. For a snack, try *'hobz biz-zejt'* (round of bread dipped in olive oil, rubbed with ripe tomatoes, and filled with a mix of tuna, onion, garlic, tomatoes, and capers) or warm *pastizzi* (flaky pastry parcel filled with ricotta or mushy peas), all washed down with award-winning local wines, Farsons Hopleaf pale ale or Cisk Lager, or a glass of Kinnie – a soda of bitter-oranges, spices and herbs unique to Malta.

Time and again, local life on the islands has been intrinsically linked to the fortunes and interests of great powers and with existential events taking place in a global setting. Clearly, these are factors that have always directly affected Malta's tourism prospects, and none more so than at this time of the pandemic and growing concerns about overtourism, climate change and the need for a sustainable approach for the regrowth of tourism.

Malta's new tourism plan that will guide the industry over the period until 2030 reflects this imperative. The strategy is based on the three-pronged approach of Recovering, Rethinking and Revitalising this important pillar of Maltese life, an opportunity allowing the country to reformat its tourism industry on a sounder footing relevant for the 21st century with a focus on 'delivery of quality services and products, the attraction of tourists who not only leave a superior economic contribution but whose interests are in parallel with all that makes the Maltese Islands diverse, unique, special and worth visiting and revisiting.'

Leadership for the tourism industry is provided by the Malta Tourism Authority, established by the Malta Travel and Tourism Service Act (1999). This private/public sector partnership's role goes beyond international marketing to include all aspects of regulating and co-ordinating tourism development for the benefit of current and future generations of Maltese people. The vision is to achieve a healthy, sustainable and equitable tourism future for the Maltese Islands based on quality, authenticity, collaboration and strong leadership. These are lofty ideals, never far away from those of the MTA's predecessors, the National Tourism Organisation of Malta (NTOM) and the Malta Government Tourist Board. What has changed is that COVID has heightened the realisation that fine words need real action. Malta and its people deserve to succeed with this 21st-century agenda for tourism, with the new SUNx Malta climate-friendly travel initiative helping to deliver sustainable tourism on a global basis.

So, this is an ancient place which has experienced immense upheavals and change but where one thing has remained constant for almost half a century, and that is the loyalty and kindness of my local counterparts who became good friends when preparing the tourism plans in the 1980s. This talented, highly committed group of then young Maltese tourism professionals have all been leaders in their country's tourism industry: Leslie Vella, Tony Ellul, Peter Portelli, Theresa Delia and Francis Albani, a few of whom are the architects of the new strategy. I am proud of what they have achieved for Malta and hope that those early days of pioneering fresh ideas may have influenced them a little in their careers.

. . . .

Left: The Gozo Citadel fortress, Victoria.

VYSOKÉ TATRY, PIENINY AND THE DUNAJEC GORGE, PREŠOV REGION, SLOVAKIA

High mountains with deep symbolism for Slovakian identity, unique to the Goral culture, with a myriad of outdoor wellness and adventure

The small landlocked Central European republic of Slovakia is at the heart of Europe, bordered by the Czech Republic, Austria, Poland, Hungary and Ukraine. A young sovereign country of just five million people, it took shape following the Velvet Revolution and the end of Communist rule in Czechoslovakia in 1989, followed by the country's dissolution (the Velvet Divorce) into two successor states. The word 'socialist' was dropped in the names of the two republics, with the Slovak Socialist Republic renamed as the Slovak Republic in July 1992, becoming a member of the European Union in 2004.

Slovakia is an understated, often underrated delight for visitors, with a remarkably diverse tourism base of historic towns, relatively unspoilt mountain regions and several national parks together with over 40 well-known traditional spa resorts, some dating back to the Middle Ages. Over the past ten years the tourism industry has come a long way, with Slovakia now ready to achieve its full potential, especially with its strong combination of culture, heritage, outdoor and wellness tourism opportunities.

My first experience of the country was in 1990, helping with tourism projects in the compact, Danube-hugging capital of Bratislava and at Piešťany, historically the most significant spa in Slovakia, located north-east of the capital in the Vah River Valley. A few years later, the UK Government's Department for International Development

Population of largest city (Poprad): 52,000
Population of wider area: 100,000
Nearest international airports: John Paul II Kraków-Balice International Airport, Vienna International Airport, Poprad-Tatry Airport, Bratislava Airport.
Key websites: www.regiontatry.sk; www.tatry.sk; www.vilajanka.sk; www.tatryspispieniny.sk; www.slovakia.travel; www.aquacity.sk
Icons: Vysoké Tatry, Pieniny National Park, Dunajec Gorge, the Gorals, Červený Kláštor, Štrbské Pleso, Rysy Mountain; Kriváň, the Grand Hotel Starý Smokovec, the Grandhotel Praha Tatranskái Lomnica, the Grand Hotel Kempinski High Tatras, Tatra Railway, Stará Ľubovňa Castle, Osturňa.

commissioned me to prepare a tourism masterplan for the Pieniny National Park, bordering with Poland in the Prešov Region, north-east of the Vysoké Tatry (the High Tatra Mountains) and five hours drive north-east of Bratislava. This gave me the honour of experiencing the extraordinary landscape of the Dunajec Gorge and allowed me to appreciate the unique folklore and hospitality of the Slovakian Goral community that live in the villages in this area on both the Slovakian and Polish sides of the river border – once divided, now connected by a bridge from Červený Kláštor in Slovakia to Sromowce Niżne in Poland since 2005.

Vysoké Tatry is part of the Carpathian Mountains, with 50 peaks over 2,000 metres, two national parks and a UNESCO biosphere reserve. Impressive credentials, but it is the deep, profound symbolism of these mountains with the national identify of the Slovak people which gives this place extra resonance. Štrbské Pleso is a pleasant, purpose-built lakeside resort community

(refurbished to host four events as part of the Winter Sports Universiade 2015) and the starting point for numerous waymarked hiking trials for Rysy Mountain, the highest accessible peak without guides, and Kriváň, the most beautiful and important mountain for the Slovakian nation. Kriváň has been celebrated in Slovakian paintings, literature and customs for centuries, featuring in the words of the Slovak national anthem, 'Lightning over the Tatras', written in 1854, and the mountain is the image used on the five euro cent coin for the country.

Along the base of the High Tatras is a string of 15 small villages collectively known as Vysoké Tatry, with a population of just 4,000 permanent residents. Today, the local authority, cultural centre and main shops are in Starý Smokovec. As the original 19th-century tourist resort, this unusual conglomeration

Above: Združenie cestovného ruchu Vysoké Tatry.

of separate and different settlements shares a common heritage and are connected by a scenic drive and railway network. The Tatra Railway is a 35-km-long narrow-gauge electric line in two parts: from Poprad via Starý Smokovec to Štrbské Pleso (29 km) and the second leg from Starý Smokovec to Tatranská Lomnica (6 km). The Tatra rack railway from Štrba to Štrbské Pleso is now under reconstruction. This rail system was initially built to help open up the High Tatras for tourism between 1906-1912 and was renovated in 1970 as part of the area's improvements to host the FIS Nordic World Ski Championships. It remains one of the most scenic, but lesser-known, rail journeys in Europe.

It was in these villages, in the period 1890-1906, that luxury, architecturally dramatic grand hotels were built to meet the increasing demand for health and wellness tourism during both summer and winter thanks to the bravery of Dr. Mikuláš Szontagh, who saw the potential for a Swiss-model

. . . .

Above: Dunajec river in Pieniny mountains.

year-round high-mountain sanatorium working in the area where sunny days and skiing were at the heart of the therapy. Later winter sports tourism emerged as a by-product of wellness, becoming the main reason to visit in the winter months.

Many of these grandiose statements of fine hospitality, such as the Grand Hotel Starý Smokovec, the Grandhotel Praha Tatranská Lomnica and the Grand Hotel Kempinski High Tatras, continue to deliver refined experiences for their contemporary clientele. The Kempinski investment reflected a growing interest in regenerating traditional products in the destination and creating new ones. Another major development was AquaCity in Poprad, the gateway city for the Tatra Mountains and host to numerous winter sports championships, although an unsuccessful candidate for the 2006 Winter Olympics, losing out to Turin.

On the north-eastern edge of Vysoké Tatry is Europe's first transborder protected area, jointly created by the Polish and Czech governments in 1932, straddling the border along the Dunajec

River. It was designated the Pieniny National Park in 1967. Pieninský Národný Park is the smallest national park in Slovakia, just 38 square kilometres of mountain and uplands. Within its boundaries are exceptional landscape features and a unique culture. The limestone gorge has been carved and sliced into seven looping meanders by the Dunajec river, connecting its Slovakian headwaters with the Baltic Sea – the only river in Slovakia to flow north. The Gorge has a unique geological structure, sheer 300-metre-high cliffs topped by the iconic skyline of Trzy Korony (the distinctive peaks of the Three Crowns) with their craggy habitats dating back to the Ice Age.

Goral villagers from both sides of the border have hereditary rights to raft down the often fast-flowing river. Originally used for transporting timber towards the Baltic seaports, they became a tourist attraction in the 19th century for nobility and their guests staying in nearby Niedzica and Czorsztyn Castles. These castles sit above the Czorsztyn Reservoir, designed to manage water flows in the Gorge. Today, convoys of wooden rafts gently carry visitors six kilometres down an awesome stretch of deep river canyon between the Slovakian villages of Červený Kláštor and Leśnica. The boatsmen, dressed in traditional Goralian costume, share stories of their heritage, folklore and the landscape. On arrival at Leśnica, the rafts are lifted out of the river and transported back to Červený Kláštor by lorry whilst the visitor can walk or cycle back along the riverbank or take a horse and carriage after a welcome snack in the village.

Červený Kláštor is a polite riverside hamlet of just 200 residents, with its Red Monastery, named because of its red cedar shingles, serving as the headquarters of the national park's management team. The Carthusian monastery dates from 1307, when legend states that Master Kokos was found guilty of murder and his penance was to build six monasteries, including this one. Abandoned in 1565, the church has been restored and is open to visitors. It is dedicated to the local eighteenth-century monk Cyprian, a revered surgeon, doctor and pharmacist who wrote *Herbarium*, a treatise on the use of herbs from the Tara Mountains for the treatment of ailments.

The small town of Spišská Stará Ves on the road from the south is the main commercial centre, with a thriving range of community association. It is the centre for a small number of characterful hotels and *penzión* and traditional wooden cottages for rent. After exiting the town, just before Červený Kláštor, a turning to the left takes you to the extraordinary nine-kilometre-long village of Osturňa in a verdant valley inhabited by less than 400 people of Goral descent and characterised by their fascinating architecture. Over half of all the village's wooden structures are recognised as national treasures. Further unusual and impressive attractions are to be found close by – the 12th-century expanse of Spiš Castle is a must-visit day out, as too the wonderfully interpreted living history open-air museum and adjacent castle of Stará Ľubovňa.

'Great places to live are great places to visit' is the recent mantra of the post-COVID tourism industry. Vysoké Tatry and especially the Goral lands of Pieniny were a delightful place to work, leaving fond memories of evenings spent with a generous, kind and receptive group of tourism and community leaders discussing new ideas for managing their visitors and sharing simple local food washed down with Tatratea, a national herbal tea mixed with alcohol that originated in the High Tatras. These memories were reignited by a recent holiday to the area and by the constant reminder of the community's gift of two decorative and highly symbolic Goral shepherd's silver-headed axes that occupy pride of place in my office.

WEST DORSET AND THE JURASSIC COAST, DORSET, ENGLAND

Local heroes, impressive fossils, cow milk vodka, knob biscuits and Dorset's own R&B

Why Sutton Bingham station ever existed at all is a mystery. With a name sounding more like a Yeoman farmer in a Thomas Hardy novel, there was only ever a hamlet here – just a mill, a farm, a church and a manor house. The station was a couple of miles from East Coker and some three miles from Yeovil Junction on the main Waterloo to Exeter railway line. A steam train ride from this tiny station was the start of one of those special always-in-your-memory days with your dad.

It was 1959; I was seven. The steam train meandered through leafy Somerset and Dorset on into Devon and the carpet loom town of Axminster. Thence a transfer to the station's middle platform to catch the Lyme Regis Light Railway branch line for the six-mile shunt over the Cannington Viaduct, through Uplyme, to its final stop at Lyme Station, perched on the northern margins of the town atop the long, steep walk down to the famous Cobb. A funicular railway line had been the tourism artery and a bustling terminus for the resort for 60 years, but this closed in 1965.

It had been my first trip to Lyme Regis on Dorset's extraordinary Jurassic Coast. The Jurassic Coast is a hugely diverse and beautiful landscape underpinned by incredible geology of global importance. In 2001 it was inscribed as a World Heritage Site by UNESCO for the outstanding universal value of its rocks, fossils and landforms and remains England's only natural World Heritage Site. The Jurassic Coast begins at Orcombe Point in Exmouth, Devon, and continues for 95 miles to Old Harry Rocks, near Swanage, Dorset. This span

GREAT BRITAIN

● DORSET

Population of Lyme Regis: 3,600
Population of wider area: 102,000
Nearest international airports: Bristol, Exeter, Bournemouth, Southampton.
Key websites: www.jurassiccoast.org; www.visit-dorset.com; www.lymeregis.org; www.tolpuddlemartyrs.org.uk; www.abbotsbury.co.uk
Icons: The Abbotsbury Swannery, Chesil Beach, Golden Cap, Black Ven, Lyme Regis, Bridport, Mary Anning, Baron Lister, Thomas Hardy, Reverend William Barnes, Dorchester, Maiden Castle, Vice Admiral Sir Thomas Hardy Monument, Poundbury, Tolpuddle Martyrs, Lulworth Cove, Durdle Door, Lulworth Estate, Cerne Abbas Giant, Dorset Knob Biscuits, Langham Estate, the Mutter Slater Band, The Yetties.

takes in four distinct geographic regions – East Devon, West Dorset, Weymouth & Portland and Purbeck. It is the stretch of West Dorset coast from Lyme Regis to Abbotsbury and its hinterland, including the county town of Dorchester, that commands attention.

A string of charming villages and small harbours hug the coastline: Burton Bradstock at the westerly end of Chesil Beach, in the beautiful Bride Valley, with its 15th-century church, West Bay, at the mouth of the River Brit great mass of the sandstone East Cliff dominating the beach, with the impressive Golden Cap, the highest point on the south coast, rising to the west. West Bay is an 18th-century harbour created for the export of rope and netting from nearby Bridport, Charmouth is the fossil hunting centre for the area, while in Eype church Bridport-born global songster PJ Harvey

recorded her 2011 Mercury Prize-winning album *Let England Shake*.

The market town of Bridport continues to thrive, bucking trends that have seen the decline of many small towns. A centre for ropemaking for centuries, in 1213 King John demanded that Bridport produce ropes and cables night and day for his army and navy, as well as ropes for gallows, which led to the term 'stabbed with a Bridport dagger' to describe a hanging. This industry, together with the sail cloth production in South Somerset, traded internationally, with Gundry Bridport Limited producing goal nets for football clubs around the world. This rope and net heritage remains active, with businesses continuing to make fishing and

Right: Seatown Beach and Golden Cap, Dorset.

sporting nets and cargo restraints.

Dorchester is the county town, the Casterbridge of Thomas Hardy's 1886 masterpiece *The Mayor of Casterbridge: The Life and Death of a Man of Character*. It retains many of the charms of an old-fashioned market centre for a rural community despite pressures to change. Daniel Defoe, in his *Tour Through the Whole Island of Great Britain* (1724), wrote, 'a man that coveted a retreat in this world might as agreeably spend his time, and as well, in Dorchester, as in any town in England', an observation that is still relevant. South-west of the town is Maiden Castle, one of the largest and most complex Iron Age hillforts in Europe at the size of 50 football pitches. Its huge multiple ramparts, dating from the 1st century BC, still tower above the surrounding countryside.

If, however, there is to be a 'capital' of the

Above: West Bay Harbour.

Jurassic Coast, it would be Lyme Regis. For the Romans this was Lym Supra Mare – the mouth of the River Lym. In 1284, Lyme was granted a Royal Charter by King Edward I, bestowing on it the title of 'Regis'. Its iconic curved harbour wall, known as the Cobb, also dates from the 13th century, creating a safe haven and generating the momentum for it to become a thriving port and centre for shipbuilding between 1750-1850. Indeed, in 1750 the port of Lyme Regis was bigger than that of Liverpool.

Numerous pubs bear testimony to the maritime trade: The Pilot Boat, The Ship Inn, The Crown and Anchor and The Royal Standard. By the mid-18th century, Lyme Regis had become a popular seaside resort attraction as many writers and painters visited, including Lord Tennyson, Hilaire Belloc, J. R. R. Tolkien, Henry Fielding, J. M. W. Turner, James Whistler and Jane Austen, who penned *Persuasion* during her time in the town between 1803 and 1804. The filming of *The French Lieutenant's Woman* in 1980, an adaptation of local author John Fowles' novel, brought a touch of Hollywood, with Jeremy Irons and Meryl Streep in residence.

Local people and their stories are the raw materials of a special place. This stretch of coastline, and Dorset in general, is littered with unconventional, slightly rebellious, always engaging ordinary people who did something extraordinary, as did Lord Joseph Lister, Baron of Lyme Regis, royal surgeon and the pioneer of antiseptics, after whom the Langmoor and Lister Gardens in the town are named.

Lyme Regis' most famous resident, however, is an understated young woman who laid the foundations for the eventual recognition of this coastline as a UNESCO World Heritage Site. This was Mary Anning, born into a poor family in Lyme Regis in 1799, whose father was an amateur fossil collector who would take his young daughter fossil hunting on local beaches then clean and sell them in their small shop. At the age of 12, Mary discovered the first complete ichthyosaur skeleton and later was the first to discover a complete plesiosaur, some of the most significant geological finds of the time. Her ichthyosaur, plesiosaur and pterosaur are displayed in London's Natural History Museum. Coincidentally, the Dinosaurland Fossil Museum in the town is housed in the church where Mary was baptised. Her story is told in the town's museum and was captured in the 2020 film *Ammonite*, starring Kate Winslet.

Another Lyme Regis character was Richard Fox MBE. In 1970 he took the same journey as I had done 11 years earlier, in his case to become the landlord of The Cobb Arms after holding the same position at The Helyar Arms, East Coker. He was instrumental in the founding of Lyme Regis Lifeboat Week, one of the biggest events of its kind, and was Lyme's town crier with his imposing frame, bushy beard and stentorian voice, becoming the World Champion Town Crier and engaged by British Airways to publicise Great Britain.

There are yet more examples of ordinary Dorset people doing the extraordinary. As the sun rose on 24 February 1834, Dorset farm labourer George Loveless set off to work, saying goodbye to his wife Betsy and their three children. They were not to meet again for years. Loveless and five fellow workers – his brother James, James Hammett, James Brine, Thomas Standfield and Thomas's son John – were charged with having taken an illegal oath and effectively forming a trade union to protest about their meagre pay. They were arrested and sentenced to seven years' transportation. Their harrowing ordeal is recounted in the Tolpuddle Martyrs' Museum in the village, where an annual festival has taken place for over a century to recognise their contribution to modern trade unionism.

Carved on a steep-sloping chalk hillside on land owned by the National Trust, just north of Cerne Abbas (one of many of Dorset's charming villages) is the world-renowned Cerne Giant, a 180 ft-high ancient chalk figure fondly regarded as another local 'character'. The origins of the Giant are a fabled mix of fact and speculation – is he a 1,500-year-old depiction of the Roman god Hercules, a pagan fertility symbol, or, because there is no known historical record before 1694, is the Giant a caricature of Oliver Cromwell?

It was Thomas Hardy, himself of this parish (born in 1840 in Higher Bockhampton), who so elegantly immortalised the essence of Dorset's rural characters, their customs and folklore, its villages, its countryside and glorious coastal scenery in his novels and poems. The Hardy Way steps beyond the border of Dorset, exploring Hardy's beloved concept of Wessex. The Dorset route of this long-distance trail visits many Hardy locations, beginning at his birthplace in the Piddle and Frome valleys and at times running parallel to the remarkable storm-created Chesil Beach to Lulworth Cove, Durdle Door and Corfe Castle. The trail ends in Stinsford churchyard, where his heart is buried in his wife Emma's grave – his body lies in Poet's Corner in Westminster Cathedral. Margaret Marande, creator of the route in 1998, has written the guidebook for the trail in association with the Thomas Hardy Society.

Hardy was also an architect, and today visitors can stay in Summer Lodge, a Georgian dower house partly designed by Hardy in the historic estate village of Evershot (appearing as Evershead in Hardy's novels), known for the legend of the three dumb sisters who were turned to stone for dancing on the Sabbath. Summer Lodge is now a delightful five-star country house hotel.

Alongside Hardy, Dorset celebrates the great writer's mentor and tutor, the Reverend William Barnes, a talented poet, mathematician, inventor and artist fluent in several languages. He was a lowly clerk and schoolmaster in his earlier life but later graduated from Cambridge University in divinity, becoming a minister in the Church of England. His poems, focused on the county's pastoral life, were all written in the Dorset dialect.

In the same way South Somerset has nurtured innovative ideas for tourist experiences, so too has West Dorset, with visitor experiences forged, often out of necessity, by pioneering local people. What about the world's only vodka made from cows' milk at a distillery in the Black Cow Distillery Bar + Kitchen in Childhay? The first bottle of Black Cow Vodka was sold in May 2012 and it is now available in 17 countries, along with their English Strawberries Vodka. The Seaside Boarding House in Burton Bradstock is a nice contemporary addition to the village, while local fisherman Harry May's deep understanding of the rhythms of the shoals of mackerel links tradition with today's issues of sustainable fishing.

Dorset born and bred is the creed of the Langham Wine Estate and Vineyard Café. The 30 acres of vineyards at Crawthorne Farm are part of a much larger agricultural estate, based on the Grade 1 listed Melcombe Manor House, just north of Dorchester. Here the micro-climate and soils of chalk, clay and flint are like those of the Champagne region of France, geology again proving critical to the Dorset experience. Justin Langham and his team have planted the three classic varieties of Chardonnay, Pinot Noir and Pinot Meunier as the raw material for their multi-award-winning, low-intervention sparkling wines. Vineyard tours, a tasting room in an old barn, exceptional local food in the Vineyard Café, clever outdoor dining and a host of music-meets-food-meets-wine events complete the range of visitor facilities.

To conclude, we are leaving Langham Vineyards chalk fields of flintstones and heading back to Bridport for a unique music experience with the Mutter Slater Band, who regularly play local pubs and other venues in the town and surrounding area. Their eclectic live sets will often include 'Heading Back to Bridport'. Formed by an old school friend, Mick 'Mutter' Slater is now based in Bridport and the band are, rightly, well-loved locally. Mutter is a veteran performer, best remembered for his quirky exploits with prog rockers Stackridge (produced by George Martin of Beatles fame). He has been hailed as having been blessed with one of the finest voices in British rock and his eponymous band now indulges his genuine passion for R&B, blues and soul, his latest album, *Field of Stone*, having received fine reviews. The Mutter Slater Band are not to be missed.

• •

Left: Summer Lodge Hotel.
Above: Dorset countryside.

WILD ATLANTIC WAY, IRELAND

Travelling on Europe's most westerly coast from the northern headlands to the southern havens and the next parish is Manhattan

This is the third destination in this book that, together with the A20 and the National Tourist Routes of Norway, breaks with the conventions that define the other 47 destinations. It is a genius of an idea. When you ask who thought of it many hands go up – success has many parents. The Wild Atlantic Way (WAW) has been instrumental in giving Ireland a much-needed contemporary position in the international tourism marketplace.

Throughout the last twenty years of the 20th century Ireland enjoyed a remarkable boom in tourism fuelled by the huge global diaspora claiming an Irish ancestry and greedy to get a taste of the old country. During this period, the Celtic Tiger's fast-growing tourism industry was given a clear direction by the national tourism body, Bord Fáilte. The emphasis was on heritage and telling the stories that the returners wanted to hear. Ancient sites, castles and historic landmarks were equipped with the accoutrements to make them attractive and accessible to these, mostly North American, tourists. New visitor centres appeared anywhere where there was a story to be told with tax-free incentives driving the creation of an army of hotels across the country. Success raged with Ireland becoming globally respected as the benchmark for successful tourism development. However, at the turn of the century it was becoming apparent that Ireland had become rather complacent about its tourism offer and over-reliant upon an ageing approach at a time when tourist demands were changing dramatically.

Length of the route: 2,500 km
Nearest international airports: Shannon, Cork, Dublin, Kerry, Ireland West Knock, Donegal, Belfast International, Belfast George Best.
Key websites: www.wildatlanticway.com; www.ireland.com
Icons: Donegal, Connemara, Doolin, Malin Head, Dingle, Killarney, Bunratty Castle, The Burren, Fungi the Dolphin, Killarney, The Ring of Kerry, The Rose of Tralee, Lahinch, Galway Bay, Aran Islands, Skellig Michael, Croagh Patrick.

Left: Beautiful view of Valentia Island Lighthouse at Cromwell Point.

The arrival of the economic crisis in 2008 further exposed the fact that tourism in Ireland needed to be re-invented and re-invigorated. Five years before the crash Fáilte Ireland had been established as the successor to Bord Fáilte, to act as the overarching tourism body, with its sister organisation, Tourism Ireland, taking on the marketing of the whole island of Ireland – including Northern Ireland. The goal of Fáilte Ireland is to provide strategic and practical support in developing and sustaining Ireland as a high-quality and competitive tourist destination by working in partnership with tourism interests and communities in order to meet these challenges. One of the early inspirational decisions was to develop Wild Atlantic Way in response to the challenges the western Ireland faced with international tourism numbers and its share of holiday visits to Ireland falling significantly over the period 2007–2010.

It is a simple concept which is exceptionally well implemented. The WAW is a 2,500 km coast road along the most westerly coast of Europe, which was launched in 2014 after two years of intensive research selecting the best route and identifying the must-see signature discovery points and attractions. It is the world's longest coastal touring route providing tourists with a classic road trip – enhanced with lots of diversions designed to allow the exploration and discovery of adjacent places off the main route. Navigating the WAW allows visitors to feel the raw power of an untrammelled Atlantic Ocean; experiences of the timeless traditions of peripheral, on-the-edge, liminal communities; and, gives access to the extraordinary beauty of a wave-ravaged coastline. It delivers exactly what its title implies, set in an Irish geography that stretches from Malin Head in Donegal's *'Gaeltacht'* (Irish speaking) Northern Headlands (characterised by glaciated valleys and megalithic sites) to County Cork's gentle southerly Haven Coast – a more sheltered, peaceful, coastline.

The WAW is organised and promoted as six, self-defining, regions. In addition to the Northern Headlands as one travels south to the Haven Coast there are the Surf, Bay and Cliff Coasts of Galway, Connemara, Clare and Kerry and on to the Southern Peninsulas where the ancient Kingdom of Kerry's finger-indented coastline merges with West Cork – the most westerly of this most westerly part of Ireland where they say that the next parish is Manhattan!

The Surf Coast stretches from Donegal town to Erris (from the Irish 'Iar Ros' meaning the western promontory) in County Mayo, recently voted Ireland's 'Best Place to Go Wild'. This is especially good for surfing, being renowned for drawing surfers from across the globe to see the fabled Prowlers wave in action as well as for international events. The Bay Coast then runs south from Erris to, what Fáilte Ireland describes as, the 'savage beauty' of Connemara, with the WAW skirting some impressive bays, including Clew Bay with its 365 islets and islands; one for every day of the year and winding around the many 'inlets of the sea' (the meaning of Connemara in Irish). The Bay Coast with its broad sandy beaches, is the place to ride horses at low tide and to kayak, kiteboard, paraglide, swim and dive. Here the Great Western Greenway has become one of the world's most scenic cycleways. Walkers can climb the sacred Croagh Patrick mountain and Twelve Bens range overlooking the Gaeltacht Aran Islands.

Galway City, 'The City of the Tribes' is the cobbled, walled capital of this part of the WAW. It is a lively, vibrant, cultural and entertainment centre as well as a popular seaside destination with beaches and a long winding promenade. It is a festival city. In July there is the, hot-ticket, seven-day Galway Racing Festival. There is also The Cúirt International Festival of Literature, (April), the Galway Sessions traditional Irish music festival, (June), the Galway Film Fleadh, (July), the world-famous Galway Arts Festival (July) and Galway International Oyster Festival (September).

The Cliff Coast between, Galway and Ballybunion includes the Loop Head Peninsula Drive which, like the Soča Valley in Slovenia, is one of the European Union's EDEN sustainable tourism destinations – and best known for its lighthouse and for the Diarmuid and Gráinne's Rock, or Lover's Leap. The sheer majesty of the Cliffs of Moher, with a 215 m vertical plunge into the ocean by their puffin-encrusted rock faces makes this one of the most visited landmarks in Ireland. Just off shore it is often said that there is a sleeping giant that has been known to inhabitants in ancient times as *Aill na Searrach* (Foals' Leap) – an enormous surf that occasionally can erupt from an area of sea just off the Cliffs of Moher known as the Aileen's. For surfers this is a rare, much sought-after, blue ribbon, ride. Legend has it that the Aileen's was the spot where seven Celtic gods transformed into seven foals and leapt into the afterlife, furious at St Patrick for bringing Christianity to Ireland.

The charming medieval market town of Ennis acts as the gateway to this part of the WAW. Sitting between Ennis and rising above the Flaggy Shore, with its delightful fishing village of Doolin famed for its traditional music scene, are the bare, fissured, karst limestone pavements of the Burren – described by the Irish poet, playwright and Nobel Literature Prize winner, Seamus Heaney, in his poem 'Postcript', as the place 'to catch the heart off guard and blow it open'. The Burren & Cliffs of Moher has achieved UNESCO-supported Global Geopark Status in recognition of the area's significant geological, ecological and cultural value. In this area the Burren Eco-Tourism Network of over 50 local businesses is now helping with this initiative and trying to regenerate the historic spa town of Lisdoonvarna, whose spa takes waters from four springs, opened in 1845, and where today the annual 'Matchmaking Festival', originally designed to help find bachelor farmers their partners, still draws 40,000 romance-seekers each September. The current matchmaker is Willie Daly, a fourth-generation doing this highly specialised job.

Each of the five Southern Peninsulas offer cliff-hugging roads, wide sandy bays and mountains dropping into fjord-fashioned seas. Each is a holiday trip in their own right: with ancient sites, UNESCO World Heritage, dolphins, extreme abseiling, Ireland's only cable car, artisan craft, food and drink producers, cookery schools and powerful stories of legendary characters – heroes in sport, politics and culture. The Dingle Peninsula and the Ring of Kerry are especially coherent as tourist experiences with Tralee, Dingle, Cahersiveen and Kilorgin being the prime stop-over opportunities. Killarney, on the north-eastern shore of Lough Leane (part of the Killarney National Park) is the County Town of Kerry and the undisputed tourism capital of the WAW. Its tourism history goes back at least 250 years when, in 1747, Lord Kenmare began to attract visitors to the town and, a hundred years later, a visit by Queen Victoria gave the town international exposure. Killarney benefited greatly from the coming of the railway in July 1853. In 1846 there were just three hotels in the town; by 1854, one year after the coming of the railway, four additional hotels opened. Tours of the Ring of Kerry, commencing and ending in Killarney, were already proving popular and remain so today with the town offering a smart array of hotels and guest houses with a multitude of live music bars, restaurants and local attractions.

Given the rich asset base along the whole 2,500 km of the WAW it would be easy for the tourism industry to rest on its laurels. Local destination groups representing tourism operators and community interests are working in collaboration with Fáilte Ireland to ensure that this doesn't happen. On the contrary they all recognise the need to continue to invest, improve service standards and deliver high-quality, highly imaginative tourist experiences. Consequently, visitor experience development plans are now being prepared for key areas along the WAW to give leadership and inspiration to everyone interested in making the WAW an on-going success.

ZADAR, DALMATIA, CROATIA

The most beautiful sunsets in the world, Croatia's oldest city and the sea organ

CROATIA

● ZADAR

Population of Zadar: 75,000
Population of wider area: 170,000
Nearest international airports: Zadar, Riejka (Krk) and Zagreb.
Key websites: www.zadar.travel; www.zadar.hr; www.falkensteiner.com
Icons: Salute to the Sun, The Sea Organ, Church of St Donatus, Nikola Bašič, Alfred Hitchcock, Falkensteiner Hotels, capital of 'Cool', Hideout Festival, Love International, St Anastaisia Bell Tower, Velebit Mountains, The Garden of Zadar, Barkajoli – the gondoliers of Zadar, Pag cheese.

Invaded, traded, placated and now celebrated. This is the story of Zadar's recent emergence as one of the world's most appealing city destinations.

Its ancient heritage now wears its contemporary vibe well, greeting international visitors with an unpretentious hospitality peppered with innovative developments alongside rich heritage and a culture of festivals and good food.

Once one of the largest cities in the Republic of Venice, Zadar is Croatia's fifth largest and its oldest, continually inhabited city. Although founded on the site of a fourth century Greek settlement, its legacy is made up of a fine Roman and Venetian heritage with its Venetian defences around the peninsula of the Old Town being inscribed on the UNESCO World Heritage list in 2017.

This is perhaps the most Croatian of all cities in the Balkans, and, despite a tortured and unsettling 200 years of civic and societal disruption, it has retained its reputation of being at the heart of the Croatian cultural and national revival with its genesis in the 19th century with the publication of the first newspaper published in the Croatian language. During 1943–1944 and the German occupation Zadar was heavily bombed by the Allies, destroying 80 per cent of the city. When Partisan troops returned the population was less than six thousand. Post-war, the city was part of the Socialist Federal Republic of Yugoslavia as the Socialist Republic of Croatia. The break-up of Yugoslavia in the early 1990s meant that attacks on the city did not end until 1995. Since then the recovery, growth and renaissance of Zadar has been truly remarkable.

Located on the north Dalmatian coast, Zadar

Above: Zadar city gate and Fosa harbour view.

is squeezed between the Adriatic and the country's largest mountain range, the Velebit Mountains – often referred to as the naked mountains because no trees grow on its west-facing karst escarpments – this is, without doubt an ancient place wedded to the sea with a great deal to offer today's traveller. It is befitting, therefore, and highly appropriate, that *'more'* in Croat means 'sea' and, certainly Zadar delivers 'more' than can be expected of a destination of its size.

As with much of Croatia, it is the Adriatic (perhaps the most human scale of all the world's oceans) that dominates the tourist experience in Zadar: from the cobalt blue of the sea to the xylophone chiming of the rigging of the boats in the harbour to the sea-born gastronomy and the 'Salute to the Sun' (see later). Indeed, born in Mostar (now Bosnia and Herzegovina) in 1932 the writer and scholar, Predrag Matvejević, best known for his 1987 non-fiction book *Mediterranean: A Cultural Landscape*, a seminal work of cultural history of the Mediterranean region, wrote that: 'The Atlantic and the Pacific are seas of distance, the Mediterranean a sea of propinquity, but the Adriatic is a sea of intimacy.'

This intimacy results from the omnipresence of islands that break down the seascape into contained and coherent vistas – and there are lots of islands. To the west, Zadar is the gateway to its own archipelago, consisting of 24 larger, inhabited islands (with crisp memorable names – Ugiljan, Iz, Olib, Ist, Pag and Rava) and hundreds of islets that punctuate this part of Dalmatia's much larger floatila of over 500 islands that stretch from the 'happy island' of Rab in the North to the Bay of Kotor, south of Dubrovnik. Surrounding the city on its landside are some of Croatia's premier-league nature and national parks (Laklenica, Plitvice, Telascia and Krka) providing a nice antidote to the dominance of the maritime scene.

For filmmaker Alfred Hitchcock Zadar made a lasting, major impact, during a fleeting visit in May 1964. During a short stay in room 204 in the classic, now closed, Hotel Zagreb he witnessed what he described as: 'the most beautiful sunset in the whole world', but, despite being captivated by the place, he never actually filmed here.

The power of tradition meeting innovation is a characteristic of the success of many of the destinations in this book. It is a crucially important factor in Zadar's inclusion in my list of great places to visit. It is present in the contemporary twist to traditional cuisine. This fusion flourishes in the abundant range and diversity of music and dance festivals in the city – giving it the title of the 'entertainment centre of the Adriatic' and the 'capital of cool'.

This hybridity is best exhibited in the remarkable 2008 dance floor designed by Croatian architect and artist Nikola Bašić, known as 'Salute to the Sun' (or 'Greetings to the Sun') – a 22 metre-wide circle is the representation of the sun. It is surrounded by smaller discs acting as other planets to create an artwork that is about communication with nature as the 300 solar-powered panels change colour as the sun sets over the Kvarner Gulf and the islands. Around the circumference of the photovoltaic is a chrome ring inscribed with the names of all the saints of churches in the Old Town and their feast dates. Adding to depth of meaning to this extraordinarily clever piece is the work of Professor Klarin from Zadar who has plotted the exact time the lightshow will start and finish every night from 2008 until 2050.

It is one of two outstanding features of Zadar's new promenade around the harbour's outer peninsula and cruise ship terminal. The second inspired creation, also by Bašić, is another fusion of creative ideas harnessing the raw energy of the natural elements. Installed in 2005 as a part of the design of the sea defences underpinning the promenade is the 'Sea Organ', located just a few metres south of his homage to the Sun. The 'Sea Organ' comprises 35 organ pipes, especially designed by experts in acoustics and sea hydraulics. They stand vertically in the steps

Zadar Waterfront and Old Town.

leading down to the sea. As the waves ebb and flow they create an harmonica effect over the pipes producing seven different musical chords with five different tones. Bašić's next challenge is to try to synchronise the sun and the waves so that the 'Sea Organ' and 'Salute to the Sun' function in harmony.

The past 15 years has seen the remarkable rise of Croatia as a leading destination, especially considering it has been less than 25 years since the break-up of the former Yugoslavia. Croatia is now ranked 27th in the World Economic Forum's 'Global Tourism Competitive Index' – a position built upon a clear national vision focusing on sustainable, high-quality, tourism experiences attracting year-round tourists interested in regional gastronomy, local culture and a relaxed lifestyle; an approach that boldly jettisoned the sun, sand and sea appeal that had driven tourism development on the Adriatic Coast throughout the period from 1970–1990. At the heart of this new approach was the creation of a new generation of local tourism destination organisations to lead, co-ordinate and deliver the national plan at the local level.

It is against this backcloth of a clear, forward-looking tourism plan for the country and its regions with a strong destination tourism organisation – the Zadar County Tourist Board providing leadership and co-ordination of a sustainable tourism plan – that gave confidence for the (then) Falkensteiner Hotel Group to look to bring its highly successful

family-owned business to Croatia (first to the Island of Krk in 2000) and then, in 2006, to the Punta Skala peninsula, Zadar.

When Maria and Josef Falkensteiner opened the seven-bed hotel in the South Tyrol in 1957 they probably had no idea how it would develop over the next 50 years but what they did have was a vision as to what makes a great hotel experience, namely: tradition meets innovation with fine gastronomy and wellness. This solid base of embracing new ideas without forgetting the roots of good hospitality has allowed their two sons, Erich and Andreas, to have a solid foundation on which they have built the Falkensteiner Michaeler Tourism Group (FMTG) with 2,000 employees in their 32 hotels and residences across six countries in Central Europe, including their cluster of five properties in Zadar. Erich Falkensteiner has recently stated that, 'the challenge is not to build a hotel, but to create a home.'

The destination of Zadar has demonstrated a clear willingness to re-imagine and re-invent itself. The tourist board and the local councils have created an environment that allows tradition and innovation to be natural partners. This value system clearly resonates with tourists and with one of Europe's leading hotel groups, who have made Zadar their home, forming a partnership that has seen a synergistic growth in the investments by the FMTG and the development of Zadar as a much respected destination in less than ten years.

ACKNOWLEDGEMENTS

Thank you to the team at Graffeg, especially the publisher's founder, Peter Gill, who wholeheartedly backed the idea for this book and shared in the risk in getting it to completion. That task was ably undertaken by the talented, patient and tolerant designer Joana Rodrigues, to the editor Daniel Williams, supported by Bethan Blake and the rest of the office in Wales. *Diolch yn fawr i chi gyd.*

Thank you to Anita Mendiratta, Sarah Freeman and Peter Greenberg for their delightful contributions to this book and their support for this project.

I would like to thank the many thousands of tourism professionals that I have had the honour to work with; there are far too many of you to mention by name. However, I would like to make a special mention of the following people: Dr Taleb Rifai (the inspirational former Secretary-General of the UNWTO); Professor Kit Carson (the wise friend and tourism guru); Stefan Puehringer (the destinations of Kitzbühel, Saalfelden-Leogang and Kufstein in Austria); K R Manfred Grubauer and Georg Steiner (Linz, Upper Austria); Marco Pointner and Hannes Reidlsperger (Saalfelden – Leogang (Austria), Tim O'Donoghue (Jackson Hole, Wyoming), Myles Rademan and Dana Williams (Park City, Utah), Patrick Torrent (Catalunya), Tomislav Popović and Denis Ivosević (Istria, Croatia); the late Jenny Prinsloo (Franschhoek Wine Valley, South Africa); Brian Johnston (Belfast City and Armagh); Harry Connolly (West Belfast); John McGrillen and Gerry Lennon (Northern Ireland and Belfast respectively); Freda Newton, Yvonne Crook and Willie Cameron (Loch Ness); Harry John (Montreux-Vevey, Switzerland); Ibon Areso (Bilbao); Alastair Dobson (Isle of Arran); Eva Stravs-Podolgar, Janez Fajfar, Misa Novak and Maja Pak (Slovenia), Lars Olsen and Claus Rex (Denmark), Francis Pauwels, Steve Chadwick and Tony Marks (New Zealand) and the visionary Claus Sendlinger (Founder of Design Hotels).

Special appreciation goes to all the destinations who helped provide the inspiration for this book, for their practical help in providing comments, photographs and for their on-going collaboration.

Wales has been my adopted home for fifty years. It is a country of considerable appeal and immense opportunity for tourism. Please take time to explore its wonderfully diverse landscape and coast; discover its great outdoors, its language and its *'croeso'*. It is well worth it. Pob lwc i Croeso Cymru / Visit Wales in all the hard work being done to develop and promote this great little country of Wales.

Finally, without the constant support, kindness and friendship of my daughters Mari and Non and especially my wife Catrin, this life-long passion for travel and tourism could not have been achieved. I am pleased to say that together we have managed to visit and enjoy most of the destinations in this book, *Diolch yn fawr iawn i chi.*

POSTSCRIPT

Tomorrow's tourists care

'After years of year-on-year growth global tourism collapsed to zero as a result of the COVID-19 pandemic. As we go to print countries that have been in lockdown for months are beginning to prepare to welcome back tourists. The tourism industry has proved to be remarkably able to bounce back from previous crisis. It has adapted and evolved over the years but COVID-19 will set unprecedented challenges for the industry to remain relevant and responsible. It will succeed but it will take time.

These are exceptional times. Many of the fragilities of the tourism industry were being exposed before January 2020 and, in many ways, COVID-19 accelerated the need for the industry to take stock of where it was going. The world of tourism was already having to consider its impact on climate change, on the lives of host communities and was actively looking at how it could play a more positive role in helping to meet the UN's Sustainable Development Goals 2030.

As tourists and tourism professionals we have a collective duty to act in a responsible and sustainable way to ensure a healthy future for travel and tourism. COVID-19 has now given us the chance to re-think tourism and to re-set all the buttons to ensure that for the generations to come the world will be a safer and even more interesting place to enjoy the benefits of tourism.

Tarutao National Park, Thailand.

PHOTO CREDITS

The author and Graffeg would like to thank the following organisations and individuals for the use of their photographs.

Page	Credit
Cover	Istria Tourism
3	David Štulc Zornik – Bovec
4	Peter Greenberg (left), Shutterstock (right)
5	iStock
6	Anita Mendiratta
7	Terry Stevens / Unsplash
9	Terry Stevens
10/11	Sarah Freeman
13	Shutterstock
14	iStock
18	iStock
21	iStock
23/25	Armagh, Banbridge and Craigavon Council
26/29	Visit Baden-Baden
30	iStock
33	Baiersbronn Tourist Board
34	F C Barcelona
37	Barcelona Turisme
38	Basel Turismus
41	Basel Turismus
42	Visit Belfast
45	Terry Stevens
46	Shutterstock
49	Shutterstock
50	Terry Stevens
52/55	iStock
57	Bilbao Turismo
60	Bled Tourism
63	Bled Tourism (top) ; iStock (below)
65	Bordeaux Tourisme & Congrés
66	Bordeaux Tourisme & Congrés
67	Bordeaux Tourisme & Congrés
68	Bregenz Turismus
70	Christiane Setz, Bregenz Turismus
72	iStock
75	iStock
76	Shutterstock
78	Unsplash
79	Unsplash
81	Unsplash
82	iStock
85	Catalan Tourist Board
86	Terry Stevens
87	Wonderful Copenhagen
89	Wonderful Copenhagen
91	Terry Stevens (top), Wonderful Copenhagen (below)
93	Visit Cornwall
94	Visit Cornwall
95	Shutterstock
96	Shutterstock
97	Visit Cornwall
99	Shutterstock
100	San Sebástian Turismo
101	San Sebástian Turismo
103	Shutterstock
105/107	iStock
109/111	Visit Fanø
113/115	Visit Flanders
117	Slovenian Tourist Board
119	Slovenian Tourist Board
121	Aran in Focus
123	Isle of Arran Ice Cream Ltd
124/127	iStock
128	iStock
131	Kitzbühel Turismus
132/133	iStock
135	Marino Trotta
137	Terry Stevens
139	Linz Turismus
141	iStock
143	Terry Stevens
144/147	Visit Inverness Loch Ness, Loch Ness by Jacobite
148/151	The Jadranka Group
153	iStock
156	Nigel Forster
159	The Retreat's Group
161	The Retreat's Group
162	Chris Warren
165	Adventure Parc Snowdonia
166/167	Zip World
168/169	iStock
170/171	iStock
173	iStock
174	Slovenian Tourist Board
177	Slovenian Tourist Board
178	Maistra Hotels and Resorts
181	Maistra Hotels and Resorts
182/185	Salfelden-Leogang Turismus
187/189	Soča Valley Tourism
191	The Newt Somerset
193	Haselbury Mill (top); Somerset Cider Brandy Company (below)
194	Terry Stevens
195	The Newt Somerset
196/199	iStock
201	Shutterstock
202	Shutterstock
203	Shutterstock
205	PromoTourismoFVG
207/209	Turku Touring
211	Visit Vadehavskysten
213	Visit Vadehavskysten
215	Vi9sit Malta
216/217	Shutterstock
218	Shutterstock
221	Shutterstock
222	Shutterstock
225	Visit Dorset
226	Visit Dorset
228	Summer House Hotel
229	Shutterstock
230	iStock
234/235	iStock
237	iStock
239	iStock

Maps by silhouettegarden.com

Every effort has been made to trace copyright holders of material and acknowledge permission for this publication. The publisher apologises for any errors or omissions to rights holders and would be grateful for notification of credits and corrections that should be included in future reprints or editions of this book.